PUBLIC ADMINISTRATION IN ANCIENT INDIA

PUBLIC ADMINISTRATION IN ANCIENT INDIA

A THESIS APPROVED BY THE UNIVERSITY OF LONDON FOR THE DEGREE OF D.SC. ECON

PRAMATHANATH BANERJEA

GYAN

Published by

GYAN

Gyan Publishing House
5, Ansari Road
Daryaganj, New Delhi-110002
Phone: 011-47034999, 9811692060
E-mail: books@gyanbooks.com

Distribution Network
gyanbooks.com
India, USA, Canada, UK, Australia

ISBN: 978-93-7447-328-3 (PB)

First Published, 1916

2nd Impression 2025

Printed at: Gyan Press, Delhi.

PUBLIC ADMINISTRATION IN ANCIENT INDIA
Author: PRAMATHANATH BANERJEA

PUBLIC ADMINISTRATION IN ANCIENT INDIA

A THESIS APPROVED BY THE UNIVERSITY OF LONDON FOR THE DEGREE OF D.Sc. Econ.

BY

PRAMATHANATH BANERJEA

M.A. (Cal.), D.Sc. Econ. (Lond.)

FORMERLY PROFESSOR OF ECONOMICS AND POLITICAL SCIENCE AT THE CITY, RIPON AND SCOTTISH CHURCHES COLLEGES OF CALCUTTA, FELLOW OF THE ROYAL ECONOMIC SOCIETY, AND AUTHOR OF 'A STUDY OF INDIAN ECONOMICS'

MACMILLAN AND CO., LIMITED
ST. MARTIN'S STREET, LONDON
1916

মাতৃদেবীর শ্রীচরণোদ্দেশে

PREFACE

The object of this book is to give within a small compass all the important facts relating to the administrative system of Ancient India. To make the account complete, a few of the political ideas of the early Hindus have been briefly noticed here. The period mainly dealt with in this work is the millennium 500 B.C. to 500 A.D., but, occasionally, references have been made to earlier and later periods. Nothing has been said here which is not supported by reliable evidence. Sanskrit passages have been transliterated in accordance with the system adopted at the Geneva Congress, which system has also been applied, with some accommodations, viz. *sh* for *ś*, *ṛi* for *ṛ*, in citation of Sanskrit terms and expressions; but, for the convenience of non-Sanskritists, all proper names have been transliterated, except for indications of vowel length, in the simple and ordinary way.

The author desires to take this opportunity to offer his best thanks to Dr. L. D. Barnett, Mr. H. B.

Lees-Smith, M.P., Prof. Rhys Davids, Dr. F. W. Thomas, Mr. B. M. Barua, and Mr. H. S. Parara for valuable suggestions received from them. He is specially thankful to Dr. Thomas and Mr. Parara, who have also assisted in seeing the book through the press.

CHAPTER VIII

PAGE

Assemblies and Councils - - - - - - - 94

CHAPTER IX

The Ministers - - - - - - - - - 106

CHAPTER X

The Subordinate Executive - - - - - 121

CHAPTER XI

Legislation - - - - - - - - - - 131

CHAPTER XII

The Administration of Justice - - - - - 141

CHAPTER XIII

Public Finance - - - - - - - - 173

CHAPTER XIV

Foreign Relations - - - - - - - 186

CHAPTER XV

The Military Organisation - - - - - 196

CHAPTER XVI

Conquest and Defence - - - - - - 219

CONTENTS

CHAPTER I

PAGE

INTRODUCTORY - - - - - - - - 1

CHAPTER II

THE STRUCTURE OF SOCIETY - - - - - - 15

CHAPTER III

THE TERRITORY OF THE STATE - - - - - 29

CHAPTER IV

THE ORIGIN AND NATURE OF THE STATE - - - 34

CHAPTER V

THE SYSTEM OF GOVERNMENT - - - - - 42

CHAPTER VI

POLITICAL DIVISIONS - - - - - - - 54

CHAPTER VII

THE KING - - - - - - - - - 63

CHAPTER XVII

PAGE

Public Works - - - - - - - - - 240

CHAPTER XVIII

Industry and Commerce - - - - - - - 257

CHAPTER XIX

Religion - - - - - - - - - - 275

CHAPTER XX

Local Government - - - - - - - 288

Appendix - - - - - - - - - 299

Index - - - - - - - - - - 300

CHAPTER I

INTRODUCTORY

IN Ancient India, the different branches of knowledge were grouped under four heads, namely, Philosophy, the Vedas, Economics, and Politics.[1] Of these, Politics was regarded as a very important—if not the most important—subject of study. The Mahābhārata says, "When the Science of Politics is neglected, the three Vedas as well as all virtues decline."[2]

The method of study pursued in ancient times was somewhat different from that generally adopted at the present day. Politics was treated more as an art than as a science; in other words, guidance in

[1] Chānakya says, "Ānvīksikī (Philosophy), Trayī (the Vedas), Vārttā (Economics), and Daṇḍanītī (the Science of Government) are the four sciences." Arthasāstra, Bk. I. ch. 1. The Mahābhārata, the Kāmandaki, and the Sukranīti follow Chānakya's classification, and use almost identical words. According to the school of the Mānavas there are only three sciences—the Vedas, Economics, and Politics; the school of Brihaspati reduces the sciences to two, namely, Economics and Politics, while that of Usanas regards the Science of Government as the only science, all other branches of knowledge being dependent on it.

[2] "Majjet trayī daṇḍanītau hatāyāṁ sarve dharmāḥ praksayeyuḥ." Mahābhārata, Sānti Parva, Sec. 63, sl. 28.

the practice of actual administration, rather than the construction of a complete and consistent system of political theories, was the object mainly aimed at in the study of the subject. Chānakya, for instance, defines Politics as "the science which treats of what is right in public policy and what is not, and of power and weakness."[1] According to the Sukranīti, a knowledge of the science "enables rulers to gain victories over their foes, to please their subjects, and to be proficient in statecraft."[2] The mode of treatment was thus more practical than theoretical; and one result of this was that the conclusions were expressed in the form not of scientific principles but of moral precepts.

Our sources of information regarding the systems of administration which prevailed in India in the ancient times and the political ideas and ideals which moulded and shaped those systems, are various. Briefly speaking, they are: the Vedas, the Hindu Epics, the Smritis, the Purānas, the religious books of the Buddhists and the Jainas, historical and dramatic literature, accounts of foreign travellers, epigraphic records, and lastly, a few treatises which deal specially with Politics.

In the Rig-Veda, many passages are met with which allude to the colonisation of the country by the Āryas, and speak of the sanguinary wars of the Āryan conquerors with the non-Āryan inhabitants

[1] Arthasāstra, Bk. I. ch. 1. [2] Ch. I. sls. 6-7.

of the country. But nothing is said about the system of administration, and very little information, beyond a few scattered hints, can be obtained from the earlier portion of Vedic literature about the political condition of India during the earliest period of her history. The later Vedic works, however, such as the Aitareya Brāhmana, the Satapatha Brāhmana, and the Atharva-Veda, are more informing in this respect.

The Rāmāyana and the Mahābhārata are not historical works in the modern sense of the term; but they give us a graphic and fairly accurate picture of the life of the Āryas in what is known as the Heroic Period of Indian history. The stories found in these Epics are largely based on real occurrences, and although the main themes of the Epics are the wars of the heroes, both of these great works present us with glimpses of the political condition of early Hindu society and of the relations between the rulers and the ruled, while not a few chapters of the Mahābhārata are specially devoted to an exposition of the duties of kings and of the rights and obligations of subjects.[1]

[1] In the Mahābhārata, a mythical account is given of the source of the Science of Politics. It is said that Brahman composed by his own intelligence a treatise consisting of a hundred thousand lessons. In it were treated the subjects of Virtue, Wealth, and Pleasure. A large portion of it was devoted to the subject of Government, that is to say, the growth, conservation, and destruction of States. This book discussed in detail the duties of the king, of the ministers, and of the people, and other kindred matters. It was first studied by Siva and abridged by him for the benefit of mankind. Further abridgments were made by Indra, Brihaspati,

The most ancient among the Smritis were in prose, and are known as the Dharma-sūtras. Only a few fragments of some of these works have yet been discovered. The Dharma-sāstras appear to have been later redactions in verse of the earlier Dharma-sūtras.[1] The most important of the Smriti works at present known are those attributed to Gautama, Āpastamba, Vasishtha, Bodhāyana, Vishnu, Manu, Yājnavalkya, and Nārada. Their purpose is to

---

Sukra, and others. Mahābhārata, Sānti Parva, Sec. 59, sl. 28, etc. The origin of the name of the science is described thus: Brahman said, "Because men are led by Government (daṇḍa), or in other words, Government leads or controls everything, therefore this Science will be known in the three worlds as the Science of Government (Daṇḍanīti)." Mahābhārata, Sānti Parva, Sec. 59, sl. 78.

[1] Considerable doubts still exist as to the dates of composition of the Vedas, the Epics, the Smritis, and the Purānas. We do not propose to enter here upon a discussion of this controversial topic, but will content ourselves with a few remarks on the subject. The hymns of the Rig-Veda are considered to have been the earliest utterances of the Āryan race, and many of them go back to a very remote period, while the bulk of the Vedic literature seems to have been composed before 1000 B.C.

Weber placed the date of composition of the Rāmāyana in the third or fourth century after Christ; but nobody accepts this view now. According to Prof. Jacobi, the Rāmāyana was composed in Kosala on the basis of ballads recited by rhapsodists throughout that district. Prof. Rhys Davids is of opinion that the date of the Mahābhārata and the Rāmāyana as Epics must be later than that of the ballad literature preserved in the Nikāyas. We are inclined to think that these Epics, originally composed in the form of ākhyana poetry about the tenth or ninth century B.C. were several times enlarged and revised, until they assumed something like their present shape in the third or second century B.C. Barth rightly remarks, "the Hindu Epic is ancient, as ancient in the origin as the earliest traditions of the nation." Indian Antiquary, 1895, p. 71.

The existing Code of Manu is perhaps not very old, but probably it was based upon a more ancient Dharma-sūtra of the Mānava school. Chānakya, in his Arthasāstra, frequently refers to this school of the Mānavas. Roughly speaking, we may say that the Sūtra works were composed between 1000 and 500 B.C., while the Dharma-sāstras were compiled between the third century B.C. and the fifth century A.D.

describe the whole of the rites and customs which ought to prevail in private, civic, and public life, and, naturally, they all devote some of their chapters to discussions of political subjects like the duties of kings, public finance, civil and criminal laws, and judicial procedure. These chapters are of inestimable value to the student of ancient Politics.

The Purānas appear to be works which were originally composed for the purpose of giving instruction to the less advanced sections of the community in all matters concerning this world and the next. Their great value from the historical standpoint lies in the fact that they contain a considerable amount of genuine historical tradition and preserve more or less correct lists of the various dynasties of kings who ruled in India from the earliest times until towards the close of the Hindu period of Indian history.[1] To the student of political science the Agni Purāna, which treats of politics in considerable detail, is specially important.

[1] Comparatively recent dates have been assigned by many scholars to the Purānas. But even Prof. H. H. Wilson admits that "a very great portion of the contents of many, some portion of the contents of all, is genuine and old. The sectarian interpolation or embellishment is always sufficiently palpable to be set aside, without injury to the more authentic and primitive material." Vishnu Purāna, Preface, p. vi. Mr. Pargiter says, "Metrical accounts of the dynasties that reigned in Northern India after the great battle between the Pāndavas and the Kauravas, grew up gradually, composed in slokas in a literary Prākrit and recited by bards and minstrels, and after writing was introduced into India, about seven centuries B.C., there would have been no lack of materials from which those accounts could have been composed and written down." Dynasties of the Kali Age, Introduction, xxvii.

A considerable amount of incidental information is supplied by the Buddhist and Jaina Sūtras, the Jātakas, the Milinda Panha, and other religious works of the two sects. Although the information obtainable from this source is small in quantity, the fact that the object of composition of these works was religious and not political lends to it a greater degree of reliability than is possessed by some of the other sources.

The purely historical literature of India at present known to us is exceedingly meagre. The Rāja-taranginī[1] of Kalhana, which treats of the Kings of Kashmir, is practically the only work in Indian literature that makes some approach to the modern conception of history. The Dīpavamsa and the Mahāvamsa contain much legendary material for history, and although not absolutely reliable in every detail as records of historical events, they are very helpful to us in elucidating some of the difficult points of Indian history and administration.[2] Much light is also thrown on the political condition of India by the writings of poets like Bhāsa and Kālidāsa, and in particular by such works as the Mudrā-Rākshasa of

[1] This work has been translated into English by Mr. J. C. Dutt, and also by Sir M. A. Stein.

[2] Prof. Rhys Davids says: "What we find in such chronicles is not indeed sober history, as we should now understand the term, but neither is it pure fiction. It is good evidence of opinion as held at the time when it was written." Prof. Geiger seems also to be of the same opinion. The approximate dates of composition of the Dīpavamsa and the Mahāvamsa were the fourth and the fifth century A.D. respectively.

Visākhadatta, Mrichchakatikā of Sūdraka, the Harsha-charita of Bāna and the Dasakumāra-charita of Daṇḍin. From some of the story books, such as the Pancha-tantra, the Brihat-Kathā, and the Kathā-sarit-sagara, we learn a great deal about the political ideas of the Hindus. In Ṭamil literature the most well-known works on the subject are the Mani-Mekalai and the Kural.

The earliest foreign travellers who left any accounts of their visits to India were the Greeks. Much of their writings consists merely of 'travellers' tales,' and as such are useless. But Megasthenes, who was attached for several years as Ambassador to the Court of Chandragupta Maurya, was a very careful observer of facts and events which came under his direct notice, and although he perhaps lacked the faculty of critical judgment, his writings still remain one of the most important sources of our information regarding the condition of the country in the fourth century before Christ. The information derived from this source is supplemented by that obtained from the historians of Alexander's Indian campaign.[1] Many Chinese pilgrims visited India during the period between the fourth and eighth centuries A.D., and the accounts left by them, especially those left by Fa Hian, Hiuen Tsiang,[2] and I-Tsing,[3] are of very

[1] Mr. McCrindle's translations have made these works very useful to the general reader.

[2] Translated by Beal. [3] Translated by Takakusu.

great use to people interested in the affairs of ancient India. Alberuni's Tārīkh-i-Hind[1] is also useful as throwing some light on the state of the country on the eve of the Mahomedan conquest.

The epigraphic records are invaluable for the elucidation of the facts of the history of India. Besides, they give us many useful hints about the political affairs of the periods to which they relate. Most of these records, however, are comparatively recent in date, and as such are not of much assistance to us. Of the earlier records, Asoka's inscriptions and the inscriptions of the Guptas are the most important. Some of the Ceylon inscriptions are of special interest in this regard. We also derive some useful information from many of the copperplate records of grants made by kings and others.

Of the works which treat specially of the subject of Public Administration, the most important is the Arthasāstra of Chānakya.[2] 'Arthaśāstra,' literally,

[1] Translated by Sachau.

[2] "The measures to be taken for the acquisition and the preservation of the earth have been described in this book." Arthasâstra, Bk. XV. ch. 1. In another passage the author says that the system of public administration has been here described for the guidance of kings. So great was the fame of this work that the name 'Chānakya' became almost a synonym for 'Political Science.' In an inscription, the Rāshtrakūta King, Govinda IV., is described as 'Chānakya-chaturmukha.' Vide Epigraphia Indica, Vol. VII. p. 36.

According to the Purānas, Chandragupta was placed on the throne by Kautılya. The Matsya, Vāyu, and Brahmānda Purānas say: "Uddharişyati tān sarvān Kautılyah." The Matsya adds: "Kautılyaś Candraguptan tu tato rājye 'bhiseksyati." The other Purānas also say practically the same thing. The Mahāvamsa says: "Then did the Brāhmana, Chānakka, anoint a glorious youth, known by name Chandagutta, as King over all

means the science of secular welfare, as distinguished from 'Dharma-śāstra,' or the science of moral and spiritual well-being. But this work treats only of Politics, for in Kautilya's opinion Public Administration was the chief means of promoting the welfare of the people. The author appears in Sanskrit literature under various names, such as Kautilya, Kautalya, Chānakya, and Vishnugupta. As Prof. Jolly puts it, " a flood of light has been thrown on the political condition of India in the very times when Megasthenes visited it, by the recent discovery of the Kautiliya Arthasastra." The author of this great work was himself a practical statesman,[1] and it bears on every one of its pages the impress of a great mind. It evinces a thorough grasp of essential principles as well as a mastery of minute details. But it is not free from defects of a very serious character. For

Jambudvīpa, born of a noble clan, the Moriyas, when, filled with bitter hate, he had slain the ninth (Nanda) Dhanananda." Geiger's Mahāvamsa, Ch. V. This story is confirmed by the Mudrā-Rākshasa. The Kathā-sarit-sagara tells us that Chandragupta obtained his throne "through the kindness of Vishnugupta."

[1] As to the authenticity of the Arthasāstra, Dr. Jolly remarks, "It can no longer be called into doubt after the learned disquisition contained in a paper published in Germany by Prof. Hillebrandt of Breslau." Dr. Jolly adds, "We consider this one of the most important discoveries ever made in the whole range of Sanskrit literature." Mysore Review, May, 1909. Vide also Über das Kautilīyaśāstra und Verwandtes by Alfred Hillebrandt (Breslau, 1908).

Mr. Shama Sastri has placed the public under a deep debt of gratitude by editing this work, and also by publishing translations of portions of it in the Mysore Review and the Indian Antiquary. I have frequently consulted Mr. Sastri's translations for the purpose of the present work. Mr. Sorabji has published a few notes on the first two books of the Arthasāstra.

side by side with words of the highest kind of wisdom, we find here emphasised the utility of time-servingness and the necessity for the subordination of ethical principles to considerations of expediency. The political doctrine preached in this book, namely, that the end justifies the means, marks a notable departure from the high moral standard of earlier times.

It strikes us as a curious coincidence that Chānakya, the greatest political philosopher of India, was the contemporary of Aristotle, the most eminent political theorist of Ancient Greece, and perhaps also a junior contemporary of Aristotle's predecessor and teacher, Plato.[1] The opinion of scholars is divided on the question whether the Arthasāstra is the work of Chānakya himself or of a school founded by Chānakya. Prof. Hillebrandt[2] holds the latter view, but Prof. Jacobi[3] advances weighty arguments to prove the individual authorship of the work. Prof. Keith suggests, "Surely one obvious solution is that Kautilya was an energetic student of the Arthasāstra, who carried his theoretical knowledge into practice, and in the evening of his days enriched the theory by knowledge based on his practical experience, and that the Arthasāstra is based on his teaching, though not by his own hand."[4]

[1] When Chānakya placed Chandragupta on the throne of Magadha in 323 or 322 B.C., he was evidently a middle-aged, if not an old, man.

[2] Über das Kautilīyaśāstra, 1908.

[3] Über die Echtheit des Kautiliya, SKPAW, 1912.

[4] Journal of the Royal Asiatic Society, January, 1916.

The author of the Arthasāstra [1] says in his Preface to the book that it is founded on all the ancient books written on the subject by the ancient teachers, and in the body of the work he criticises the views of many political theorists, such as Usanas, Brihaspati, Bharadvāja, Parāsara, Visālāksha, and Pisuna, and of the schools founded by these teachers. The names of these teachers and of some others also occur in the Mahābhārata. But at present we know nothing of their writings beyond what is contained in the Smritis. It is not improbable, however, that some of their works will be discovered in future and will add considerably to our knowledge of the polity of Ancient India.[2] Of political works now known to

[1] Kautilya has sometimes been compared to Machiavelli. But this comparison does not seem to be a very happy one. There is no doubt that both these great writers wrote for the guidance of princes, and that both favoured a subordination of ethical principles to considerations of expediency. But the points of similarity do not extend any further. In intellectual acumen and in comprehensiveness of outlook, Kautilya far surpasses his Italian rival. Moreover, the Hindu author was also a practical statesman of the first rank to whose guidance and advice Chandragupta owed the foundation and consolidation of a pan-Indian Empire; while the practical experience of the Florentine diplomat was limited to a few years' service in a subordinate department of the State. Lastly, Kautilya's political ideas continued to be accepted by many generations of kings and statesmen as safe guides in their work of actual administration, but Machiavelli's Prince and other works were valued merely as abstract treatises and never influenced to any considerable extent the current of political events. If any European politician can be compared to Chānakya, it is Bismarck.

[2] Dr. F. W. Thomas of the India Office Library has obtained possession of a copy of a small MS. work entitled 'Brihaspati Sūtra.' He is now editing and translating this work, and has kindly permitted me to consult it. This work appears to be comparatively modern, but probably it contains some of the traditional ideas of the Bārhaspatya school of Politics.

us besides the Arthasāstra, the most notable are the Nītisāra of Kāmandaki, the Nītivākyāmrita of Somadeva Sūri, and the Nītisāra which is attributed to Sukrāchārya.[1] All these works seem to have been based, to a greater or less extent, on the Arthasāstra. The Kāmandaki-nīti was probably composed in the third or fourth century A.D., and may be regarded as a metrical version of certain portions of the Arthasāstra. The Nītivākyāmrita also, like the Kāmandaki, closely follows the Kautiliya in its treatment of political topics. It appears to have been composed in the tenth century.[2] In the Sukranīti are to be found passages which occur in the Kāmandaki, but it also contains matter which is not to be found in the earlier books. The date of compilation of the bulk of the book may be placed in the ninth or tenth century after Christ, but some portions are evidently more modern.[3] Mention may also be made of a few other books of comparatively recent dates, which, though not important in themselves, show the continuity of the political system of the Hindus.

[1] Very little is known about the authors of these books. Dr. Rajendralala Mitra held the opinion that Kāmandaki was a Buddhist, and that his work was composed some time before the fifth century A.D. Sukrāchārya, the reputed author of Sukranīti, is supposed to have been the preceptor of the Demons (Daityas). He is also known by other names, such as Usanas, Kavi, Bhārgava, Maghābhava, etc.

[2] Somadeva Sūri wrote his 'Yasastilaka' in Saka 881 (959 A.D.).

[3] Gustav Oppert's opinion that the work was composed anterior to the composition of the Mahābhārata is entitled to no weight. The truth seems to be this, that the work in its present shape was compiled from several ancient works on Politics.

The Yuktikalpataru, ascribed to King Bhoja, was probably composed in the eleventh or twelfth century.[1] The Nītimayūkha is a portion of Nīlakantha's Bhāskara, compiled in the seventeenth century. Nothing is known about the authorship or the probable date of the Nītiprakāsikā, attributed to Vaisampāyana, but the detailed description which it gives of the weapons used in warfare shows that it is a recent work.[2] Abul Fazl, in his Ayeen-i-Akbery (written in the sixteenth century) gives a short summary of Hindu polity (Rajneet) and law (Beyhar) which is very interesting.

There is a large number of books and manuscripts in the British Museum, in the India Office Library, and in the Libraries at Oxford and Cambridge which profess to give the teachings of Chānakya, but none of them are of any use to the student of Political Science.[3] A manuscript has, however, been recently found in the Oriental Manuscripts Library of Madras, entitled 'Chānakya-sūtra,'[4] which looks like an

[1] Several kings bearing the name of Bhoja are to be found in history, and it is not known to which of them it refers. Bhoja, King of Dhara, is supposed to have lived about the end of the tenth or the beginning of the eleventh century, and is said to have been not only a great patron of learning but himself the author of several learned works. This book has not yet been printed, but a manuscript copy exists in the Bodleian at Oxford, and a few copies are known to exist in India.

[2] In 1881 Gustav Oppert published this work at Madras, but the authenticity of the work has not yet been established beyond all doubt.

[3] Eugene Monseur published some years ago a few of these works in a volume which contains the Nīti-Sataka, Nīti-Sāstra, Laghuchānakya-Rājanītī-Sāstra, Vriddha-Chānakya-Rājuhnīti-Sāstra and Chānakya-Sloka.

[4] A copy of this MS. is now in the possession of Mr. F. W. Thomas.

abridgment of a few chapters of the Arthasāstra. The style of this work is akin to that of the Nītivākyāmrita of Somadeva Sūri, and it probably belongs to the same period as the latter work.

CHAPTER II

THE STRUCTURE OF SOCIETY

WHEN the primeval Āryas left their original cradle-home—we do not exactly know where it was, whether in Persia, or in Central Asia, or in the regions farther north—and entered on their journeys in different directions, they had already passed out of the nomadic and pastoral stages of civilisation. The dawn of history thus finds the Indo-Āryans settled on the banks of the Seven Rivers (Sapta-Sindhavaḥ), leading a civilised life, practising agriculture and some of the simpler kinds of manufacture, and adoring whatever is sublime and beautiful in Nature.

The Āryas of the land of the Seven Rivers (now known as the Punjab) were divided into a number of tribes or nations (janāḥ).[1] Each tribe or nation, again, was subdivided into a number of clans (viśaḥ), the members of which claimed their descent from a common ancestor, real or mythical. The different

[1] The Āryas of the Punjab are often alluded to in the Rig-Veda as the five nations or tribes (pañca-janāḥ). For the meaning of the term see Chap. VI., footnote.

tribes lived, as a rule, on terms of amity and peaceful neighbourliness, and each clan was united with the others by a tie of kindred and a sense of common interest. Occasionally, envy and jealousy led to quarrels and internecine wars, but such occasions were few and far between.[1]

In the early Vedic Age, the structure of society was very simple. There were no class distinctions, and each person was the full equal of every other.[2] But as time went on, and the struggle with the non-Āryans became keener, it was found necessary to devise some system which would keep the Āryas distinct and separate from the Dasyus,[3] and would, at the same time, increase the political, industrial, and intellectual efficiency of the Āryas themselves.

Several theories exist about the origin of the caste-system. But it seems reasonable to hold that the

[1] A careful reading of the Rig-Veda gives the reader the impression that although the wars of the Āryas with the Dasyus were very frequent, internecine wars among the Āryas themselves were rare.

[2] Even the Mahābhārata, the great book of orthodox Brahmanism, admits, "There is no real distinction between the different orders. The whole world at first consisted of Brāhmanas. Created (equal) by Brahman, men have in consequence of their acts become distributed into several classes." Sānti Parva. Sec. 188, sl. 10. The description given in the Rig-Veda of the rise of the four castes from the mouth, the arms, the thighs, and the feet respectively of Brahman, is merely figurative, but in later times the Brāhmanas used this passage to prove their superiority to the other classes.

[3] Originally, the term 'Dasyu' meant 'non-Āryan,' and was similar in signification to the Gr. word 'barbarian.' But as many of the non-Āryan tribes disturbed the Āryas in the performance of their sacrifices and carried off their cattle, the term gradually acquired a sinister meaning. The other epithets which the Āryas applied to the aboriginal tribes were 'Yakshas,' 'Rākshasas,' 'Nāgas,' 'Vānaras,' and 'Kinnaras.'

first beginnings of the system are to be found in the sharp colour line[1] which distinguished the fair-complexioned Āryas from the dark-skinned non-Āryan races of India. Very little is as yet known about the origin of the pre-Āryan inhabitants of the country. But they are said to have belonged mainly to two races, the Kolarian and the Dravidian, who had probably come into India from outside at some remote period of history.[2] Some of the tribes belonging to these races were fairly civilised, while others were at a very low stage of civilisation. The Āryan conquerors, conscious of their higher powers of intellect, and proud of their superior culture, despised the less civilised non-Āryans, and detested their superstitious customs and practices; and in order to preserve the purity of the Āryan blood, they prohibited all intercourse with the non-Āryan races.

During this time other factors were at work to introduce social distinctions into the Āryan community itself. As civilisation grew, the needs of life became more varied and complex, and this necessitated a division of duties among the people. The

[1] The constant use of the term 'varna' in Sanskrit literature suggests that colour was the chief ground of distinction. The following reference in the Tibetan Buddhist 'Dulva' to the caste-system is interesting: "Then those whose complexion was clear said to the others, 'Why, I have a fine complexion, whereas you are dark,' and thus were established distinctions.' The Life of Buddha, derived from Tibetan works, translated by Rockhill, p. 3.

[2] Some scholars think that the Kolarians came into India from the north-east, and the Dravidians from the north-west. The Dravidians are believed to have had affinities with the people of the First Babylonian Empire, and, in fact, to have belonged to the same race.

continuous and unceasing struggle with the aboriginal races compelled the Āryas to set apart the hardiest portion of their community for the exclusive occupation of war. Then, as engagement in warfare was found incompatible with devotion to learning and the arts of peace, the most intellectual among the Āryas formed themselves into a separate class, while the general mass of the people began to devote their energies exclusively to agriculture, industry, and trade. The members of a clan were originally designated by the collective name of *vis*, but in the course of time this name was reserved for the common people, while those who distinguished themselves either in learning or in war were raised above the general level, and became Brāhmanas and Kshatriyas (or Rājanyas). Lastly, those among the Dasyus who submitted to the Aryan conquerors and were admitted into the pale of Āryan society came to be known as Sūdras. Thus arose the caste-system.

The origin of the caste-system can be traced back to the early Vedic times,[1] but it was not until a much later period that it became well established. Intermarriages were not prohibited in early times, and

[1] Dr. Muir, many years ago, collected a number of passages from the Vedas in his Original Sanskrit Texts, which point to the existence of distinctions within the Aryan community in the Vedic Period. The fact that the social divisions of the early Persians were very similar to the castes of India leads us to think that the beginning of the system can be traced back to the period when the Indo-Āryans had not yet separated from their kinsmen, the Perso-Āryans.

famous Rishis sometimes married the daughters of kings. The division into classes in these times depended more upon occupation, character, and attainments than upon birth.[1] But as the Vedic Age glided imperceptibly into the Brahmanic Period, the caste-system was more fully organised, and by about the eighth or seventh century B.C. it became almost completely stereotyped. In the fourth century B.C., according to Megasthenes, "no one is allowed to marry out of his own caste or to exchange one profession or trade for another, or to follow more than one business."[2] This, however, was the caste-system in its simple form. In the course of time, *anulom* and *pratilom* marriages and an ever-increasing diversity of occupations gave rise to innumerable mixed castes, until there was developed that complex mass of social divergences with which we are at the present day familiar, and to which the term caste-system is now—not very properly—applied.

[1] In the Buddhist books there are many references to persons who changed their professions without losing caste. In the time of the Mahābhārata mixed marriages were infrequent, but not absolutely impossible. The Sukranīti, a comparatively recent work, says, "It is not by birth that men became Brāhmanas, Kshatriyas, Vaisyas, Sūdras and Mlechchas; but the distinctions arose in accordance with their qualifications (guṇa) and occupation (karma)." The Bhagavad-Gītā also mentions guṇa and karma as the determining factors in the division of men into castes.

[2] Megasthenes, Fragment XXXIII. (McCrindle's Trans.). According to Megasthenes, the population of India was divided into seven parts, namely, (1) philosophers, (2) husbandmen, (3) herdsmen and hunters, (4) traders and manual labourers, (5) fighters, (6) overseers, and (7) councillors. This division is substantially correct; and if we put (1) and (7) in one group, (3) and (4) in a second, and (5) and (6) in a third, the classification would exactly correspond with that given by Kautilya.

A review of the caste-system is important to the student of ancient Indian polity in this that it affected the status of the citizens and their duties as members of the body politic. From the commencement of the Brahmanic Period until recently, the position of a man in relation to society, and his duties, both public and private, always depended more upon the importance of his class, than upon his individual capacity and character. The duties of the different castes are thus defined by Manu: of the Brāhmanas,—teaching, studying, offering sacrifices, officiating at sacrifices, charity and acceptance of gifts; of the Kshatriyas,—protection of the people, charity, performing sacrifices, study, and want of attachment to pleasures; of the Vaisyas,—cattle-rearing, agriculture, charity, performance of sacrifices, study, trade and money-lending; of the Sūdras,—service of the three orders.[1] To this list Chānakya adds agriculture, arts, and crafts as the occupations of the Sūdras;[2] and Vishnu mentions all industrial arts (sarva-śilpāni)[3] as being within their province. In the Mahābhārata,[4] also, similar duties are assigned to the members of the different castes.

[1] Manu-Samhitā, I. 88-91. The other Smriti works also mention the same or similar duties for the different orders.

[2] Arthaśāstra, Bk. I. ch. 3.

[3] Vishnu Smriti (ed. by J. Jolly), ch. 2.

[4] Sānti Parva, Sec. 72. The Great Epic enumerates the following as the duties common to all classes: the suppression of wrath, truthfulness of speech, justice, forgiveness, begetting children on one's wedded wives, purity of conduct, avoidance of quarrel, and maintenance of dependents.

With the establishment of the caste-system the Brāhmanas, by virtue of their position and intellectual attainments, gradually gained an ascendancy over the other classes in society. And this ascendancy was won and maintained not only in matters of religion and learning, but also in politics and statecraft.[1] They were, in fact, looked upon as the natural guardians of society. They were the councillors of the king, and the chief officers of state, both executive and judicial. "To them," says Megasthenes, "belong the highest posts of government, the tribunals of justice, and the general administration of public affairs."[2]

But this ascendancy had not been won without a struggle. Although the contest was not always bloody, yet there appears to be some truth in the story of Parasu-Rāma who is said to have cleared the earth of the Kshatriyas "thrice seven times." It does not, however, seem that the Brāhmanas had always the best of the business, and possibly the failure of the appeal to force led them to adopt milder methods for the attainment of their object. The allegory of Mitra and Varuna in the Satapatha-Brāhmana correctly represents the final rapproche-

[1] The Brahmanical books give an exaggerated importance to the Brāhmanas, and push their claims to absurd lengths. "The Brāhmaṇa is the lord of the entire creation, for he sprang from the head of Brahmā, and he is the eldest of all created beings." Manu, I. 92. And again, "Everything that exists in the Universe belongs to the Brāhmanas in consequence of his birth and precedence." Mahābhārata, Sānti Parva, Sec. 72, sl. 10.

[2] Megasthenes, Fragment XIII.

ment between the two classes. "Mitra is the priesthood, and Varuna, the nobility; and the priesthood is the conceiver, and the noble is the doer. . . . So the two united."[1] But they did not unite on an exactly equal footing, for we are told that "it is quite proper that a Brāhmana should be without a king, but were he to obtain a king, it would be conducive to the success (of both). It is, however, quite improper that a king should be without a Brāhmana, for whatever deed he does, unsped by Mitra, the priesthood, therein he succeeds not."[2] Gautama says, "Kshatriyas who are assisted by the Brāhmanas prosper, and do not fall into distress." And further, "A king and a Brāhmana, deeply versed in the Vedas, these two uphold the moral order of the world."

It is thus evident that the Brāhmanas and the Kshatriyas were the two most important classes in the early Indian society. The general superiority of the Brāhmanas over the Kshatriyas was admitted to some extent, but the influence of the former class in the State was not quite exclusive.[3] Even in the sphere of religion their supremacy was not absolutely undisputed. For we find that in the sixth century

[1] Satapatha Brāhmana, IV. 1, 4, 1-4.

[2] Satapatha Brāhmana, IV. 1, 4, 6. In another passage the Brāhmana is compared to truth, and the Kshatriya to life.

[3] It is difficult, however, to fully agree with Prof. Hopkins when he says, "Brahmanism has always been an island in a sea. . . . It did not even control all the Āryan population." Quoted with approval by Prof. Rhys Davids in Buddhist India, p. 152.

B.C., two of the greatest religious reformers of India—Vardhamāna Mahāvīra and Gautama Buddha—belonged to the Kshatriya caste; and throughout the period known as the Buddhist Age, the superiority of the Brāhmanas was challenged by men belonging to the other classes. With the decline of Buddhism, however, the ascendancy of the Brāhmanas became complete. But though in these latter days the Brāhmanas gained an unassailable position as religious and social leaders, they lost the political influence they once possessed as an organised community. Individual Brāhmanas continued to fill high offices in the State, but as a body they never again became a factor of any great importance in the administration of the country.

A few words may be said here in regard to a system connected with the caste-system. This was the Āsrama-dharma. Under this system there were four stages in the life of every person belonging to the three higher grades, namely, student (Brahmacārin), householder (Gṛihastha), hermit (Vānaprastha), and ascetic (Parivrājaka).[1] This system undoubtedly tended to promote the efficiency of society, but it was not free from practical difficulties; and it does not seem that the rules laid down in regard to this institution were ever very strictly observed.

We now pass on to the second important feature of early Indian society—the family. Man is a

[1] The duties of the different orders are described in detail in the Dharma-sūtras and Dharma-sāstras. Kautilya also devotes some space to the subject.

gregarious animal, and in the very earliest stages of social evolution, the family—and not the individual —was the unit of society.[1] From this starting-point social progress seems to have taken place concurrently in two distinct—and, in fact, opposite—directions. One movement led to the formation of larger and still larger associations, such as the clan, the tribe, and the village, culminating in the State. The other movement consisted in the gradual emancipation of the component parts of the family, thus giving rise to the individual. And this, we may take it, was what happened in India as in other countries.

From very early times, the reverence for family ties was firmly established and held sacred in India. The family was like a small communistic society, bound together by the tie of natural affection, holding in joint possession the means of production, and enjoying the fruit of labour in common.[2] All acquisitions were joint property, and all expenses were paid out of the common fund. The Joint Family was, in fact, very similar to the *societas universorum bonorum* of the Romans. The father was the head and protector of the family. But just as the dependent members owed their duties to the father, so

[1] Some sociologists hold that the tribe was the earliest type of social aggregation, and that the family was a later development. But this view does not seem to be quite correct.

[2] Kautilya says, "With the exception of the sleeping rooms, all parts of the house shall be open to all members of the family." Arthaśāstra, Bk. III. ch. 8.

the father was bound by obligations to the rest of the family. Unlike the Roman paterfamilias, the father of the Indian family had no powers of life and death over the subordinate members. The family was not his property. Every individual member of the family had a locus standi in the law-courts and the other departments of the State; and the government could, if it thought fit, deal direct with every member of the family without the intervention of the head. As regards the family property, the father was the manager, rather than the owner, of it. The family collectively was the owner, and the father had powers to deal with it only as the representative of the family; but even here his powers were not unlimited.

The members of the family were the father, the mother, sons, daughters, daughters-in-law, brothers, sisters, and other dependent relations. Slavery, such as existed in olden times in other parts of the world, was unknown in India. Megasthenes emphatically asserts, "None of the Indians employ slaves."[1] And, again, he says, "All Indians are free, and not one of them is a slave. The Lakedaemonians and the Indians are so far in agreement. The Lakedaemonians, however, hold the Helots as slaves, and these Helots do servile labour; but the Indians do not even use aliens as slaves, and much less a countryman of their own."[2] This was perfectly true,

[1] Fragment XXVII. Also Fragment XLI. [2] Fragment XXVI.

and yet there existed in Ancient India a class of persons who were not completely free. This class was known as the Dāsas. The word 'Dāsa' is a variant of the word 'Dasyu,' and, originally, the Dāsas consisted of the non-Āryans who were captured in war.[1] To this class were afterwards added the issue of Dāsas and those who were deprived of their freedom as a judicial punishment. The number of Dāsas was never very large, and no Ārya could be a Dāsa.[2] Trading in Dāsas was prohibited,[3] and any Dāsa could purchase his freedom by paying a reasonable price.[4] The Dāsas were members of the family of their masters, and their condition was very different from that of the slaves in ancient Rome. In Roman law, a slave was nothing better than the chattel of his owner, and the penalty for the killing of a slave was the same as that for killing a four-footed beast. In India, on the other hand, a Dāsa had the protection of the courts, and any ill-treatment of a Dāsa was visited with severe punishment.[5] Moreover, the emancipation of a Dāsa was always considered as a virtuous act, which produced the happy result that

[1] Manu mentions seven different classes of Dāsas. VIII. 415.

[2] Arthasāstra, Bk. III. ch. 13. [3] Ibid.

[4] Kautilya prescribes a heavy fine for any person who refuses to emancipate his Dāsa on the latter offering the ransom-money. Bk. III. ch. 13. Manu, on the other hand, is, like Aristotle, a believer in the doctrine of natural slavery. "A Sūdra," says he, "though emancipated by his master, is not released; since that is innate in him, who can free him from it?" VIII. 414.

[5] Arthasāstra, Bk. III. ch. 3.

the institution died out in India at an early period, and Hindu society was rid of an evil which continued to disfigure other civilised societies for a much longer time and in a much more degraded form.

The third important feature of the early Indian society was the village system. The village was in ancient times—as it is still to some extent—the basis of the social structure of the country. A village was an aggregation of families, and was composed of various classes following divers occupations. The bond, which united the villagers together, were some or all of the following: common blood, common property, common production and distribution, common institutions, or merely common interest. The villagers did not necessarily trace their lineage from a common ancestor, and, very often, the connections of the villagers outstripped the limits of the village. The village lands were held in private ownership, but pastures, plains, and forests were enjoyed in common. Transfers of property to outsiders were permitted, but only with the consent, explicit or implied, of the villagers.[1] All fines went to the common fund of the village, and every person was bound to co-operate in all works tending to the common benefit of the villagers and in the getting up of public amusements. The village thus had a sort of corporate life in the times of Manu and

[1] Arthaśāstra, Bk III. ch. 9. Relatives, neighbours, and creditors had the right of pre-emption in respect of lands which were to be sold. Ibid.

Chānakya, but it seems that it was not until a much later date that village communities, such as they existed at the time of the rise of the British power, came into existence.

CHAPTER III

THE TERRITORY OF THE STATE

In the last chapter we discussed the social environment of the State; in the present chapter we shall briefly describe its physical surroundings.

Territory is the material basis of the State, and its importance was fully understood in Ancient India. Chānakya discusses in full the excellent qualities of a territory. In his opinion a territory should be extensive; self-supporting; capable of supporting outsiders (besides inhabitants) in times of distress; capable of defending itself and of repelling enemies; powerful enough to guard itself against neighbouring kings; free from rocky, marshy, desert, and uneven tracts; devoid of robbers, wild beasts, and jungles; beautiful; containing fertile fields, mines, valuable products, elephant forests, and pasture lands; strong; containing hidden passages; full of cattle; not dependent upon natural rainfall for the supply of water; possessed of land-routes as well as waterways; rich in many kinds of commercial products; capable of bearing the burden of taxation; inhabited by industrious agriculturists; full of children and of persons belonging to the inferior orders; having a loyal and honest population.[1] So also Manu says, "Let him (the King) settle in a country which is open and has a dry climate, where grain is abundant, which is chiefly (inhabited) by Āryas, not subject to epidemic diseases (or similar troubles), and pleasant, where the vassals are obedient and his own (people easily) find their livelihood."[2]

The chief points which are important in considering the relation of a territory to the State are its size, climate, and nature of the soil. These three constitute what may be called the natural environment of a State, and it will not perhaps be out of place to say a few words here in regard to each of them. Throughout the long period of Indian history the size of the territory of a State varied with the circumstances. Some Kings ruled over only a few square miles of territory, while others controlled extensive empires. When the Āryas first settled in the Punjab, each tribe occupied a small extent of territory. The nature of the country, intersected as it was by large rivers and mountain spurs, favoured the establishment of a large number of separate and independent communities. But with the growth of the national forces, the size of the territory tended to grow. The extent of territory had also an important bearing on the constitution of the govern-

[1] Arthasāstra, Bk. I. ch. 6. [2] VII. 69.

ment. So long as the territory was small, the form of administration was more or less democratic; but as the size of the territory grew large, it was found necessary to adopt a system in which political powers were concentrated in the hands of the Head of the State assisted by a Council of Ministers and a trained bureaucracy. The strength of a large State became manifest to the people when they saw how easily Chandragupta, with his vast resources, succeeded in inflicting a defeat on Seleukos Nikator, as contrasted with the ease with which Alexander had only a few years before devastated and conquered the small States of the Punjab.

But as extensive territories have their obvious advantages, they have their drawbacks. In the hands of a weak ruler, great size makes the State cumbrous and helpless, and is a source of impotence rather than of strength. Readers of Indian history know that a large territory could be controlled only by an Asoka or a Vikramāditya, and that as soon as the guiding hand of the strong and capable ruler was withdrawn, the fabric of the large State always fell into pieces.

Climate and the nature of the soil determine in a very large measure the prosperity or adversity of a country as well as the physical and moral characteristics of its people. The effects produced by these factors in the ancient Punjab are thus described by Megasthenes:

"The inhabitants having abundant means of subsistence exceed in consequence the ordinary stature, and are distinguished by their proud bearing. They are also found to be well skilled in the arts, as might be expected of men who inhale a pure air and drink the very finest water. And while the soil bears on its surface all kinds of fruits which are known to cultivation, it has also underground numerous veins of all sorts of metals, for it contains much gold and silver, and copper and iron in no small quantity, and even tin and other metals, which are employed in making articles of use and ornament, as well as the implements and accoutrements of war. . . . In addition to cereals, there grows throughout India much millet, which is kept well watered by the profusion of river-streams, and much pulse of different sorts, and rice also, and what is called bosphorum, as well as many other plants useful for food, of which most grow spontaneously. . . . It is accordingly affirmed that famine has never visited India, and that there has never been a great scarcity in the supply of nourishing food."

We thus find that the ample material resources yielded by the land in the shape of crops and minerals enabled the people to develop a healthy civilisation. The rigour of the climate of the Punjab, combined with the moderately fertile quality of the soil, made the early settlers a race of valiant warriors and industrious agriculturists, and fostered the growth of a strong and manly population. But as the Āryas spread to the other parts of India, they met with a climate which was exceedingly mild and a soil which yielded rich harvests without requiring much labour; and these facts, while, on the one hand, they favoured intellectual activity, on the other, disposed the people to indolence and love of ease.

CHAPTER IV

ORIGIN AND NATURE OF THE STATE

PHILOSOPHERS in all ages and of all countries have loved to speculate on the origin of the State, and it would be a matter for surprise if we were told that the Āryan sages of India did not exercise their imagination on so inviting a subject. As a matter of fact, however, we know that Indian philosophers did devote some attention to this matter, and that although their speculations were not elaborated with the same minuteness of detail as those of some of the European theorists, they would not perhaps be entirely devoid of interest to the student of political philosophy.

The origin of the State has been thus described in the Mahābhārata :

In the early years of the Krita Yuga, there was no sovereignty, no king, no government, no ruler. All men used to protect one another righteously. After some time, however, they found the task of righteously protecting each other painful. Error began to assail their hearts. Having become subject to error, the perceptions of men became clouded, and, as a consequence, their virtues began to decline. Love of acquisition got hold of them, and they became covetous. When they had become subject to covetousness, another passion, namely wrath, soon possessed their minds. Once subject to wrath, they lost all consideration of what ought to be done and what should be avoided. Thus, unrestrained license set in. Men began to do what they liked and to utter what they chose. All distinctions between virtue and vice came to an end. When such confusion possessed the souls of men, the knowledge of the Supreme Being disappeared, and with the disappearance of the highest knowledge, righteousness was utterly lost. The gods were then overcome with grief and fear, and approached Brahmā for protection and advice. Brahmā then created by a fiat of his will a son named Virajas. This son, born of the energy of Brahmā, was made the ruler of the world.[1]

This imaginary picture of the ante-political condition of man and of the circumstances which necessitated a State organisation, appears to us as specially interesting when we remember that similar pictures have also been drawn by European thinkers of a later age.[2] Besides, this description of the birth of

[1] Mahābhārata, Sānti Parva (Rājadharma P.), Sec. 59.

[2] Cf. Milton's view as expressed in his Tenure of Kings and Magistrates, where he says that all men were born free, that wrong sprang up through Adam's sin, and that to avert their own complete destruction, men agreed

the State, fanciful as it is, embodies the belief which many people had, and still have, in the divine origin of the State. The State, according to this theory, is neither a voluntary association of men nor the natural result of the workings of human instinct and reason, but is a thing imposed upon human beings for their general good by a power superior to their own. It is "the immediate work of God." Manu is another exponent of the belief in the divine origin of the State. He says, "When these creatures, being without a King, through fear dispersed in all directions, the Lord created a King for the protection of the whole creation."[1] But the view of the less

"by common league to bind each other from mutual injury and jointly to defend themselves against any that gave disturbance to such agreement."

Cf. also Locke, who regards the state of nature as "a state of perfect freedom to order their actions, and dispose of their possessions and persons as they think fit, within the bounds of the law of Nature." Two Treatises of Government, Bk. II. ch. 2.

In the opinion of Hobbes, "The Finall Cause, End, or Designe of men (who naturally love Liberty and Dominion over others), in the introduction of the restraint upon themselves (in which we see them live in Commonwealths), is the foresight of their own preservation, and of a more contented life thereby; that is to say, of getting themselves out from that miserable condition of Warre, which is necessarily consequent to the naturall Passions of men, when there is no visible Power to keep them in awe, and tye them by feare of punishment to the performance of their covenants, and observation of those Laws of Nature . . ." Leviathan, Ch. XVII.

The circumstances which impelled individuals to organise themselves into the State are thus described by Rousseau: "I assume that men have reached a point at which the obstacles that endanger their preservation in the state of nature overcome by their resistance the forces which the individuals can cast with a view to maintaining himself in that state. Then this primitive condition can no longer subsist, and the human race would perish unless it changed its mode of existence." Social Contract, Bk. I. ch. 6.

[1] Manu, Ch. VII. sl. 3.

spiritually-minded, but more practical, Chānakya is different. He is a believer in the human creation of the State. "When the weak," says he, "began to be oppressed by the strong, the people made Vaivasvata Manu their King, and fixed one-sixth of the produce of the soil and one-tenth of merchandise as his remuneration."[1] Chānakya adds: "In the absence of a government people behave like fish, the strong devouring the weak, but protected by a government, they flourish."[2]

Divergent as are the views of the two schools in some of the most essential particulars, there are two points on which they agree. Both schools hold (i) that the State had its origin in necessity, and (ii) that the object of its establishment was the common weal.[3]

Speculation, however, is not of much help to us in ascertaining the origin of the State. Neither does our present knowledge of history assist us in any considerable degree in this matter. Perhaps the ultimate origin of the State in India, as elsewhere,

[1] "Matsyanyāyābhibhūtāḥ prajā Manuṁ Vaivasvataṁ rājānaṁ cakrire." Arthasāstra, Bk. I. ch. 13. The Vāyu Purāna, on the other hand, says, "After the Manvantara, (Brahmā), with the concurrence of the Gods, bestowed the Kingship of the world on the great Vaivasvata." Ch. XXIII. sl. 1.

[2] This view is favoured in the Buddhist religious books. Vide the story in the Tibetan Dulva about the origin of the Kingship.

[3] Cf. Aristotle's famous lines: "If all communities aim at some good, the State or political community, which is the highest of all, and which embraces all the rest, aims, and, in a greater degree than any other, at the highest good." Politics, Bk. I.

is to be found in human nature. History, although unable to trace the origin of the State, gives us considerable aid in following its development. It tells us that men lived in India, as in most other countries, in some form or other of organised society from very early times. We know as yet very little of the condition of the pre-Āryan races of India, but the little knowledge that we do possess enables us to assert that some at least of these early inhabitants not only lived an organised political life, but even developed a fairly efficient system of public administration. It was, however, at the hands of the Āryans that the Indian State seems to have received its full development. The primitive Āryan State was perhaps based upon the family. It is probable that the family in the process of evolution grew into the clan, the clan expanded into the tribe, and finally, the tribe was absorbed in the State. The head of the family became the chief of the clan, then the leader of the tribe, and ultimately the ruler of the State. Although, however, the beginnings of the Indian State were connected with the family, the clan, and the tribe, the purely political idea gradually became more and more clear and dominant, with the result that in the course of time the State outgrew its original limitations, and became national. We do not know for certain at what period of time the patriarchal and tribal stages were passed in India, but the opinion may be hazarded that the national

State had become firmly established in most parts of India many centuries before the commencement of the Buddhist period.

We now pass on to a consideration of the nature of the State as it existed in the Hindu period of Indian history. This may be considered under five heads, namely, (1) the character of the State as an institution, (2) the sphere of State-action, (3) the extent of the power of the State, (4) the differentiation of functions in the State organisation, and (5) the rights of individuals in the State.

In many ancient countries the State, in the earlier stages of its development, was theocratic; but in India, although the social organisation contained within its bosom the Brahmanic theocracy and was to a large extent dominated by it, the State itself never became a theocracy in the proper sense of the term. This becomes evident when we consider a few broad facts. First, the ruler was never regarded as the head of religion. Secondly, the primary object of the State was not spiritual salvation, but social well-being. Thirdly, law, mingled as it was with religion and morality, was the chief source of the authority of the State. And lastly, the political status of individuals was independent of their religious beliefs and convictions.

The sphere of State-action was in the earliest period very limited. The State was then, in fact, what political scientists term a 'Police-State.' Security against foreign invasions and the maintenance of internal order summed up the activities of the State. The first step towards a higher type seems to have been taken when the State assumed the administration of justice. And as society became more complex with the progress of civilisation the sphere of State-activity tended gradually to extend, until about the sixth or fifth century A.D. it embraced almost the entire life of the people. Under the Emperor Asoka the State closely approximated to the highest type of a Culture-State, its aim being to secure the maximum well-being of the people in every department of life.

During the period of the extension of the sphere of State-activity, the power of the State also tended to grow, but State-sovereignty in India never became quite absolute. The conception of political sovereignty as "independent, indivisible, perpetual, inalienable power" was never developed here to the same extent as in Ancient Greece or in Modern Europe.

As for the differentiation of functions, we find that during the earlier stages of political growth, the same persons exercised various powers. But with the growth of the sphere of State-action and the increase of the authority of the State, it was found necessary to separate the different kinds of functions; and, as time went on, this separation was carried further and further, until in the fully-developed State it was as complete as it reasonably could be.

The great drawback of the State in Ancient India was that the rights of man as man were not fully recognised. Individuals had rights and duties not as component parts of the body politic but as members of estates or classes in society; and consequently, as we have already seen in a previous chapter, the rights and obligations varied according to the class to which the individuals belonged.

CHAPTER V

THE SYSTEM OF GOVERNMENT

As we saw in the last chapter,[1] during the Vedic and Brahmanic periods the country was divided into a large number of independent States, some of them exceedingly small, others of a moderate bulk, but none having any considerable size. The systems of Government which prevailed in those States differed from one another in many respects. Some of them were governed by Princes, while others were Oligarchies or Republics. The Vedic literature contains references to non-monarchical forms of government.[2] In the Mahābhārata also we find mention of kingless

[1] In the Aitareya Brāhmana occur the terms 'Svarājya' and 'Vairājya,' which Mr. K. P. Jayasval translates as 'self-governing country' and 'kingless State.' From the context, however, the right meanings appear to be 'independent kingdom' and 'extensive kingdom.' The terms 'Virāj' and 'Svarāj' occur in Brihaddevatā, VIII. 107, but there the meaning is not very clear.

[2] Prof. Macdonell says: "It is quite clear that the normal, though not universal, form of government in early India was by Kings, as might be expected in view of the fact that the Āryan Indians were invaders in a hostile territory: a situation which, as in the case of the Āryan invaders of Greece and of the German invaders of England, resulted almost necessarily in strengthening the monarchic element of the constitution." Vedic Index, Vol. II. p. 210.

states. The Vrishnis, for instance, formed an Oligarchy ruled by many chiefs, of whom Krishna was one.[1] In fact, almost all the Indian nations of these times possessed popular institutions of some type or other.[2]

At the time of the rise of Buddhism, there were a number of independent tribes, living either under the republican or the oligarchic system of government.[3] In the Republics, the affairs of State were discussed and decided in the tribal assemblies, and the executive power was in the hands of the leaders (mukhyas), who also acted as commanders in war. In regard to the system of government prevailing among the Sākiyas, Prof. Rhys Davids, one of the greatest Buddhist scholars of modern times, says: "The administrative and judicial business of the clan was carried out in public assembly, at which young and old were alike present in their common Mote Hall (Sanghāgāra) at Kapilavastu.[4] A single chief—how

[1] It is interesting to note that while Krishna, one of the great leaders of this clan, was with the Pāndavas in the Great War, the clan as a body fought on the side of the Kurus.

[2] Zimmer sees traces in one passage of the Rig-Veda that in times of peace there was no King in some States, the members of the royal family holding equal rights. Macdonell's Vedic Index, II. p. 216.

[3] Prof. Rhys Davids says: "The earliest Buddhist records reveal the survival, side by side with more or less powerful monarchies, of republics with either complete or modified independence." Buddhist India.

[4] Prof. Rhys Davids adds: "It was at such a parliament, or palaver, that King Pasenadi's proposition [i.e. the request for a bride from the Sākiya clan] was discussed. When Ambattha goes to Kapilavastu on business, he goes to the Mote Hall, where the Sākiyas were then in session. And it is to the Mote Hall of the Mallas that Ānanda goes to announce the death of the Buddha." Buddhist India, p. 9.

and for what period chosen we do not know—was elected an office-holder, presiding over the sessions, and if no sessions were sitting, over the State. He bore the title of Rājā, which must have meant something like the Roman Consul, or the Greek Archon." [1] In an Oligarchy, the conduct of the administration was in the hands of the members of the ruling family.[2] The most striking instance of an Oligarchy was that of the Lichchavis, whose chiefs were all called 'Rājās.'[3] The free Lichchavi clans were very powerful, and they played an important part in the social and political life of India in the sixth century B.C., and for many centuries afterwards.[4]

Even as late as the date of Alexander's invasion many of the nations of the Punjab lived under democratic institutions. The Ambashthas (Sambastai), for instance, "were a people inferior to none for numbers or for bravery. They dwelt in cities in which the democratic form of government prevailed." [5] Curtius mentions a tribe called Sabarcae, "a powerful Indian tribe where the form of Government was democratic, and not regal." [6] The Kathanians, the Oxydrakai,

[1] Buddhist India, p. 9.

[2] "Kulasya vā bhaved rājyam." Arthasāstra, Bk. I. ch. 17.

[3] Arthasāstra, Bk. XI. ch. 1. In the Buddhist books we are told that there were 7707 chiefs of the Lichchavis, all of whom were called 'Rājās.'

[4] The chief clans at the time of the rise of Buddhism were: (1) Lichchavis, (2) Sākiyas, (3) Bhaggas of Sumsumāra Hill, (4) Bulis of Allakappa, (5) Kālāmas of Kesaputta, (6) Koliyas of Rāmagāma, (7) Mallas of Pāvā, (8) Mallas of Kusinārā, (9) Moriyas of Pippalīvana, (10) Videhas of Mithilā.

[5] Ancient India, Alexander's Invasion (McCrindle), p. 292. [6] Ibid.

the Adraistai, and the Malloi, who offered stout resistance to the advance of Alexander, also lived under a democratic form of government. When the Malloi tendered their submission to Alexander, they told him that "they were attached more than any others to freedom and autonomy, and that their freedom they had preserved intact from the time Dionysos came to India until Alexander's invasion."[1]

Some of the other nations had an aristocratic form of government with a President at the head of the administration. At the city of Nysa, the administration was in the hands of three hundred wise men. When Alexander requested the Nysians to send with him one hundred men from their governing body, their President replied: "How, O King! can a single city, if deprived of a hundred of its best men, continue to be well-governed?"[2] It was reported to Alexander that "the country beyond the Hyphasis was exceedingly fertile, and that the inhabitants were good agriculturists and lived under an excellent system of internal government, for the multitude are governed by the aristocracy who exercised their authority with justice and moderation."[3]

In other States, there was a King who was assisted by an assembly of elders or 'heads' of families. Diodoros speaks of a Patala as "a city of great note, with a political constitution drawn on the same lines

[1] Arrian, Anabasis (McCrindle), p. 154.

[2] Ancient India (McCrindle), p. 81.

[3] Ibid.

as the Spartan; for in this community the command in war vested in two hereditary Kings of two different houses, while a Council of elders ruled the whole State with paramount authority."

Chānakya also mentions many powerful oligarchies. From him we know that the Lichchivikas, Vrijjikas, Mallakas, Madrakas, Kukuras, Kurus, and Pānchālas were ruling oligarchies,[1] while the Kshatriya clans of the Kāmbojas and Surāshtras were engaged in agriculture, industry, and the profession of arms.[2]

But although the non-monarchical forms of government existed down to the fourth century A.D.,[3] many forces had been at work for several centuries past to make monarchy the prevailing form of administration in the country.[4] The most important of these factors was a great increase in the size of the State. As the Āryas moved eastward from the Punjab, the territory of the State tended steadily to grow. Now,

[1] "Rājaśabdopajīvinah." Arthasāstra, Bk. XI. ch. 1.

[2] Ibid. It is not very clear whether the second generation of the Nandas, consisting of eight kings, ruled as a family oligarchy, or reigned in succession. In Mudrā-Rākshasa, the great family (vipula kula) of the Nandas is compared to the clan of the Vrishnis. Act II.

[3] In a few parts of the country, these institutions lasted till the third or fourth centuries of the Christian Era, but in these later days they never played any important part in Indian history. In the Mandasor Inscription of Kumāragupta and Bandhuvarman (sixth century A.D.), the Mālavas are referred to as living under a republican form of government (Mālavānāṁ gaṇasthityā).

[4] The Sukranīti, at a comparatively recent date, says: "There should be only one head in the State, not many. Nor should a State ever be without a head." This idea must have grown up several centuries before the Christian Era.

it must have been found very difficult to manage the affairs of large kingdoms by means of popular institutions at a time when the representative system had not yet been invented.[1] Popular freedom had thus gradually to give way before the advance of the imperial idea. And when the success of Alexander's invasion made manifest the weakness of a system of small independent States, the people probably welcomed, or at least submitted to, Chandragupta's attempt to establish a centralised imperial government. Chandragupta had thus comparatively little difficulty in absorbing within the empire of Magadha all the States of Northern India, and this establishment of an imperial rule meant the sweeping away of all the free institutions of the country. In the words of the historian, Chandragupta "changed the name of freedom to that of bondage, for he himself oppressed with servitude the very people he had rescued from foreign dominion."[2]

Chandragupta was not the first monarch to aspire to the title of 'Samrāt' or 'King of Kings.' The people for many centuries previously had been familiar with the Chakravarti or Suzerain idea. The later Vedic literature abounds with references to paramount

[1] One of the chief causes of the substitution of the monarchical for the republican form of government in Rome was the great increase in the size of the territory governed from Rome.

[2] Justin, XV. 4 (McCrindle). It is a curious coincidence that the small States of Northern India were absorbed in the Magadhan Empire about the same time that the Macedonian Empire destroyed the independence of the City States of Ancient Greece.

rulers (Adhirāja, Samrāt, Sārvabhauma, etc.). The Aitareya Brāhmana and the Satapatha Brāhmana give detailed descriptions of the ceremonies that were to be performed by paramount sovereigns. According to tradition Trasadasyu, the grandson of Kutsa of Vedic fame, was the first to assume the title of Emperor, and Bharata was the first monarch to bring the whole country under the influence of Āryan civilisation. In the Mahābhārata we read of Jarāsandha's ambition to become a paramount sovereign, of his defeat by the Pāndavas, of Yudhishthira's Digvijaya (conquest of all the quarters) and assumption of the imperial title. It should be remembered however, that what these powerful monarchs of old aimed at was the establishment, not of an imperial rule, but of a sort of nominal supremacy over the other Kings. And one chief object of these endeavours was to bring a large part of India together by binding the Kings in a sort of alliance for offensive and defensive purposes with the strongest among them as the nominal suzerain. Ajātasatru and Mahāpadma Nanda endeavoured to bring large tracts of country under their rule, but it was Chandragupta who for the first time succeeded in bringing under one direct authority the entire country from Afghanistan to the Bay of Bengal, and from the Himālayas to beyond the Vindhya mountains. For a thousand years after the establishment of Chandragupta's supremacy, India witnessed a continual struggle for imperial suzerainty made in different parts of the country and attended with varying degrees of success.

The control of this imperial system of course necessitated the use of a complex machinery of administration. Such a machinery was invented and brought into use by Chandragupta with the help of his Prime Minister, Chānakya, and afterwards improved upon by Asoka. Under this system, the home province was under the control of the central executive, while the distant provinces were administered by Viceroys or Governors sent out from the capital. In Asoka's time there were four or five such provinces besides Magadha which formed the home province. The provinces were divided into districts and sub-districts with suitable officials in charge of them. Chānakya mentions 'gopas' and 'sthānikas' as the country officials. In Asoka's edicts occur the terms 'mahāmātras,' 'prādeśikas,' and 'rājūkas.' In some of the later inscriptions we find mention of 'maṇḍaleśvaras,' 'rāja-sthānīyas,' 'uparikas,' and 'vishayapatis.' Besides these officers, there were 'antaḥpālas,' or wardens of the marches, to guard the boundaries of the kingdom.

A constant touch was kept up with the distant provinces by means of a regular system of correspondence, and also with the assistance of a class of inspecting officers or 'overseers,' whose duty it was to watch all that occurred and to make reports to the Central Government. Portions of the Empire were, it seems, ruled by local Rājās [1] who enjoyed varying degrees of independence. Some of them only owed a nominal allegiance to the Suzerain Power. There were others who paid the annual tribute and were liable to be called upon to assist in case of a war with foreign Powers, but were practically independent of control so far as their internal affairs were concerned. The administration of the less important Princes was probably subject to some sort of supervision by the imperial government.

The system of government may be described as a limited monarchy. There were various checks on the authority of the monarch. The King had to abide by the law as laid down in the Sāstras or embodied in the customs of the country. In the practical work of administration he was guided by his ministers, who occupied an important position in society and wielded the real power in the State.[2] Then, there was the influence of the learned Brāhmanas as a class, who were looked upon by the people as the natural guardians of society. With these checks operating on the governmental system it was very difficult for a king to have his own way in the administration of the country. Occasionally, under a strong and capable ruler like Asoka or Harshavardhana, the government might resemble a paternal

[1] Chānakya advises conquerors to place a scion of the royal family on the throne of a conquered country, and to leave the internal administration in his hands.

[2] Vide Arthasāstra, Bk. I. ch. 7; also Bk. I. ch. 9

despotism,[1] but it was very rarely that the power of the King was quite absolute.[2] The Sāstras he regarded as embodying a sort of political constitution as well as ethical law, and the ancient system of government may thus be called a constitutional monarchy. It must, however, be remembered that the devices by which the monarch's authority was kept within proper limits were more moral than political. The most suitable term which can be used to describe the system appears in our opinion to be 'Sachivatantra.'[3] The different parts of the governmental machinery of this system will be described in some detail in the next few chapters.

The efficiency of administration, of course, varied in the different States and at different times. As might be expected, under good kings and capable ministers a high standard of success was attained, while incompetent administrators not unoften found it difficult to maintain peace and security in the land and brought trouble and misery to the people. On the whole, however, it seems that the administration was efficient. It was founded, as the Chinese traveller,

[1] In the Kalinga Rock Edict Asoka says: "All men are my children, and just as I desire for my children that they enjoy every kind of prosperity and happiness in both this world and the next, so also I desire the same for all men."

[2] Vide Sukranīti, Ch. II. sl. 4.

[3] The term 'sachivāyatta-tantra,' that is to say, a form of government in which real power exists in the hands of the Ministers, is found in Mudrā-Rākshasa. Under favourable conditions, such a government answered to Aristotle's description of an aristocracy, that is to say, government by the wisest.

Hiuen Tsiang, noticed, "on benign principles"; and the results of good government were to be seen in the happiness and prosperity of the people, the growth of literature, arts, and sciences, and the development of a high order of civilisation.

A few words may here be said about a form of government which came into existence towards the end of the Hindu period of Indian history. This system prevailed among the Rajputs, and was preeminently a martial system. It had some analogies with the Feudal Monarchy of Europe in the Middle Ages. How it came into existence we do not exactly know, but it seems that during the turmoil of the eighth and ninth centuries A.D., the Rajput clans made themselves masters of some parts of the country. The leader of the clan became the owner of the conquered land, and divided it among his followers as a reward for military services. All vassals held land from the Prince on condition of military service and fidelity. The chief vassals formed the Great Council of the King, and were summoned on important occasions, generally for military purposes. The Prince, with the aid of his Civil Council and the Ministers of the Crown, conducted the central administration and promulgated all legislative enactments which affected the rights and interests of the entire community. In the Crown Demesnes justice was administered by Chabootaras (Terraces of Justice). Local Government was in the hands of the chiefs, who were assisted by their domestic councils composed of the greater sub-vassals, the Pradhān (Premier), the Mayor of the household, the priest, the bard, and two or three of the most intelligent citizens. The chiefs administered their own justice, and in the internal administration of the chiefs' estates, the government officers seldom interfered. Besides, each town and village had its own council or chotia elected by the citizens, who helped the Nagarseth (City Magistrate) and the village headman in the discharge of their local duties.[1]

[1] Vide Tod's Rajasthan, Vol. I. In regard to the merits and defects of the system, Col. Tod says: "It is a system full of defects; yet we see them so often balanced by virtues, that we are alternately biassed by these counter-acting qualities; loyalty and patriotism, which combine a love of the institutions, religion, and manners of the country, are the counterpoise to systematic evil. In no country has the system ever proved efficient." Vol. I. p. 148 (first edition).

CHAPTER VI

POLITICAL DIVISIONS

FROM very early times down to the fourth century B.C., the country was divided into a large number of independent States—Kingdoms, Oligarchies, or Republics. In the Vedic Age, there was a large number of tribes who inhabited the Punjab. The most important of these tribes were the Pūrus, the Yadus, the Turvasas, the Druhyus, and the Anus.[1] As the Āryans advanced eastward and southward the number of Āryan States steadily increased, either by the establishment of new administrations or by the re-modelling of the pre-Āryan governments then existing.

In the Brahmanic period, the chief nations were the Kurus, the Pānchālas, the Kosalas, the Kāsis, and the Videhas. The Kurus and the Pānchālas were so intimately connected with each other that they practically formed one nation. The Kosalas, the Kāsis,

[1] Mahābhārata, Ādi (Sambhava) Parva, Sec. 82. It is not exactly known whether all these tribes were Āryan, or some of them were composed of mixed races.

and the Videhas formed a sort of confederacy, and their relations with the Kuru-Pānchāla peoples perhaps were not always very friendly. The Kuru-Pānchālas occupied the middle country (madhya-deśa), while the other three nations occupied the country to the east.[1]

The Pāli Pitakas mention sixteen great countries (Mahā-janapadāḥ). In the sixth century B.C. they were:

(1) Anga, near modern Bhagalpur, with capital Champā;

(2) Magadha, or South Behar, with capital at Rājagriha and afterwards at Pātaliputra;

(3) Kāsi, with capital at Kāsī, modern Benares;

(4) Kosala, with capital at Srāvastī on the borders of Nepal;

(5) Vrijji, the country of the Vajjians, who were composed of eight confederate clans, of whom the Lichchavis and the Videhas were the most powerful. The capital of the Videhas was Mithilā, and that of the Lichchavis, Vaisalī;

(6) The country of the Mallas, who were divided into two independent clans, and whose territory was on the mountain slopes to the east of the Sākiya land;

[1] Cf. Macdonell's Vedic Index, I. p. 154.

Pancha-janah, the five peoples, are mentioned under various names in Vedic literature. Who are meant by the five is very uncertain. According to Zimmer, the five tribes of the Anus, Druhyus, Yadus, Turvasas, and Pūrus are meant, and Macdonell seems to incline to this view. In the Brihad-Devatā, several different meanings of the term are given.

(7) Cheti, the country of the Chedis, who perhaps had two distinct settlements, one in Nepal and the other to the east or south-east of Kosambī;

(8) Vatsa or Vamsa, of which Kosambī was the capital. It lay north of Avantī and along the banks of the Jumna;

(9) The country of the Kurus, with its capital at Indraprastha, near modern Delhi;

(10) The country of the two Pānchālas, to the east of the land of the Kurus, with capitals at Kāmpilya and Kanauj;

(11) The Matsya country, to the south of the Kurus and west of the Jumna;

(12) The country of the Surasenas, with its capital at Mathurā, to the south-west of the Matsya country and west of the Jumna;

(13) The country of the Arsakas, on the banks of the Godāvarī, with its capital at Potana or Potali;

(14) Avantī, afterwards called Mālava, with its capital, Ujjayinī;

(15) Gandhāra (modern Kandahar), including Eastern Afghanistan and North-western Punjab, with its capital, Taksha-silā;

(16) Kāmboja, the country near modern Sindh, with its capital at Dvārakā.[1]

This list is not at all exhaustive. The whole of South India is ignored, and so also the greater part

[1] Vide Vinaya Texts, VII. 1, 1, footnote, and Rhys Davids, Buddhist India.

of the Punjab. Of the States mentioned in Buddhist books, Kosala was at first the paramount power, but its glory sank as Magadha rose into prominence, and at last it became subject to the latter.

Our knowledge of the political divisions of India in the fourth century B.C. is derived from the Greek accounts. These accounts inform us that, at the time of Alexander's invasion, the Punjab was occupied by a large number of independent nations, the most important of whom were called by the Greeks the Assakenoi, the Glausai, the Kathaioi, the Oxydrakai, and the Malloi. Besides these, there were two large kingdoms ruled over by Ambhi and Poros respectively. To the east were situated the countries of the Mandei, the Malli, the Modogalingae, the Modobae, the Molindae, the Colubae, and others. The Saurasenas were an important nation and possessed two large cities, Methora and Cleisobora. The region of the Ganges was inhabited by two powerful nations, the Prasii and the Gangaridae.[1] "The Prasii," says Megasthenes, "surpass in power and glory every other people, not only in this quarter, but one may say in all India."[2] The Calingae (the three Kalingas) were also a powerful race, who had their capital at Parthalis. To the south, the most important country was that of the Āndhras, a powerful race which possessed numerous villages, and thirty towns defended by walls and towers.

[1] Alexander's Invasion (McCrindle).

[2] Megasthenes, Fragment LVI.

The greater part of the peninsula of Gujrat was occupied by the Saurāshtras, who had some fine cities. Near the extreme south were the Pāndyas, "a race ruled by women."[1] Besides these, there were the aboriginal tribes who lived chiefly on the hills.

In the Rāmāyana, Dasaratha, speaking of the extent of his sway, mentions the following States :

> "Mine are the tribes in eastern lands
> And those who dwell on Sindhu's sands.
> Mine is Surashtra far away,
> Sauvira's realm admits my sway ;
> My hest the southern nations fear,
> The Angas and the Vangas hear.
> And as lord paramount I reign
> O'er Magadh and the Matsya's plain,
> Kosal and Kasis' wide domain
> All rich in treasures of the mine
> In golden corn, sheep, goats, and kine."[2]

The Mahābhārata gives a long list of over two hundred names of nations and tribes who dwelt in India or in countries bordering on it.[3] In the Vishnu-purāna we find the following list of the important nations inhabiting Bhārata-varsha : "The Kurus and the Pānchālas in the middle district ; the people of Kāmarūpa in the east ; the Pundras, the Kalingas, the Magadhas, and the southern nations in the south ; in the extreme west the Saurāshtras, the Sūras, the

[1] Megasthenes, Fragment LVI.
[2] Rāmāyana (Griffith's trans.), Bk. II. ch. 10.
[3] Mahābhārata, Bhishma Parva.

Bhīras and the Arbudas; the Karūshas and the Mālavas dwelling in the Pāripātra mountains; the Sauvīras, the Saindhavas, the Hūnas, the Sālvas, the Sākalas, the Madras, the Rāmas, the Ambasthas, and the Pārasīkas in the Punjab, and in the territory comprising north-western India and modern Afghanistan.[1] This list, however, fails to render us much assistance, as we do not know what period of history it refers to. Perhaps a portion of the list refers to an early period, while some names are later additions.

In early times, the States were generally small in size. In the Heroic Age, the conquests of the warrior-kings added considerable territories to their dominions. But it seems that the movement towards the formation of extensive kingdoms did not begin until about the eighth or seventh century B.C. Once started, however, the movement steadily grew in strength. Thus we find that the Kingdom of Magadha had its territories augmented under rulers like Bimbisāra, Ajātasatru, and Mahāpadma Nanda, until it became the largest State in Northern India. And its progress did not stop there.

Soon after the departure of Alexander from India, Chandragupta, with the help of his minister, Chānakya, succeeded in bringing the whole of Northern India under his imperial control, and the empire of his grandson Asoka included the entire continent of India with the exception of the countries of Chola,

[1] Vishnu Purāna, Bk. II. ch. 3.

Pāndya, Keralaputra and Satiyaputra lying to the extreme south of the peninsula.[1] But this vast fabric fell into pieces not long after Asoka's death. The centre of political predominance then shifted to the Āndhra country, which succeeded in bringing under its sway the whole of the Deccan as well as a considerable part of Northern India. In the fourth century after Christ, Samudragupta and his son Chandragupta Vikramāditya revived for a time the lost glory of Magadha by re-establishing the Magadhan empire. The dominion under the direct control of the early Gupta Emperors comprised almost the whole of Northern India, while many of the kingdoms in the other parts of the country were attached to the Empire by bonds of subordinate alliance. The Gupta Empire was broken up by the incursions of the Huns in the latter part of the fifth century A.D., and the Gupta Kings sank into the position of local Rājās, ruling over a limited extent of territory. Yasodharman of Mālava was the next ruler to aspire to the position of an imperial sovereign.[2] In the seventh century, the political suzerainty of Northern India passed to Kanauj under Harshavardhana,

[1] Mr. Vincent Smith says: "Asoka's empire, therefore, comprised the countries now known as Afghanistan, as far as the Hindu Kush, Baluchistan, Makran, Sind, Kachh (Cutch), the Swat valley, with the adjoining regions, Kasmir, Nepal, and the whole of India proper, except the extreme south, Tamilakam or Tamil Land. His dominions were far more extensive than British India of to-day, excluding Burma." Asoka (second edition), p. 81.

[2] Yasodharman claimed to be the lord of Northern India from the Brahmaputra to the Arabian Sea and from the Himālaya to Mount Mahendra.

whose victorious arms and wise statesmanship gathered together for the last time the scattered fragments of the North-Indian Empire.[1] In the country beyond the Vindhyas, the Chālukyas had already founded a powerful empire, and in the eighth and ninth centuries after Christ they fought with another great nation, the Rāshtrakūtas, for imperial dominion over the Deccan with varying success. In the ninth and tenth centuries the Pāla Kings of Bengal made themselves masters of large territories, and some of them assumed titles of paramount sovereignty.[2] The Cholas in South India rose into prominence in the tenth century, and under Rajendra Chola they succeeded in conquering not only the whole of South India, but also Kalinga and Ceylon. In the meanwhile, the Rājpūts had appeared on the scene and had occupied Kanauj, Delhi, and Central India, and founded settlements in the country called

[1] According to the Rājataranginī, Lalitāditya-Muktāpīda of Kasmir in the eighth century undertook a dig-vijaya, and became paramount sovereign over a large part of Northern India. But this account seems to be greatly exaggerated. Bk. IV.

[2] The Bhagalpur grant of Nārāyana-Pāla asserts that the second Pāla King, Dharma-Pāla, acquired the sovereignty of Mahodaya (Kanauj) by conquering Indrarāja and others, but bestowed it on Chakrāyudha, the monarch who had been deposed by Krishnarāja, the Rāshtrakūta King. The same event is referred to in the Khalimpur charter of Dharma-Pāla himself, which says: "With a sign of his eyebrows gracefully moved, he made over to the illustrious King of Kanyakubja his own golden water-pitcher of coronation, lifted up by the delighted elders of Pānchāla, and acquiesced in by the Bhoja, Matsya, Madra, Kuru, Yadu, Yavana, Avantī, Gandhāra and Kirāta Kings, bent down while bowing with their heads trembling." Quoted by D. R. Bhandakar in Epigraphia Indica, Vol. VII. p. 27. Another Pāla King claims to have exterminated the Hūnas and to have extended his sway over the whole of Northern India.

after them 'Rājasthān.' The new as well as the old nations fought with one another for supremacy, but no King after Harsha seems to have succeeded in establishing a stable empire in any part of India. The country thus continued to be governed by a number of independent or semi-independent rulers, until the conquest of India by the Mahomedans deprived the people of their liberty, and brought about a rearrangement of the political boundaries of Indian States.

The history of the variations of political boundaries in India is full of interest to the student of public administration. The success achieved on several occasions in establishing an imperial government for the whole or a large part of India, and the failure to maintain such an empire, show that while the people were striving after an imperial unity, the physical difficulties in the way of its realisation were too great to be easily overcome before the advent of the contrivances of modern science.

CHAPTER VII

THE KING

We have already seen that in ancient times there existed in India several distinct forms of government, and that in the course of time monarchy succeeded in practically supplanting all the other forms.[1] Kingship came henceforward to be regarded as an essential part of society. The limbs of the body politic were said to be seven, namely, (1) the King (Svāmī), (2) Ministers (Amātya), (3) Territory (Janapada), (4) Forts (Durga), (5) Treasury (Kosa), (6) Army (Daṇḍa), and (7) Allies (Mitra);[2] and of these the monarch became the most important limb. In the Mahābhārata, the people are strongly advised to elect and crown a King, for "in a country without

[1] According to tradition, Prithu, the son of Vena, was the first king of men. Vide Satapatha Brāhmana, V. 3, 5, 4, and also Mahābhārata, Sānti Parva. The names of many Kings are mentioned in the Vedic literature; of these, Ikshvāku, Santanu, Sudās, and Trasadasyu were perhaps the most famous. There are many words in Sanskrit which denote a 'king,' but the words most often used are 'rājan' and 'nṛpati.'

[2] The idea of the seven elements of the State occurs in the Arthasāstra (Bk. VI. ch. 1), and in the Mahābhārata, as also in such comparatively recent works as the Kāmandaki, the Mahāvamsa, and the Sukranīti.

a King, there can be no sacrifice."[1] The evils of the absence of this institution are thus described in the Great Epic:[2] "As all creatures would sink in utter darkness if the Sun and the Moon did not shine, so men would have no light to guide their steps by, if the King did not rule. Without a King the position of men would be like that of a herd of cattle without a herdsman. If the King did not exercise the duty of protection, the strong would forcibly appropriate the possessions of the weak. All kinds of property, and even wives, sons, and daughters would cease to exist. Every part of the country would be overrun by robbers; all restrictions about marriage would cease; agriculture and trade would fall into confusion; morality would be lost; the Vedas would disappear; sacrifices would no longer be performed; society itself would cease to exist; famine would ravage the country; and all kinds of injustice would set in."

In the Vedic times, Kingship seems often to have been elective.[3] The following hymn of the Rig-Veda

[1] Mahābhārata, Sānti Parva.

[2] Mahābhārata, Sānti Parva, Sec. 68, sls. 8-31.

[3] Prof. Macdonell says, "Zimmer is of opinion that while the Vedic monarchy was sometimes hereditary, as is indeed shown by several cases where the descent can be traced, yet in others the monarchy was elective, though it is not clear whether the selection by the people was between the members of the royal family only or extended to members of all the noble clans. It must, however, be admitted that the evidence of the elective monarchy is not strong. As Geldner argues, all the passages cited can be regarded not as choice by the cantons (viś), but as acceptance by the subjects (viś): this seems the more probable sense. Of course, this is no

suggests the elective character of Kingship in the early ages: "I have brought thee forward; remain in the midst; may all thy subjects desire thee! May thy dominion never fall away from thee! . . . And may Indra make the subjects devoted to thee alone and bringers of tribute."[1] Hymn III. 4, of the Atharva-Veda is more explicit. "Let the people (viśaḥ) choose unto Kingship (Rājya) thee these five divine directions; rest at the summit of royalty, at the pinnacle (kakud); from thence formidable, share out good things to us."[2] Another hymn of the Atharva-Veda runs thus: "Like a human Indra, go thou away; for thou hast concurred in accord with the castes."[3]

As Kings were elected by the people, they were sometimes deposed by the people.[4] This is suggested by the Rig-Veda hymn quoted above which also occurs in the Atharva-Veda.[5] The following hymn refers to the restoration of a King: "Let thine opponents call thee, thy friends have chosen (thee)

---

proof that the monarchy was not sometimes elective; the practice of selecting one member of the family to the exclusion of another less qualified is exemplified by the legend in Yāska of the Kuru brothers, Devāpi and Santanu." Vedic Index, Vol. II. p. 211.

[1] Rig-Veda, X. 173.

[2] Atharva-Veda, III. 4. The translation of the passage is as given by Whitney.

[3] Atharva-Veda (Whitney), III. 4.

[4] "Royal power was clearly insecure: there are several references to Kings being expelled from their realms, and their efforts to recover their sovereignty." Vedic Index, II. p. 213.

[5] Atharva-Veda, VI. 87.

against (them); Indra and Agni, all the gods, have maintained for thee security (kshema) in the people (viś)."[1]

Gradually, however, the system of election gave place to a hereditary Kingship. By the time, possibly of the later Vedic literature,[2] and certainly of the Rāmāyana and the Mahābhārata, the succession of the eldest son of the last ruler had become the general rule. But the memory of the elective Kingship lingered. That the people were not unfamiliar in the Buddhist period with the idea of an elected King is shown by the story told in the Pancha-guru Jātaka of the Kingship being offered to the Bodhisatva by the people.[3] The tradition of 'Mahāsammata'[4] (accepted by all), the first king, referred to in the

[1] Atharva-Veda, III. 3.

[2] 'Daśa-purusa-rājya,' occurring in the Satapatha-Brāhmana, suggests that hereditary rule had already become almost well established.

[3] Cf. Jātaka Stories, Bk. I. 32.

[4] In the Dulva, an interesting story is told of the rise of kingship in India. The story runs thus: After private property had come into existence, it happened one day that one person took another's rice without his consent as if it was his own. Then the people thought, "Let us, in view of what has just happened, assemble together, and choose from our midst those who are the finest looking, the largest, the handsomest, and let us make them lords over our fields, and they shall punish those of us who do what is punishable, and they shall recompense those of us who do what is praiseworthy, and from the produce of our fields and of the fruits we gather, we will give them a portion." So they gathered together, and made one of themselves lord over their fields with these words: "Henceforth thou shalt punish those of us who deserve punishment and recompense those of us who deserve recompense, and we shall give thee a portion of the produce of the fields and of the fruits we gather." From his receiving the homages of all he was called 'Mahāsammata'; and as he was lord over the fields and kept them from harm he received the name of 'Protector of the fields' or Kshatriya, and as he was a righteous man and wise, and one who brought happiness to mankind with the law, he was called 'Rājā' (King). The

Tibetan 'Dulva' and in the Ceylonese 'Mahāvamsa' also recalls the elective character of early Kingship.

Even after the hereditary principle had become fully established, the formal offer by the people of the sovereignty to the King was for a long time held essential.[1] Ancient tradition and history also speak of occasional departures from the hereditary principle.[2] When the person who claimed the crown by right of hereditary succession appeared to be unsuitable for the office of King, or was disqualified by reason of any special defect, another member of the royal family was placed on the throne.[3] Devāpi, for instance, being afflicted with skin disease, declined the sovereignty, and the subjects anointed Santanu King. So also, according to the Mahābhārata, Dhritarāshtra, being blind, was passed over in favour of his younger brother, Pāndu. Again, in troublous times it was often found necessary to appoint a strong man as King in preference to a weak or minor claimant, although the latter might have the best right according to the hereditary principle. In such cases, it seems, the people, not unnaturally, claimed

---

life of the Buddha derived from the Tibetan Works (Rockhill), p. 7. This theory of a compact between the King and the people is to be found in other books in somewhat different forms. See also Mahāvamsa, Ch. II.

[1] Vide Brihaddevatā, VII. 157.

[2] Chānakya says: "Except in times of danger (āpadah anyatra) the rule that sovereignty descends to the eldest son is (to be) respected." Arthasāstra, Bk. I. ch. 17.

[3] Brihaddevatā, VIII. 1. Vide also Mahābhārata, Adi Parva, Sec. 141, sl. 25.

a voice in the appointment of the King. So also, in cases of disputed succession, the views of the people were taken into account. Thus, when the succession was in dispute between Yudhishthira and Duryodhana, the people declared in favour of the former.[1] But more often, it was perhaps the reigning sovereign who nominated his successor. Samudragupta, for instance, on account of his valour and administrative ability, was nominated by his father, Chandragupta, to succeed him to the throne.[2] On some occasions it was the Ministers who made the choice.[3] After the treacherous assassination of Rājyavardhana by the King of Pundra, the Prime Minister Bhandi, with the concurrence of the Council of Ministers and the approval of the people, placed Harshavardhana on the throne.[4] Not unoften, physical force was the ultimate arbiter in settling questions of disputed succession. To avoid an appeal to force, a partition of the Kingdom was in some instances agreed upon.[5]

[1] "Vayaṁ Pāṇḍava-jyestham abhisincāmaḥ," Ādi Parva, Sec. 141, sl. 27. And again, in sl. 32, Duryodhana tells Dhritarāshtra: "The citizens want Pāndava (i.e. Yudhishthira) as their lord, passing over you and Bhishma." From the Mahāvamsa account it seems that Asoka was not the eldest son of Bindusāra; but, as he stood high above his brothers "in valour, splendour, might and wondrous powers," he succeeded in raising himself to the throne. Vide Mahāvamsa (Geiger), Ch. V. The Mahāvamsa story, however, is not worthy of credence in all details.

[2] Vide Gupta Inscriptions (Fleet).

[3] Vide Arthasāstra, Bk. V. ch. 6.

[4] See post, Ch. IX.

[5] That a division of the Kingdom was not looked upon with much favour is shown by the following remark of Sukra: "No good can arise out of the division of a Kingdom. By division the States become small, and thus are liable to be easily attacked by the enemy." Ch. I. sl. 346.

The partition which took place between the Kauravas and the Pāndavas was the result of the conciliatory policy adopted by Dhritarāshtra on the one side and Yudhishthira and his brothers on the other. In comparatively modern times, a partition of the Kingdom of Nepal is known to have taken place between two dynasties, and these ruled simultaneously, having their respective capitals in different parts of the same city.[1]

The succession was limited to males, and as a consequence, the history of Āryan India does not furnish us with many names of female sovereigns. Almost the only instances of reigning queens come to us from Kasmir and Ceylon. Diddā of Kasmir[2] and Lilāvatī of Ceylon[3] were practically the only female rulers who occupied any places in Indian history. Both of them were widows of kings, and it was the unsettled condition of the times which raised them to their royal positions.

The Kings, as a rule, belonged to the Kshatriya caste, but history furnishes us with the names of some Kings who belonged to the other castes. Mahā-

[1] Vide Corpus Inscriptionum Indicarum, Gupta Inscriptions, p. 188. The Lichchavi family ruled contemporaneously with the Thākurī family.

[2] Vide Rājataranginī, Bk. VI. The only other reigning queen of Kasmir was Sugandhā.

[3] Vide Epigraphia Zeylanica and the Mahāvamsa. Three other queens reigned in Ceylon, namely, Anulā, Sivali, and Kalyānavatī. Queen-consort Sūryamatī was the virtual ruler of Kasmir during the reign of her husband Ananta.

Megasthenes speaks of the Pāndyas as "a race ruled by women."

padma Nanda, the founder of the Nanda dynasty, was the son of the last Sisunāga King by a Sūdra woman. Chandragupta also claimed his descent from the Magadhan royal family through a Sūdra mother.[1] The Sunga and Kānva monarchs were probably Brāhmanas. The Kings of Gandhāra, at the time of Fa Hian's visit and later, belonged to the Brāhmana caste. Hiuen Tsiang speaks of the King of Matipura as a Sūdra. It is suggested by Dr. Fleet that the Guptas of Magadha belonged to the Vaisya caste,[2] but his argument does not seem to be very convincing.

After the establishment of a hereditary Kingship there grew up the theory of the divine origin of the institution. This theory is first hinted at in the later Vedic literature, and afterwards elaborated in the Epics, the Smritis, and the Purānas. The Atharva-Veda [3] and some of the Brāhmanas [4] contain the germs of the theory, and it is soon developed

[1] In Mudrā-Rākshasa, Chānakya always addresses Chandragupta as 'Vrishala' (*i.e.* Sūdra). Rākshasa, the Prime Minister of the Nanda Kings, addressing the goddess of royal power in a soliloquy, asks: "Was there no chief of noble blood to win thy fickle smiles, that thou must elevate a base-born outcast to imperial sway?" Act II. (Wilson's trans.)

[2] Fleet, Gupta Inscriptions.
In the Satapatha-Brāhmana we are told: "Unsuited for kingship is the Brāhmana." In the Mahābhārata, the King is always described as a Kshatriya, but we find that Drona, a Brāhmana, was a king.

[3] Atharva-Veda, III. 3; III. 4; and IV. 22.

[4] In the Satapatha-Brāhmana, not only the King, but the Kshatriya class is described as having a divine origin. "And as to why a Rājanya shoots, he, the Rājanya, is manifestly of Prajāpati (the Lord of creatures): hence while being one, he rules over many." V. 1, 5, 14.

into a sort of political principle. Manu says, "When these creatures, being without a King (arājake), through fear dispersed in all directions, the Lord created a King for the protection of the world, taking (for that purpose) eternal particles (mātran) of Indra (the King of the gods), of Anila (Wind), of Yama (the god of death), of Arka (the Sun), of Agni (the Fire), of Varuna (the Rain-god), of Chandra (the Moon), and of Kubera (the god of wealth)."[1] So, the Mahābhārata says, "No one should disregard the King by taking him for a man, for he is really a high divinity in human form. The King assumes five different forms according to five different occasions. He becomes Agni, Āditya, Mrityu, Vaisravana, and Yama."[2] And again, "it is on account of his divine origin that the multitude obey his words of command, though he belongs to the same world and is possessed of similar limbs."[3]

Thus, the King in India was invested with something like a divine halo, but it was only a righteous monarch who was regarded as divine.[4] The Hindu

[1] Manu, VII. 3-4. [2] Mahābhārata, Sānti Parva, Sec. 68, sls. 40-41.

[3] Mahābhārata, Sānti Parva.

[4] The King was not a 'devatā' but only a 'nara-devatā.' The Sukraniti says, "An unrighteous King is a demon (Raksho'msah)." The Sukraniti divides Kings into three classes, namely, Sāttvika, Rājasika, and Tāmasika. "The King who observes his own duties, protects his subjects, performs all sacrifices, leads his army against his enemies, is charitable, forgiving and brave, and has no attachment to things of this world is a Sāttvika, and he attains salvation. That King who is the reverse of a Sāttvika King, who is devoid of pity, is full of pride and envy, and is untruthful is a Tāmasika King, and he goes to hell. A Rājasa King is one

King's claim was very different from the divine right—"the right divine to govern wrong," to use the words of a famous historian—which was claimed by the monarchs of Europe in the latter part of the Middle Ages. Kingship in India was a political office, and not the sphere of power of a fortunate individual. The King was the chief of the nation, and not the owner of the territory over which he ruled. The State existed for the well-being of the people, and the King held his position as the head of the State only in so far as he was expected to further such well-being.[1] Whatever might be the character of the monarchy on the surface, there is no doubt that at bottom the relations between the ruler and the ruled were contractual. It was in return for the services he rendered to the people that he received their obedience and their contributions for the maintenance of royalty. If it was the duty of the subjects to obey their King,[2] it was the duty of the King to promote the welfare of his subjects. The conception of the King as the servant of the State was one of

---

who is vain, greedy, attached to objects of enjoyment, whose deeds are different from his words and thoughts, who is quarrelsome, who is fond of low company and intrigue, who is self-willed and regardless of the rules of Ethics and Politics; such a bad King after death reaches the state of the lower animals and of inanimate things." Ch. I. sls. 30-34.

[1] Cf. Mahābhārata, Sānti Parva (R.P.), Sec. 59, sl. 70, where the protection of the citizens and the promotion of the welfare of the State are considered to be the two duties of the King. In the Rig-Veda, the King is described as the protector of the people (gopā janasya).

[2] The Nītivākyāmrita says: "The royal command should never be disobeyed by anybody." Ch. XVII.

the basic principles of political thought in Ancient India. Thus Bodhāyana says: "Let the King protect (his) subjects, receiving as his *pay* a sixth part (of their income)."[1] So also, Chānakya says: "As Kings are remunerated by the people, it is their duty to look to the interests of the State."[2] In comparatively modern times, the Sukranīti expresses the same view. "(Brahma) created the King to be the servant of his subjects, and he is remunerated by a share of the produce. He assumes the character (of King) only for protecting (his subjects)."[3] When the King failed to perform the duties of his office or injured the interests of society, the subjects were held absolved from their obligations. "A King," says the Mahābhārata, "who is unable to protect, is useless. If the King fails in his duties, any person, no matter to what caste he belongs, may wield the sceptre of government."[4] The Sukranīti offers the following advice: "If the King is an enemy of virtue, morality, and power, and is unrighteous in conduct, the people should expel him as a destroyer of the State. And for the preservation of the State the Purohita (High Priest) should, with the consent of the people, place in his seat a member of the (royal) family who may be possessed of virtue."[5]

[1] Bodhāyana, I. 10, 1: "Ṣaḍbhāga-bhrto rājā rakset prajām."
[2] Arthasāstra, Bk. II. [3] I. 255.
[4] Sānti Parva, Sec. 78, sl. 36. Vide also Manu, VII. 111-112.
[5] Ch. II. sls. 234-235.

The powers of the King were limited. The idea of an autocratic (svatantra) ruler was not very congenial to the Hindu mind. An eminent writer on legal philosophy remarks: "Among the Āryan peoples there has never arisen that despotism which blots out man as in Egypt, Babylon, China, and among the Mussulman and Tartar tribes—or if it has appeared it has not been of long duration."[1] This remark is as true of the Āryan people of India as of the Āryan races of the west. The King in India was never regarded as being "above the law."[2]

It was the duty of the King always to act according to the rules laid down in the Sāstras, and in the practical application of these rules he had to follow the advice of the great Officers of State and, in cases of difficulty, to accept the guidance of the learned Brāhmanas.[3] The Aitareya Brāhmana prescribes the following oath for the King: "Whatever good I

[1] Miraglia, Comparative Legal Philosophy, quoted in N. C. Sen Gupta's Origin of Society in India.

[2] That the idea that the King was not above the law had a firm root in the minds of the people is made clear by the following story heard by Hiuen Tsiang about King Bimbisāra. In order to prevent fires in the capital, which had become rather frequent at the time, the King passed an ordinance to the effect that any person in whose house a fire should break out, would be banished to the "cold forest." One day a fire broke out in the Royal Palace. Then the King said to his Ministers: "I myself must be banished"; and he gave up the government to his eldest son and retired to the forest saying, "I wish to maintain the laws of the country. I therefore myself am going into exile." Buddhist Records, Bk. IX.

[3] Manu says: "Let the King, after rising early in the morning, worship the Brāhmanas, who are well versed in the threefold sacred science and learned (in polity), and follow their advice." VII. 37.

may have done (during my life), my position (in the next world), my life and my progeny be taken from me if I oppress you."[1] The Mahābhārata tells the King: "Take the oath in mind, word and deed, namely, I shall always look to the welfare of the country regarding it as the Supreme Being. Whatever is law and whatever is prescribed by the rules of Ethics and Politics, I shall always abide by. I shall never be independent."[2] "In governing his kingdom," says Manu, "let him (i.e. the King) always observe the rules (vidhāna): for a King who governs his kingdom well, easily prospers."[3] The Nītivākyāmrita is very emphatic as to the necessity of the King following the advice of his Ministers. It says: "He is not a King who acts without (or against) the advice of his Ministers."[4] The Sukranīti goes further in its condemnation of the independent action of a monarch when it remarks: "That King who does not listen to the advice of the Ministers is a robber (dasyu) in the disguise of a King, and is a thief (apahāraka) of the wealth of his subjects."[5] And it adds: "When the King acts independently (of his ministers) he brings ruin upon himself; he is deprived of his sovereignty and is turned out of

[1] VIII. 4, 1, 13. I am indebted for this suggestion to an article in the Modern Review of Calcutta (1913) contributed by Mr. K. P. Jayasval.

[2] Sānti Parva, Sec. 59. [3] Manu, VII. 113.

[4] Somadeva Sūri's Nītivākyāmrita, Ch. X.: "Na khalvasau rājā yaḥ mantriṇo 'tikramya vartate."

[5] II. 257.

the State." [1] It should, however, be noted that in the latter part of the Hindu Period of Indian history, the power of the monarch was much greater than in the earlier, and that such increase of power did to some extent receive the sanction of the writers on Law and Politics; but at no time was the royal power, in theory at least, quite absolute. In practice, it is true, some Kings acted in an autocratic manner, but this must be regarded as a usurpation and abuse rather than a normal exercise of authority.

In the people lay the strength of the King, and it was their well-being to which he was expected to devote his constant attention. It was held unrighteous and inexpedient to excite popular discontent. The duties of the King, according to the Mahābhārata,[2] were: (1) to please the people; [3] (2) to protect them; (3) always to seek their welfare; (4) to establish all his subjects in the observance of their respective duties; (5) to punish wrongdoers; and (6) to practise the virtues of promptitude, energy, truthfulness, self-restraint, humility, righteousness, fortitude, and compassion. The following passage,

[1] The Sukranīti adds: "The King who performs his duties in accordance with the rules of the Sāstras and practises self-control, becomes happy in this world and in the next." I. 123.

[2] Arthasāstra, Bk. V. ch. 6. Mahābhārata, Sānti Parva (R.P.), Sec. 68.

[3] The advice to the King to please the people occurs again and again in the Rāmāyana, in the Mahābhārata, and in works like the Arthasāstra, the Kāmandaki, and the Sukranīti. The Mahābhārata derives the word 'rājan' from 'ranj' (to please). The real meaning of the word, however, seems to be 'one who shines.'

which occurs in the Milinda-panha, also gives us an idea of what the people thought to be the duties of the King. It runs thus: "The sovran overlord gains the favour of the people by the four elements of popularity (viz. liberality, affability, justice, and impartiality). . . . The sovran overlord allows no robber bands to form in his realm . . . travels through the whole world even to its own boundary, examining into the evil and the good . . . is completely provided with protection, both within and without."[1]

Translated into the language of modern Politics, these and other similar accounts would mean that the chief duties of the King were three-fold, namely, executive, judicial, and military. The King was the executive head of the State and the chief custodian of political authority,[2] and as such the most important of his duties was to preserve peace and security in the realm.[3] It was as his servants that the State officials worked for the prevention of crimes and enforced the observance of the laws of the kingdom. All officers of the State were appointed and removed—directly or indirectly—by the King; they acted according to his commands, and were accountable for the exercise of their functions to him. The administration of justice was carried on

[1] Questions of King Milinda (Rhys Davids), VII. 3.

[2] Kautilya says: "The King is the centre of the State (Kūṭa-sthānīya)." Arthasāstra, Bk. VIII. ch. 1.

[3] In the Satapatha-Brāhmana, the Kings are described as the realm-sustainers, "for it is they who sustain realms." IX. 4, 1, 3.

in the name of the King, and sometimes he himself presided over the Royal Court of Justice.[1] It was he who gave effect to the judgments of the Law Courts, and exercised his prorogative of mercy in suitable cases. Though legislation was not among the powers entrusted to the King, yet royal edicts, at least so far as they related to administrative business, had the force of laws.[2] The King was also the supreme commander of the military forces of the country, and, not unfrequently, he personally led the army on the field of battle.[3] The fame of a victorious warrior was much coveted by Kings of old, and there were not a few among them who were renowned far and wide for their prowess in battle.[4] Among the minor duties of the King may be mentioned the guardianship of infants and the custody

[1] See the Chapter on the Administration of Justice for a fuller treatment of this subject.

[2] Cf. Macdonell, Vedic Index, II. p. 214. "There is no reference in early Vedic literature to the exercise of legislative activity by the King, though later it is an essential part of his duties."

[3] "Kings should acquire proficiency in Dharmasāstra, Arthasāstra, Nītisāstra, and in the arts of war. It is their paramount duty to fight and to do their utmost to win." Rāmāyana, Sundara Kānda, Sec. 48, sl. 14. According to Manu, "not to turn back in battle" is one of the best means for a King to secure happiness. VII. 88. Manu further says: "A King must not shrink from battle." That Manu's advice was followed in practice by Kings even in comparatively modern times is shown by the following extract from an inscription from Belgaum (1204 A.D.): "All the folk applaud him for his love for the spirit of liberty, a course (enjoined) by Manu associated with the triple domain, a nature by which he captured foemen's fastnesses . . . glorious was Kārtavīrya."

[4] See the Chapter on Conquest and Defence, in which this subject has been fully dealt with. The inscriptions found in different parts of India are full of the records of victories won by warrior-Kings.

of the property of minors and others who were unable to take care of their own things.[1] The King was also, in a sense, the head of the society. He was the protector, though not the head, of religion;[2] and in his executive capacity he guided, and to some extent controlled, the religious and moral life of the people.

The chief possessions of a King which, according to Chānakya, would enable him to properly perform his duties were: Noble birth, godlike intelligence, valour, ability to see through the eyes of experienced persons, love of virtue, truthfulness, straightforwardness, gratefulness, comprehensiveness of outlook (sthūla-laksha), enthusiasm, want of procrastination, resoluteness of spirit, and a Council of a fairly large size (akshudra-parishatka). Chānakya also mentions the following as the most important of the regal qualities: profound knowledge; good memory; a strong mind; enthusiasm for work; versatility; ability to confer rewards and inflict punishments; capacity to guard against dangers and calamities; dignity; foresight; readiness to avail one's self of opportunities; ability to decide upon peace and war and to take advantage of the weak points of an enemy; ability to be humorous without loss of dignity; freedom from passion, wrath, greed, obstinacy, fickleness, and hatred; possession of a

[1] Gautama, X. 48; Vasishtha, XVI. 7-9; also Agni Purāna, Ch. CCXXII.

[2] Asoka, however, made himself almost the head of the Buddhist Church. Some of the Kings of Ceylon also assumed something like supreme authority over the Church.

smiling countenance; and observance of customs enjoined by aged persons.[1]

The Mahābhārata lays down the following thirty-six principles for the guidance of the King: The King should observe duties without malice and wrath; acquire wealth without persecution; never abandon kindness; pursue pleasure without attachment; utter what is agreeable; be brave without being boastful; be liberal; show prowess without cruelty; make alliances, avoiding those that are wicked; never act with hostility towards friends; never employ persons not devoted to him as his spies and secret agents; ever accomplish his objects without persecution; never disclose his purposes before persons that are wicked; speak of the merits of others but never of his own; take wealth from his subjects but never from those that are good; never employ or take the assistance of persons that are wicked; never inflict punishment without careful enquiry; never disclose his counsels; give away his wealth but not to covetous persons; repose confidence in others, but never in those who have injured him; never cherish malice; protect his wedded wives; be pure; never be melted by compassion; without pride pay respect to those that deserve it; serve his preceptors and seniors with sincerity; worship the gods without pride; seek prosperity, but never do anything that brings disgrace; wait (upon

[1] Arthasāstra, Bk. VI. ch. 1.

his seniors) with humility; be clever in business, but always wait for the proper moment; comfort men, and never send them away with empty speeches; never abandon a person who has once been taken into favour; never strike in ignorance; having slain a foe, never indulge in sorrow; display wrath, but only when there is an occasion; be mild, but never to those who have offended." [1]

Every morning it was the custom for the King to repair to the Assembly Hall and enquire into the grievances of the people.[2] A good and wise King was expected to regulate his daily business according to a fixed time-table. Chānakya advises the King to divide the day and the night into eight equal

[1] The following extract from Abul Fazl's summary of the duties of a King, according to Hindu Polity, is interesting as showing that the principles were widely known for long ages and that they were meant to be acted upon: "It is incumbent on a monarch to divest himself of avarice and anger by following the counsels of wisdom and not to debase himself by the commission of any of the crimes described above. If he unfortunately suffers injury from others it behoves him to be moderate in his resentments. It is his indispensable duty to fear God; to be just and merciful to himself, and to excite the like disposition in others; to pay particular respect to men of exalted rank, and behave with kindness and condescension towards subjects of every description. He should be ambitious to extend his dominions; and protect his subjects from the oppressions of his officers, from robbers and other evil doers, proportioning the punishment to the offence. In everything that concerns himself he should be patient, and forgiving of injuries." Gladwin, Ayeen Akbery, p. 492.

[2] In one of the Ajantā paintings, the King is represented as seated on the throne with his usual female attendants behind him, and his Prime Minister seated on a low stool in front of him. A crowd in front is lodging a complaint against one who seems to be brought as a criminal. Fergusson and Burgess, Cave-temples of India, p. 313. From the Mudrā-Rākshasa, we know that Kings used to be guarded by female attendants (pratihārī).

parts each, and to arrange the daily duties in the following manner: [1]

I. Day-time:

(1) Deliberation upon the means of defence.

(2) Enquiry into the grievances of the people.

(3) Bath, meal, and study.

(4) Receiving accounts from cashiers and other officers.

(5) Meeting of the Privy Council.

(6) Recreation or taking Counsel with Ministers.

(7) Supervision of the elephant force, the cavalry, and the armoury.

(8) Consultation with the Commander-in-Chief about military matters.

II. Night-time:

(1) Receiving reports from the spies.

(2) Bath, meals, and study.

(3), (4), and (5) Sleep.

(6) Reflection upon the Sāstras and upon Kingly duties.

(7) Taking counsel with Ministers and sending out spies.

(8) Performance of religious ceremonies.

[1] Arthasāstra, Bk. I. ch. 19. Chānakya says that this division should be made with the help of water-clocks (nālikā) or by observing the size of shadows (chhāyāpramānena). The Sukranīti also gives the King similar advice, but the time-table suggested therein is somewhat different. The twenty-four hours of the day and night are to be divided into thirty parts (muhūrtas), thus: Consideration of income and expenditure, 2 muhūrtas; Bath, 1; Religious observances. 2; Physical exercise, 1; Distribution

It is not to be supposed that this time-table was followed in its entirety by any King, but there is little doubt that many monarchs performed their daily duties in accordance with a more or less fixed routine. But all monarchs, it seems, attended to urgent business at any hour of the day.[1]

The standard by which Kings were judged in Ancient India was thus very high. This standard could only be reached, when, in the words of Plato, "philosophers are Kings, or the Kings and Princes of this world have the spirit and power of philosophy, and political greatness and wisdom melt in one."[2] Fortunately, tradition and history do furnish us with examples of such philosopher-kings in India. Tradition enshrines the memories of Rāma and Yudhishthira as the highest ideals of virtuous monarchs. Kālidāsa depicts Dilīpa as a great and wise King who always found his happiness in that of his subjects.[3] In historical times, rulers like Asoka and Harshavardhana

of rewards, 1; Receiving accounts from Officers of State, 4; Dinner, 1; Reflection on old and new events, 1; Consultation with judges, 1; Hunting and sport, 2; Parade of troops, 1; Religious observances, 1; Evening meal, 1; Business with spies, 1; and sleep, 8. Vide also Manu, VII. 145, etc., and Agni Purāna, Ch. CCXXXV.

[1] Kautilya says: "All urgent business he must attend to at once, and never put off, for when postponed, they will prove difficult or even impossible of accomplishment." Arthasāstra, Bk. I. ch. 19. According to Hiuen Tsiang, Harshavardhana "divided each day into three portions. During the first he occupied himself with the business of government; during the second he practised himself in religious devotion without interruption." Buddhist Records (Beal), Bk. IV. p. 216.

[2] Plato's Republic (Jowett), V.

[3] Raghuvamsa.

are known to have worked strenuously and unceasingly for the well-being of the State.[1] Asoka was an ascetic on the throne, whose principle of government was "protection by the Law of Piety, regulation by that Law, felicity by that Law."[2] "For the welfare of all folk," said Asoka, "is what I must work for—and the root of that again is in effort and the dispatch of business. And whatever exertions I make are for the end that I may discharge my debt to animate beings, and that while I make some happy here, they may in the next world gain heaven."[3] Though Asoka worked exceedingly hard, he never felt full satisfaction in his effort and dispatch of business, and therefore he made the arrangement that "at all hours and all places—whether I am dining, or in the ladies' apartments, in my bedroom, or in my closet, in my carriage, or in the palace gardens—the official Reporters should report to me on the people's business, and I am ready to do the people's business in all places."[4] Harsha also, like Asoka, was a royal ascetic. He personally supervised the affairs of his vast empire, and for the transaction of State business was incessantly on the move through his wide

[1] Kāmandaki says that the King should try his best to promote the welfare of the State in every possible way. Ch. VI. sl. 3; also Mahābhārata, Sānti Parva.

[2] Rock Edict I.

[3] Rock Edict VI. Asoka adds: "For this purpose have I caused this pious edict to be written, that it may long endure and that my sons and grandsons may exert themselves for the welfare of all folk."

[4] Rock Edict VI.

dominions.[1] Of him the admiring foreign traveller records, "His qualifications moved heaven and earth; his sense of justice was admired by Devas and men. . . . His renown was spread abroad everywhere, and all his subjects reverenced his virtues."[2] "Through him," says the poet, "the earth does indeed possess a King (rājanvatī)."[3]

But while there were rulers who approached the grand ideal of what Kings should be, the majority of monarchs must have been men of the average type. And some of them even fell below the average. Indian history unfortunately preserves accounts of

[1] Hiuen Tsiang says: "If it was necessary to transact business, he employed couriers who continually went and returned. If there was any irregularity in the manners of the people of the cities, he went amongst them. Wherever he moved he dwelt in a ready-made building during his sojourn. During the excessive rains of the three months he would not travel thus. . . ." Buddhist Records, Bk. IV. King Harsha was visiting different parts of the country, when he came to know of Hiuen Tsiang's presence in Kāmarūpa. In one of the Ceylon inscriptions we find that King Nissanka Malla not only "constantly viewed with the eyes of spies his own kingdom," but went on a tour of inspection through the three Kingdoms of Ceylon, visiting the villages, towns, cities and palaces difficult of access through water, hills, forests and marshes." Epigraphia Zeylanica, Vol. II. No. 1713.

[2] Life of Hiuen Tsiang, p. 83. And again, "He is virtuous and patriotic; all people celebrate his praises in songs." Ibid.

[3] Harsha-charita, Ch. II. Bāna describes Harsha in the most eulogistic terms: "This, then, is the Emperor Śrī Harsha, that union of separate glories (tejasāṁ rāśiḥ), of noble birth, of befitting name, the lord of the earth bounded by the four oceans—the surpasser of all the victories won by all Kings of ancient times." Ch. II. And again, "No reign has been stainless except that of Harsha, King of Kings, sovereign of all countries." Ch. III. I have in the main followed the translation of Cowell and Thomas. Devānampiya Tissa of Ceylon is described in the Mahāvamsa as "the dispenser of happiness to his own subjects bearing the profoundly significant title of Devānam-piya (the beloved of the gods), exerting his powers to the utmost, and making Lankā overflow with rejoicings." Ch. XI.

Kings whose incompetency and misdeeds brought destruction upon themselves and ruin on their country. Diodorus speaks of the King of Gangaridai as "a man of quite worthless character, and held in no respect." [1] Some Kings lived a life of dull idleness and ease, and were fond of a disgusting sort of pomp and luxury. Curtius says: "The luxury of their Kings, or, as they call it, their magnificence, is carried to a vicious extent without a parallel in the world." [2] "When the King," records the historian, "condescends to show himself in public, his attendants carry in their hands silver censers and perfume with incense all the road by which it is his pleasure to be conveyed. He lolls in a golden palanquin garnished with pearls which dangle all around, and is robed in fine muslin embroidered with purple and gold. Behind his palanquin follow men-at-arms, and his bodyguards. The palace is adorned with gilded pillars clasped all around by a vine embossed in gold, while silver images of those birds which most charm the eye diversify the workmanship." [3]

Nor were all Kings equally righteous in conduct. Some were greedy, not a few were tyrannical. "Kings are grasping," says Milinda, "the princes might, in

[1] Alexander's Invasion (McCrindle), p. 282.

[2] Curtius, McCrindle's Alexander's Invasion, p. 188.

[3] Alexander's Invasion (McCrindle). As a rule, when the King went on procession he rode an elephant. The retinue of a Rājā is given in one of the cave-paintings at Ajantā. There he is described as going out on a large elephant with the Umbrella of State over his head and the ankuśa in his hand. Burgess, Buddhist Cave Temples.

the lust of power, subjugate an extent of territory twice or thrice the size of what they had, but they would never give up what they already possessed."[1] Again, Nāgasena says, "Some people have left the world in terror at the tyranny of Kings."[2] The Rājatarangini, while it describes in glowing terms the splendid achievements of Lalitāditya and the beneficent administration of Avantivarman, also records the cruelty of Tārāpīda, the fiscal exactions of Sankaravarman, and the misrule of Harsha.

The position of a King in ancient times was not a very easy one. In the Sanskrit drama Mudrā-Rākshasa, Chandragupta is made to describe the difficulties of the King's position in these words:

"How irksome are the toils of State to those
Who hold their tasks as duties.[3] Kings must have
Their own desires, and for the general good,
Forego their own advantage. But to lose
My own for others' benefit makes me a slave,
And what would slaves know of sincere regard?
Fortune makes Kings her sport, and vain the hope
To fix the fickle wanton in her faith.
She flies the violent, disdains the mild,
Despises fools, the wise she disregards,
Derides the cowardly, and dreads the brave."[4]

[1] Questions of King Milinda, IV. 22.

[2] Questions of King Milinda, II. 1, 6.

[3] "Rājyaṁ hi nāma rājadharmānuvrtti-paratantrasya bhūpater mahad apritisthānam." Mudrā Rākshasa, Act III.

[4] Mudrā Rākshasa, Act III. (Wilson's trans.). Some of these lines are practically a quotation from Kāmandaki's Nītisāra, Ch. VI. sl. 15.

Besides, the King's life was constantly threatened by plots. Chānakya describes in detail the measures that had to be taken to ensure the safety of the King.[1] Although Strabo perhaps went a little too far when he asserted that the King at night was obliged from time to time to change his couch for fear of treachery, yet there can be little doubt that "in the midst of all the gold and glitter, and in spite of the most elaborate precautions, uneasy lay the head that wore the crown."[2]

Kings were of various grades, and were known by different titles according to their renown and extent of territory. The Sukranīti says that a ruler who receives a revenue of more than one lakh and less than three lakhs of silver karshas without oppressing his subjects, should be called a Sāmanta; one with an income of over three but below ten lakhs, a Māṇḍalika; one with up to twenty lakhs, a Rājā; up to fifty lakhs, a Mahārāja; up to a crore, a Svarāt; up to fifty crores, a Samrāt; and he who rules the whole earth should be known as a Sārvabhauma.[3] It is not to be supposed, however, that the terms were ever used in these strict senses.

[1] Arthasāstra, Bk. I. ch. 21. Vide also Kāmandaki and Sukranīti. Manu says: "Let him mix all his food with medicines (that are) antidotes against poison, and let him always be careful to wear gems which destroy poison." VII. 218. Hiuen Tsiang describes an attempt on the life of King Harshavardhana at the end of the great religious festival at Prayāg. Vide Buddhist Records (Beal).

[2] Vincent Smith, Early History of India (1904), p. 11.

[3] II. 181-187. Besides these, in the inscriptions we come across some other terms, such as 'Mahāmaṇḍalesvara' and 'Mahāsāmanta.'

It was the custom for the would-be King to go through a period of apprenticeship as Crown Prince (Yuvarāja). On his attaining the proper age, the heir-apparent received a special inauguration.[1] Great importance was attached to the training of a Crown Prince in order that when he ascended the throne he might be able to discharge the duties of Kingship properly. As a knowledge of Politics was regarded as indispensable for Kings,[2] instruction in that science was imparted to him by distinguished professors and administrators.[3] But what was more important was that he received practical training in the art of administration by being associated with the actual work of government.[4] The Crown Prince was an important member of the Great Council, and, very often, he was the Governor of a Province or a Commander of the Army.[5] Asoka, for instance, held the position of Governor in two provinces in succession

[1] The main plot of the Rāmāyana commences with Dasaratha's preparations for inaugurating Rāma as Crown Prince. In the Mahābhārata, Yudhishthira is inaugurated as Yuvarāja.

[2] According to the Sukranīti, a knowledge of Political Science was held absolutely essential for a King. "The primary duties of the King are the protection of his subjects and the punishment of wrong-doers; but neither of these duties can be performed without the help of the Nītisāstra." Ch. I. sls. 14-15; see also Kāmandaki.

[3] Kautilya says: "The Prince should be instructed by professors and practical administrators (vaktṛprayoktṛbhyaḥ)." Vide also Agni Purāna, CCXXV.

[4] "In the Mahāvamsa, Vijaya is described as a Prince Regent whose mal-administration led to discontent and ultimately to his own banishment. The Crown Prince used to have his own Minister whose title was 'Kumārāmātya'." We come across this term in many of the inscriptions.

[5] Arthasāstra, Bk. I. ch. 17.

during the lifetime of his father. Samudragupta acquired his renown as a warrior while he was still a Prince.[1] Rājyavardhana was sent by his father King Prabhākara-vardhana as the Commander-in-Chief of the army to fight against the Huns.[2] If the Crown Prince showed conspicuous ability, he was sometimes chosen to act as a sort of Sub-King (Uparāja) or Prince Regent with almost all the powers of a Sovereign. Occasionally, an old King would retire from the worries of Kingship and abdicate in favour of the Crown Prince.[3]

So much about the institution of Kingship. We shall conclude this chapter with a short description of some of the ceremonies connected with Kingship. Great importance was in early times attached to those ceremonies. The most important of the sacrifices performed by Kings were Rājasūya, Vājapeya, Asvamedha, and Aindra Mahābhisheka. The Rā a-sūya or Consecration sacrifice is thus described in the Satapatha-Brāhmana: First of all, hymns are

[1] Vide Gupta Inscriptions (Fleet). [2] Vide Harsha-charita.

[3] In the Rājatarangini, we read accounts of such abdication. Yudhishthira's abdication is thus described in the Mahābhārata: "Yudhishthira arranged that Parīkshit should rule in Hastinapura. He summoned all his subjects and informed them of his intentions. The citizens as well as the inhabitants of the provinces, hearing the King's words, became filled with anxiety and disapproved of the proposal. 'This should never be done,' said they to the King. But he at last succeeded in persuading the people to sanction his proposal. Then Yudhishthira and his brothers and Draupadī all cast off their ornaments and clothes, wore the bark of trees, and set out for the forest." Mahāprasthānika Parva, Sec. I.

Nissanka-Malla of Ceylon, for instance, is described in an inscription as a Sub-King before his accession to the throne.

chanted, and prayers are offered to the gods with libations of soma. Then a throne-seat is brought for the King which the Priest (Adhvaryu) spreads before him with the words, "This is thy Kingship," whereby he endows him with royal power. He then makes him sit down, with the words, "Thou art the ruler, the ruling lord!" whereby he makes him the ruler, ruling over those his subjects. Then he says, "Thou art firm and steadfast!" whereby he makes him firm and steadfast in the world. Thereupon taking hold of the sacrificer by the right arm, the Adhvaryu mutters, "May Savitṛ quicken thee for (powers of) quickening (ruling). . . . Quicken him, O Gods, to be unrivalled. Quicken him, O Gods, so as to be without an enemy,—for great chiefdom, for great lordship, for the ruling of men." He then presents the sacrificer to the people with the words, "This man, O ye (people), is your King, Soma is the King of us Brāhmanas." Then the Priest sprinkles him with water and utters mantras. He then invests the King with the consecration garments, and hands to him a bow and three arrows with the words, "Protect ye him in front! Protect ye him behind! Protect ye him from the sides! Protect ye him from all quarters!" Thereupon he makes him pronounce the *avid* (announcement) formulas. He thus announces him to Prajāpati, to the priesthood, to the nobility, to Mitra and Varuna (the upholders of the Law), to Heaven and Earth, and to the deities, and they approve of his consecration, and approved by them he is consecrated.[1]

Another sacrifice was the Vājapeya, which used originally to be performed by a King who aspired to the imperial title. "By performing the Rājasūya one becomes King (Rājā), and by the Vājapeya, Emperor (Samrāt); and the position of the King is (obtained) first, and thereafter that of Emperor."[2] In later years, however, the Vājapeya seems to have lost its importance and to have become a sacrifice preliminary to the Rājasūya.

The Asvamedha[3] sacrifice was performed by Kings who were successful in Digvijaya, or conquest of all quarters. A horse was let loose with the words, "Go thou along the way of the Ādityas!" It was allowed to roam about for a year, and was guarded by armed warriors. During the year oblations, amounting to sixteen nineties, were offered by the sacrificer; and when the horse returned unmolested at the end of the year, a grand assembly was held of all the Kings and chiefs of the country, and in their presence the horse was sacrificed. In the Heroic

[1] Satapatha-Brāhmana (Eggeling), Bk. V. The Rājasūya sacrifice of Yudhishthira is described in Mahābhārata, Sabhā Parva (Rājasūyika P.), Secs. XXXIII.-XXXVI. On this occasion, the greatest Rishis are said to have officiated as priests, and all the great Kings and chiefs are said to have been present.

[2] Satapatha-Brāhmana, IX. 3, 4, 8.

[3] The Satapatha-Brāhmana says: "Prajāpati produced the sacrifice. His greatness departed from him, and entered the great sacrificial priests." XIII. 1, 1, 4. Prof. Eggeling remarks on this passage: "The Asvamedha is thus the immolation (or emptying out) of his own self, so to speak."

Age, the Asvamedha was performed by Kings who succeeded in extending their suzerain power over a large part of India.[1] In historical times, it was revived by Samudragupta, the great conqueror of the fourth century A.D.

The Aitareya Brāhmana gives great importance to the Aindra-Mahābhisheka, which, it says, was performed by great rulers like Janamejaya, Sāryāta, Satrujit, Visvakarman, Sudās and Marut, each of whom succeeded in conquering the whole world. "A Kshatriya who is consecrated with this Aindra Mahābhisheka conquers all conquerors, knows all the worlds, becomes superior to all Kings, gains renown and majesty, becomes self-created and self-ruled, after conquering empires, countries ruled by the Bhojas (i.e. powerful monarchs), independent countries, extensive kingdoms, great overlordships, principalities, extensive dominions, and sovereignties; and after death, having gained all desires ascends Heaven, and overcomes death." [2]

[1] "Let him who holds royal (i.e. imperial) sway perform the horse-sacrifice, for, verily, whosoever performs the horse-sacrifice without possessing power, is swept away." Satapatha-Brāhmana, XIII. 1, 6, 3. Vide description of Yudhishthira's Asvamedha sacrifice in the Māhabhārata.

[2] Aitareya Brāhmana, ch. 39. Another ceremony mentioned in the Aitareya Brāhmana is the Punarabhisheka. The Realm-sustaining oblations described in the Satapatha-Brāhmana were also offered by Kings.

CHAPTER VIII

ASSEMBLIES AND COUNCILS

THE system of conducting public administration by means of an Assembly of the people prevailed in India in the early Vedic times. Hymn 191 of Mandala X. of the Rig-Veda is addressed to Saṁjñāna (agreement in assembly) and runs thus:

"Assemble, speak together: let your minds be all of one accord,
As ancient gods unanimous sit down to their appointed share.
The place is common, common the assembly, common the mind, so be your thoughts united.
A common purpose do I lay before you, and worship with your general oblation.
One and the same be your resolve, and be your minds of one accord.
United be the thoughts of all that all may happily agree." [1]

The following hymn of the Atharva-Veda also relates to the work of the Assembly:

(Be) all the quarters (disah) like-minded, concordant: let the Assembly (samiti) here suit (klp) thee fixed.[2]

[1] Rig-Veda (Griffith's trans.).

[2] Atharva-Veda (Whitney). Many other hymns of the Atharva-Veda relate to the work of the Assembly; one such hymn is: "Fixed (dhruva),

The Assembly was of two descriptions,—the Samiti and the Sabhā. The Samiti appears to have been a general assembly of the people convened on an important occasion, such as the election of a king.[1] The less formal, and more commonly convened, Assembly was the Sabhā. The Assembly deliberated upon State business of all kinds, executive, judicial, and military.

The popular assembly was a regular institution in the early years of the Buddhistic Age. When Ajātasatru, wishing to destroy the Vrijjikas, sent his Prime Minister, Varshakāra, to the Buddha, the Buddha asked his chief disciple, "Have you heard, Ānanda, that the Vajjians hold full and frequent assemblies?" "Lord, so I have heard," replied he. "So long,

with a fixed oblation, do we lead down Soma, that Indra may make the clans (viśaḥ) like-minded, wholly ours." VII. 94.

[1] Vide Griffith's Rig-Veda, footnote to Bk. X. Hymn 191.

According to Ludwig, the 'Sabhā' was an assembly not of all the people, but of the Brāhmanas and Maghavans (rich patrons), while the 'Samiti' included the entire people, primarily, the viśaḥ. In Zimmer's opinion the 'Sabhā' was the village assembly. Prof. Macdonell is unable to accept either view, and agrees with Hillebrandt in holding that the Sabhā and the Samiti cannot be distinguished. Vedic Index, II. pp. 427-430.

Prof. Macdonell adds: "The King went to the assembly just as he went to the Sabhā. That he was elected there, as Zimmer thinks, is as uncertain as whether he was elected at all. But there are clear signs that concord between King and assembly was essential for his prosperity." P. 431.

E. W. Hopkins says: "The earliest assembly for adjusting political affairs in Āryan India was the clan-assembly called sabhā (compare German Sippe) . . . In the Epic we find the Sabhā to be an assembly of any sort. It may be a judicial one, or court of law; it may be a royal one, the King's court; it may be a social gathering for pleasure; and finally it may, in its older meaning, be a political assembly." Journal of the American Oriental Society.

Ānanda," rejoined the Blessed One, "as the Vajjians hold full and frequent assemblies, so long may they be expected not to decline but to prosper."[1] And the Buddha added the following other conditions which would ensure the welfare of the Vajjian confederacy. "So long, Ānanda, as the Vajjians meet together in concord, and rise in concord, and carry out their undertakings in concord, so long as they enact nothing not already established, abrogate nothing that has been established, and act in accordance with the ancient institutions of the Vajjians as established in former days—so long as they honour and esteem and revere and support the Vajjian elders and hold it a point of duty to hearken to their words . . . so long may the Vajjians be expected not to decline but to prosper."[2]

How the deliberations of these assemblies were conducted, and whether the proposals were submitted to votes, or the decisions were in accordance with the general sense of the assembly, we do not exactly know. But as the rule of majority was not unknown, it is probable that the decisions of the majority prevailed.[3] Nor do we know in what

[1] Mahā-parinibbāna Suttanta (Rhys Davids and Carpenter's Dīgha-Nikāya), I. 4; also Rhys Davids, Buddhist Suttas.

[2] Ibid.

[3] Chānakya says that in case of a difference of opinion (dvaidhībhāve), the decision of the larger number of honest persons (bahavaḥ śuchayaḥ) shall prevail. This refers to the work village meetings for the arbitration of boundary disputes, but it is probable that this rule applied also to the decisions of other assemblies. Again, regarding the procedure of the King's Council, Chānakya says that the decision of the majority should prevail.

manner the president of such an assembly was appointed. But there is no doubt that the appointment was made in view of his age, attainments, and character.

It was not only in republican States, but also in States in which the monarchical form of government prevailed, that the popular assemblies were important in ancient times. Gradually, however, their importance diminished, and they fell ultimately into disuse. Three causes seem to have combined to produce this result, namely, the increase of the territory of the State, the growth of the King's power, and the stereotyping of the caste-system. When the size of the State grew large, it was found impossible to bring together the entire people; and as the representative system was unknown at the time, the meetings of the popular assemblies became more and more infrequent, until at last the assemblies ceased altogether to meet. The growth of the King's authority led to the substitution of the Great Council (Rāja-sabhā, Rāja-samiti) and the Privy Council (Mantri-parishat) of the King for the ancient meetings of the folk. Lastly, the influence of the fully developed caste-system led to the break-up of the national assembly into many religious and caste associations, to which in course of time were added trade and guild unions (pūga, śreṇi, etc.).

The Royal Assembly or the Great Council of the King sat every day. The chief business transacted in this Assembly was to receive and consider the petitions of the people in regard to their grievances.[1] It also discharged the functions of the Final Court of Appeal in the State.[2] Matters of general policy affecting the well-being of the State were also sometimes considered in this Assembly.[3] The members of the Assembly were the Crown Prince, the Ministers and other high officials, the Commander-in-Chief, the King's relatives, the subject rulers, the nobles, and such other persons as were invited to attend.[4] "The Members of the Royal Assembly," says Vishnu, "should be men who are well-born, possessed of capacity and devoted to the King's interest, who can look with an equal eye upon friend and foe, and who cannot be drawn away from the path of duty by desire, anger, fear, or greed."[5]

Members (Sabhācarāḥ, Sabhāsadaḥ) had their allotted seats in the Assembly Hall.[6] Great im-

[1] Vide ante, Chapter VII. Vide also Sukranīti, Ch. I. sl. 32.

[2] Vide the chapter on the Administration of Justice.

[3] Vide Sukranīti, Ch. I. sl. 352. It was before a meeting of the Royal Assembly or Great Council that Dhritarāshtra placed his proposal for making peace with the Pāndavas, who had married the daughter of Drupada, king of the Pānchālas, and had been taking steps for the recovery of their lost kingdom. The description of this meeting and of the speeches made by the members of the Assembly for and against the proposal gives us an excellent idea of the procedure of the Royal Assembly.

[4] The Nītivākyāmrita says: "No one should enter (i.e. sit in) the Assembly who is not an officer or who has not been invited to attend." Ch. XXIV.

[5] Vishnu (Jolly's Sanskrit text), Ch. III.

[6] Sukranīti, Ch. I. sl. 353, etc. The Mahābhārata gives an imaginary picture of the Assembly-halls of Indra, Yama, Varuna, Kubera and Brahmā in Sabhā Parva, Secs. VII.-XII.

portance was attached to decorous and courteous behaviour on the part of the members. Mutual conversations were forbidden, and no member was allowed to interrupt another in the midst of his speech.[1] As a rule, members spoke only when called upon to do so, but on an emergent occasion or in case of an impending danger to the State, a member was permitted to address the Assembly without a request from the King. "It is the duty of a member of the Assembly," says Chānakya, "to offer the King the best advice. When his opinion is sought, he should express his views boldly and without regard to the opinions of the other members. He should always speak with due regard to the interests of the State, and in conformity with the principles of righteousness and expediency. He should never speak ill of the other members of the Assembly, nor ascribe any motives to their actions. He should never indulge in statements which are unworthy of a member of the Assembly, or of which he has no direct knowledge, or which are incredible or false."[2] The Sukranīti advises members of the Assembly to use words "which are pleasant (priya), true (tathya), and conducive to the welfare of the State (pathya)."[3]

[1] 'Vākyāpakṣepanam.' Arthasāstra, Bk. V. ch. 4.

[2] 'Asabhyam,' 'apratyakṣam,' 'aśraddheyam,' 'anṛtam.' Arthasāstra, Bk. V. ch. 4. According to Chānakya, a member is not justified in attacking other members even when he has himself been attacked.

[3] Sukranīti, Ch. I. sls. 121, 122.

The procedure adopted at meetings of the Royal Assembly seems to have been somewhat different from that at other meetings. No votes were taken, but all matters were decided by the King, with the advice of the Ministers and in accordance with the general sense of the Assembly. On ceremonial occasions, Grand Assemblies were convened. Such a Grand Assembly was held by Yudhishthira on the occasion of his entry into the newly-built capital of Khandava-prastha, when all the renowned sages, the great Kings, and the powerful chiefs of India were invited to attend.[1]

Before any important administrative step was taken, the matter was discussed and decided in the Council of Ministers (Mantri-parishat).[2] This Council was composed of the great Officers-of-State and a few other members who held no office. The size of the Council varied according to circumstances. The school of Brihaspati held that the number of Councillors should be sixteen, Usanas thought it should be twenty, while, in the opinion of Manu, twelve were sufficient. Chānakya was in favour of a fairly

[1] Mahābhārata, Sabhā Parva. The Mahāvagga mentions a grand Assembly of Bimbisāra, King of Magadha, attended by eighty thousand overseers of his township. Fifth Khandaka (Rhys Davids and Oldenburg).

[2] Arthasāstra, Bk. I. ch. 14. Somadeva Sūri uses almost identical words in his Nītivākyāmrita (Ch. IX.). In Kāmandaki the term 'Mantra-maṇḍala' is used for the Council.

Hopkins says: "As the popular assembly became the Kingly 'court' (rājasamiti), so the duties of that assembly became transferred to the 'councillors' or private ministers of the King." Journal of the American Oriental Society.

large Council,[1] but he thought that the actual number of members should depend upon the needs of the State.[2]

The necessity for the meeting of the Council is briefly described by Visālāksha in the words, "the decision of a single mind can never lead to success." Chānakya says: "The work of government relates to three kinds of things,—those that can be perceived, those that cannot be perceived, and those that can be inferred. To know what is not known, to make certain what is known, to clear away doubts regarding what is susceptible of two opinions, and to infer the whole from the part,—for all these purposes, deliberation with ministers is necessary. Therefore, the King should deliberate with men who are wise."[3]

The subjects for discussion at a meeting of the Council included everything which affected the interests of the State. In particular, Chānakya mentions five subjects, namely, the measures to be taken

[1] 'Akṣudrapariṣatka' is regarded by Chānakya as one of the great qualities of a King.

[2] Arthasāstra, Bk. I. ch. 14. Indra's Council consisted of one thousand Rishis and, therefore, he was called "the thousand-eyed."

Abul Fazl, describing the Hindu system of government, says: "In affairs of moment, it is not advisable to consult with many, because that to be qualified to give advice on such occasions requires fidelity, liberality of sentiment, valour and circumspection, qualities that are seldom found united in one person . . . They (i.e. the ancient Hindu monarchs) found it the safest way to join with the prime minister a few wise and experienced men, and to require each to deliver his opinion in writing, to be separately canvassed and debated upon." Ayeen-i-Akbery (Gladwin), pp. 493-494.

[3] Arthasāstra, Bk. I. ch. 15. Somadeva Sūri in his Nītivākyāmrita follows Chānakya and uses practically the same language.

to commence work, the command of men and things for carrying out an object, the appropriate time and place of action, the precautions to be taken against possible dangers, and the means by which final success is to be achieved.[1] The success of deliberation in Council, according to Somadeva, is "the attainment of large results at small expense." [2]

Meetings of the Council were presided over by the King himself, and probably in his absence, by the Prime Minister.[3] The procedure adopted at a meeting of the Council was this: First a measure was introduced by the president.[4] Then the opinion of each member in order was heard.[5] Lastly, a sort of general discussion took place. If the members were unanimous, well and good; if not, the decision of the majority prevailed.[6] Brihaspati says: 'That counsel is best which is taken unanimously, under the guidance of policy, by wise councillors. Where, at first of divers opinions, they are afterwards unanimous, that is middling. Where there is broiling and reproach, one being for right, one for interest, . . . tears on the one part, anger on the other, that is

[1] Arthasāstra, Bk. I. ch. 15.

[2] Nitivākyāmrita, Ch. X.

[3] On the death of Rājyavardhana, the Prime Minister Bhandi presided at the meeting convened for the purpose of selecting a new King. Vide Harshacharita.

[4] "Pūrvaṁ svāminā kārya-nivedanam." Brihaspati Sūtra, IV. 37 (ed. F. W. Thomas).

[5] "Yat punar yathākramam ekaikasya mataṁ śrotavyam." Ibid. IV. 40.

[6] "Yad bhūyiṣṭhā brūyus tat kuryāt." Arthasāstra, Bk. I. ch. 15.

the worst."[1] Ministers were required to observe the strictest secrecy in regard to the subjects of discussion as well as the decision of the Council, and every precaution was taken against the disclosure of secrets.[2] Debates in the Council were perhaps sometimes lengthy, but Chānakya expresses himself as opposed to prolonged discussions,[3] and urges that no time should be lost in taking action after a decision has been arrived at in the Council.

The Council was the chief administrative authority in the kingdom. The King was supposed not to do anything without the consent of the Council.[4] All ordinances were perhaps sanctioned by the Council. It possessed immense powers, and enjoyed a great deal of independence. In exceptional cases, it had even the power to elect the King.

In treating of this subject we have so far confined our attention to Northern India. But it was not in that part of the country alone that the system of government by assemblies and councils prevailed. In the Kerala State in South India, during the first and second centuries of the Christian Era, there were five assemblies,

[1] Brihaspati Sūtra, IV. 34-36.

[2] Kāmandaki, Ch. XXI. sls. 65-66. Mahābhārata, Āsramavāsa Parva, Sec. V., and Sukranīti, ch. I. sl. 351. The Nītivākyāmrita says: "No unauthorised person should be allowed to be present at meetings of the Council."

[3] "Na dīrgham mantrayet." Arthasāstra, Bk. I. ch. 15. The Nītivākyāmrita says: "Ministers must not quarrel among themselves nor indulge in mutual conversation." Ch. X.

[4] Cf. Chānakya-sūtra, "Mantra-sampadā hi rājyaṁ nīyate."

namely, (1) the Assembly of the People, which consisted of representatives of the people summoned from various parts of the State, and which acted as a check on the King ; (2) the Assembly of the Priests, which directed the religious ceremonies of the State ; (3) the Assembly of Physicians, which acted as a sort of Board of Public Health ; (4) the Assembly of the Astrologers, which fixed auspicious times for the public ceremonies ; and (5) the Assembly of the Ministers, whose chief duties consisted in the collection and disbursement of revenue and the administration of justice.[1]

From the Ceylon inscriptions we learn that in that island all measures were enacted by the King-in-Council, and all orders were issued by, and under the authority of, the Council. In the Vevala-Katiya Inscription of Mahinda IV.,[2] for instance, we find the following : "... Goluggam Raksam Kudasenu, Meykappar Kuburgamu Lokohi, Katiri Agbohi, and Kundala Arayam ; all these lords who sit in the Royal Council, and who have come (together) in accordance with the mandate delivered (by the King-in-Council), have promulgated these regulations." When any grant was made by the State to any individual or body, a Council Warrant of Immunity was issued. In the Madirigiriya Pillar inscription of

[1] Vide Chillapa Adikāram, and Mani-Mekalai, quoted by P. S. Rama-Krishna Iyer in his Polity and Social Life in Ancient Kerala.

[2] Epigraphia Zeylanica, Vol. I. No. 21.

Kassapa V. (980-990 A.D.),[1] we find the following passage: "Whereas it was (so) decreed by the Supreme Council, we, all of us, Officers-of-State, namely, . . . (five names) . . . have come . . . by Order and granted this Council Warrant of Immunity to the area . . ." Sometimes Pillars of Council Warranty [2] were set up to inform people of the privileges granted to religious or other institutions. The appreciation of the importance of the Council by monarchs is shown by the Slab Inscription of Queen Līlāvatī [3] where she says: "By creating a Council of wise, brave, and faithful ministers, she has freed her own kingdom from the dangers (arising) from other kingdoms."

[1] Epigraphia Zeylanica, Vol. II. No. 6.

[2] Vide Pillar-inscription of Dappula V., Ep. 2. Vol. II. No. 8.

[3] Epigraphia Zeylanica, Vol. I. No. 14.

CHAPTER IX

THE MINISTERS

THE Central Administration was conducted by the King with the assistance of a number of Ministers or Chief Officers-of-State. "Government," says Kautilya, "can be carried on only with the assistance of others. A single wheel does not move (the car of administration). Therefore, the King should appoint ministers, and act according to their advice."[1] Manu says: "Even an undertaking easy (in itself) is (sometimes) hard to be accomplished by a single man; how much (harder is it for a King), especially (if he has) no assistant (to govern) a kingdom which yields great revenues."[2]

Great importance was attached in ancient days to the proper selection of Ministers. A Minister was chosen not only in view of his capacity and character, but also of his family connections. The fittest person to be a Minister was he who was "a native of the country; born of a high family; influential; learned in the arts and sciences; possessed of wisdom and

[1] Arthasāstra, Bk. I. ch. 7. [2] Manu, VII. 55.

foresight; endowed with a good memory; capable; eloquent; intelligent; possessed of enthusiasm, endurance, dignity and grandeur; pure in character, devotedly attached (to the interests of the State); endowed with excellent conduct, strength, health, and boldness; devoid of procrastination and fickleness of mind; of a loving nature; and not of a disposition to excite enmity."[1] This was the ideal measure of the qualities of a Minister, and one who made a close approximation to this ideal was considered as a Minister belonging to the highest class. A Minister whose qualifications fell short of the ideal measure by a quarter was of the middling type; while he who possessed only one-half of the qualifications, belonged to the inferior class.[2] The Mahābhārata also lays down a very high standard of ministerial qualifications. "The person," says the great Epic, "who achieves celebrity, who observes all restraints, who never feels jealous of others, who never does

[1] Arthasāstra, Bk. I. ch. 9.

[2] Ibid. "According to Vishnu, men should be selected as ministers who are honest, devoid of greed, careful, and possessed of capacity." Ch. III. The Nitivākyāmrita also discusses the qualifications of ministers (Chs. X. and XI.). Manu says: "Let him appoint seven or eight ministers whose ancestors have been royal servants, who are versed in the sciences, heroes skilled in the use of weapons and descended from good families who have been tried." VII. 54. The Kural says:

> "The King, since counsellors are monarch's eyes,
> Should counsellors select with counsel wise."
>
> Pope's trans. Bk. II. ch. 45.

And again:

> "A minister must greatness own of guardian power, determined mind,
> Learn'd wisdom, manly effort with the former five combined."
>
> Bk. II. ch. 64.

an evil act, who never abandons righteousness through lust, or fear, or covetousness, or wrath, who is clever in the transaction of business, and who is possessed of wise and weighty speech, should be the foremost of Ministers . . . Persons well-born, and possessed of good behaviour, who are liberal and never indulge in brag, who are brave and respectable, learned and full of resources, should be appointed as subordinate Ministers in charge of the different departments." [1]

Ministers were, as a rule, selected from the ranks of learned Brāhmanas who, according to Megasthenes, formed a separate class and who advised the King or magistrates of self-governed cities in the management of public affairs. "In point of numbers," says the Greek writer, "it is a small class, but it is distinguished by superior wisdom and justice, and hence enjoys the prerogative of choosing governors, chiefs of provinces, deputy governors, superintendents of the treasury, generals of the army, admirals of the navy, controllers, and commissioners who superintend agriculture." [2]

Chānakya, in his Arthasāstra, gives an interesting

[1] Sānti Parva, Sec. 80, sls. 25-27.

Cf. Plato's conception of the character of the guardians of the State: "Truth was his leader whom he followed, always and in all things, and his other virtues were courage, magnificence, apprehension, and memory." Republic, Bk. VI. Cf. also Aristotle: "These are the qualifications required in those who have to fill the highest offices—(1) first of all, loyalty to the established constitution; (2) the greatest administrative quality; (3) virtue and justice of the kind proper to each form of government." Politics, V. 9.

[2] McCrindle, p. 212.

summary of the discussions of the older teachers in regard to the question, namely, what sort of persons should be made ministers. We give a translation of this passage below :

"The King," says Bharadvāja, "should employ his fellow-students as his Ministers, for they can be trusted by him inasmuch as he has personal knowledge of their honesty and capacity." "No," says Visālāksha, "for, as they have been his playmates, they would disregard him. But he should employ as ministers those whose secrets are known to him." Parāsara says, "The fear of betrayal is common to both, and under the fear of the betrayal of his own secrets, the King may follow his Ministers in their good and bad acts. Hence he should employ as Ministers those who have proved faithful to him under difficult circumstances." "No," says Pisuna, "for this is devotion but not intellectual capacity. He should appoint as ministers those who, when employed in financial work, show as much as, or more than, the usual revenue, and are of tried ability." Kaunapadanta says: "That would not do; for such persons are devoid of other ministerial qualifications; he should employ as Ministers men whose fathers and grandfathers have been Ministers; such persons, because of their knowledge of past events and of a long-standing relationship with the King, will, though offended, never desert him." "No," says Vāta-vyādhi, "for such persons, having acquired complete dominion over the King, usurp the King's powers. He should, therefore, appoint such new men as are proficient in political science." "No," says the son of Bāhudanti, "for a man possessing only a theoretical knowledge of the science and having no experience of practical politics is likely to commit serious blunders when employed in the work of actual administration. Hence he should employ as ministers, men who are born of a high family, and are possessed of wisdom, purity of purpose, bravery and loyalty. Ministerial appointments should depend only on qualifications." Chānakya gives his own view in those words : "There is an element of reasonableness in each of these opinions ; the fitness of a Minister should be considered in view of the work he is called upon to undertake." [1]

The general duties of Ministers, according to the Agni Purāna, consisted in "deliberating upon the measures of the State, taking steps for the success of undertakings, preparing for all future contingencies, supervising the royal exchequer, drafting civil and criminal laws for the realm, checking encroachment by any Foreign Power, taking steps for arresting the progress of disturbances, and protecting the King and the country." [2]

The number of Ministers depended upon the needs

[1] Arthasāstra, Bk. I. ch. 8. The Nītivákyāmrita also discusses this matter in Ch. 18.

[2] Agni Purāna, CCXLI. sls. 16-17.

of the State. Chānakya is in favour of a small cabinet. "He (the King) shall consult," says Chānakya, "three or four Ministers. The advice of a single Minister does not lead to satisfactory results in complicated cases. (Besides,) a single Minister proceeds wilfully and without restraint. If the King has two Ministers, he may be overpowered by their combined action, or imperilled by their mutual dissensions. But with three or four Ministers, he will never come to any serious grief, and will always arrive at satisfactory conclusions. With Ministers more than four in number, he will come to a decision only after a great deal of trouble, and it will be very difficult to maintain secrecy of counsel."[1] According to Manu, the number of Ministers was to be seven or eight.[2] The Nītivākyāmrita is of opinion that there should be three, five, or seven ministers; "unanimity of opinion being difficult to obtain, the number should be uneven."[3]

The Sukranīti mentions ten chief Ministers, namely, Purodhas (Priest), Pratinidhi (Regent), Pradhāna (Premier), Sachiva (Minister of Finance), Mantri (Councillor), Prāḍvivāka (Chief Judge), Pandita (Legal Minister), Sumantraka (Minister of Peace and War),

[1] Arthasāstra, Bk. I. ch. 15. Cf. also Nītivākyāmrita.

[2] Manu, VII. 54.

[3] Ch. X. Somadeva Sūri adds: "A large number of Ministers, by the combined effect of their separate abilities, increase the efficiency of the government. When, however, one Minister possesses all the faculties necessary for the proper administration of the kingdom, there is no harm in having only one or two Ministers." Ch. X.

Amātya (Secretary of State), and Dūta (Ambassador).[1] In Milinda-panha, we find mention of six chief Officers-of-State, namely, the Commander-in-Chief, the Prime Minister, the Chief Judge, the High Treasurer, the Bearer of the Sunshade of State, and the State Sword-bearer.[2]

The Prime Minister (Pradhāna, Sarvārthaka,[3] Sarvādhikāra,[4] Agrāmātya,[5] Mahāmātya,[6] or simply Mantri[7]) was the highest Officer-of-State and the real Head of the Executive. He was in general charge of the affairs of the State, and sometimes he undertook in addition the duties of a particular department, such as the Foreign Office. Another important Minister was the Purohita (the High Priest), who was always held in the highest regard. In the Aitareya Brāhmana, the Purohita is called the "Protector of the State" (rāshṭra-gopa).[8] Chānakya says:

[1] Sukranīti, Ch. 1.

[2] "And again, O King, just as there are a hundred or two of officers under the King, but only six of them are reckoned as Officers-of-State—the Commander-in-Chief, the Prime Minister, the Chief Judge, the High Treasurer, the Bearer of the Sunshade of State, and the State Sword-bearer. And why? Because of their royal prerogatives." Questions of King Milinda (Rhys Davids), IV. 1, 36.

[3] The term 'Sabbatthaka' (Minister in general) occurs in Questions of Milinda, IV. 8, 26; it correctly indicates the nature of the work of the Prime Minister.

[4] This term is found in the Rājatarangiṇī.

[5] The term 'agrāmātya' occurs in a Ceylon inscription.

[6] In the Mahāparinibbāna-suttanta, Vassakāra is described as 'Magadha-mahāmatta.'

[7] Kautilya uses the word 'Mantri' in the sense of 'Prime Minister.'

[8] The passage may be freely translated thus: "A King who has a learned Brāhmana as his Purohita and Protector of the State, makes alliances

"As a disciple follows his preceptor, as a son obeys his father, as a servant obeys his master, so should the King obey the Purohita."[1] The Nītivākyāmrita says: "The Prime Minister and the Purohita are the father and mother of the King." Sometimes, these two offices were combined in the person of one minister.

The other chief Officers-of-State (Amātya, Sachiva, or Mahāmātra) were in charge of particular departments.[2] Of these, the most important were the Collector-general (Samāhartā) and the Treasurer-general (sannidhātā). It was the duty of the former to collect the revenues of the State from various sources, such as the taxes levied on lands, the income from mines, forests, pasture lands, and fishing, and the tolls received from the trade-routes.[3] The Treasurer-general was the custodian of the moneys of the State. He received into the treasury the King's revenues, and had custody of the precious metals, jewellery, and valuable property of all other kinds.

with foreign Kings, destroys his enemies, conquers Kshatriyas with the help of Kshatriyas, and enjoys power with the assistance of an army; the people (visah) become favourable to him, and give their unanimous support to him." Ch. XI.

[1] Cf. Bodhāyana, I. 10, 8, "Tasya śāsane varteta."

[2] Chānakya says: "Having divided the spheres of their respective powers in view of the different kinds of work to be performed, and the time and place of their performance, such persons should be appointed as Officers-of-State and not (merely) as Councillors." Arthasāstra, Bk. II. Ch. 8. The term 'mahāmātra' occurs in the Arthasāstra as well as in Asoka's Edicts.

[3] Arthasāstra, Bk. II. ch. 6.

It was also his duty to see to it that no part of the income of the State was misappropriated by the officers of any of the departments.[1] Another important officer was the Minister of War and Peace, whose duty it was to maintain communications with Foreign Powers and to decide which of the expedients of foreign politics was the most suitable at any particular moment.[2] The Chief Judge presided over the Royal Court and was also a sort of Minister of Justice. The Commander-in-Chief, it seems, held the position of a Minister, although the Nītivākyāmrita objects to his being a Councillor,[3] and the Sukranīti omits him from the list of Ministers. Sometimes a separate Minister was appointed to have charge of the Royal Seal,[4] and the fact that the concurrence of the Keeper of the Seal was essential in all important matters of State made his position one of great dignity and importance.

Each Minister managed the affairs of his own department, and all the Ministers collectively formed a sort of Cabinet for purposes of combined action. But it seems that the responsibility of the Ministers

[1] Arthasāstra, Bk. II. ch. 5. [2] Agni Purāna, Ch. 220.

[3] "Commanders of the army should not be members of Council (mantrādhikārinah), for each of these, viz. the favour of the King, membership of the Council, and the profession of arms is sufficient to turn a man's head, not to speak of a combination." Ch. X.

[4] "Just, O King, as an official who is anxious for the Seal (mudda-kāmo), and for the office and custody thereof, will exert himself to the attainment of the Seal by sacrificing everything in his house—property and corn, gold and silver . . ." Questions of Milinda (Rhys Davids), IV. 8, 9.

was individual and not collective. Chānakya draws a distinction between the Cabinet (mantriṇaḥ) and the Council of Ministers (mantri-parishat). The Council thus seems to have been the Cabinet of Ministers enlarged by the addition of members who held no portfolios. Chānakya advises the King to consult both these bodies on important occasions. The King had also the power to consult the Ministers individually as well as collectively. To ensure that each Minister should become familiar with all kinds of work, and to prevent any Minister from growing too powerful, an interchange of places in the Ministry was ordered from time to time.

The Ministers were, of course, directly responsible for the due performance of their duties to the King. But they had also a sort of indirect responsibility to the people. This is illustrated by the story told by Hiuen Tsiang about Vikramāditya, King of Srāvastī. This King was very charitably inclined, and he largely supplied the wants of the poor, the orphans, and the bereaved. One day he ordered his Ministers to distribute daily five lakhs of gold coins. On this, the treasurer, fearing that the resources of the State would soon be exhausted, said to the King: "Your treasury will thus be emptied, and then fresh imposts will have to be laid, until the resources of the land be also exhausted, then the voice of complaint will be heard and hostility be provoked. Your Majesty, indeed, will get credit for charity, but your Minister will lose the respect of all."[1] The story current at Hiuen Tsiang's time about Asoka's Minister[2] refusing to comply with the King's wish to give away all his possessions in charity, also shows that the Ministers recognised some responsibility to the people. And they were held responsible not only for their own actions but also for those of the King. This theory of Ministerial responsibility is clearly expressed in the following passage in the Sanskrit drama, Mudrā-Rākshasa: "When anything wrong is done by the King, the fault is of the Minister; (for) it is through the negligence of the driver that an elephant goes mad."[3] So, when Rājyavardhana was treacherously assassinated, the Ministers told Harshavardhana that they were to blame for the misfortune, for they ought not to have allowed Rājyavardhana to go to a foreign King's camp unguarded.[4]

The Ministers possessed great powers in the State even in normal times; but during the minority of a King or when the King happened to be a weak man, their powers were immense. When the throne fell vacant, they played the role of King-makers.[5] Chāṇakya, for instance, placed Chandragupta on the throne of Magadha.[6] From the poet-historian Bāna as well

[1] Buddhist Records (Beal), Bk. II. [2] Hiuen Tsiang (Beal), Bk. VIII.

[3] Act III. [4] Harshacharita, Ch. VI.

[5] In the Satapatha Brāhmana some of the state officials are called 'king-makers' (rāja-kṛtaḥ).

[6] Cf. the Vāyu and the other Purānas, "Chandraguptaṁ rājye Kauṭilyaḥ-sthāpayiṣyati." See ante, Ch. I.

as from Hiuen Tsiang we know how a successor was appointed to Rājyavardhana, King of Kanauj. We are told that Bhandi, the Prime Minister, called a meeting of the Ministers and said to them: "The destiny of the nation is to be fixed to-day . . . Because he (Harsha) is attached to his family, the people will trust in him. I propose that he assume the royal authority. Let each one give his opinion on the matter, whatever he thinks." Then the chief Ministers exhorted Harsha to take authority, saying: "The opinion of the people as shown in their songs, proves their real submission to your qualities. Reign, then, with glory over the lands."[1] From the Ceylon inscriptions we learn that the Ministers elected Līlāvatī as Queen of Ceylon, and afterwards deposed her. In the temporary absence of a King, the Ministers ruled the country—as a rule, very wisely and well.[2]

Although every Minister occupied a responsible position, it was the Prime Minister who was mainly responsible for the good government of the country.[3] Unless the King happened to be a man of exceptional

[1] Vide Hiuen Tsiang's Travels and Harshacharita.

[2] In the Mahāvamsa it is said that the ministers governed the Kingdom of Ceylon righteously for one year after the death of Vijaya, and on the arrival of his nephew from India, they invested him with the sovereignty of Lanka. Ch. IX. The Chānakya-sūtra contains the following passage: "If there are good ministers, the affairs of a State can be managed even without a King."

[3] Abul Fazl, describing the Hindu system of government, says: "Him (the Prime Minister) he (the King) must consult on all occasions with implicit confidence, and intrust with the executive power." Ayeen-i-Akbery (Gladwin), p. 493.

ability, the Prime Minister was the real ruler of the State. "All activities," says Chānakya, "depend upon the Prime Minister, such, for instance, as the accomplishment of the works of the people, the security of the Kingdom from foreign aggression and internal troubles, remedial measures against calamities, colonisation, improvement of the soil, maintenance of the army, and the collection and disbursement of the State revenue."[1] According to Bharadvāja, the Prime Minister was the most important person in the State—even more important than the King himself, for, says Bharadvāja, "in the absence of the Prime Minister, the King is absolutely incapable of doing any work, like a bird deprived of its wings." Chānakya, however, would place the Prime Minister as next to the King, for "the King appoints the Ministers, and he can replace a bad Minister by a good one."[2]

The influence exercised by an able Prime Minister over a King is well illustrated by the relations between Chānakya and Chandragupta, as depicted in Mudrā-Rākshasa. The Emperor is there described as a person who is absolutely helpless without the guidance of the Prime Minister. He never undertakes any measure, great or small, without the advice of Chānakya. So great is the Emperor's regard for his Minister that whenever the two meet, Chandragupta greets Chānakya by touching the latter's feet.

[1] Bk. VIII. ch. 1. [2] Arthasāstra, Bk. VIII. ch. 1.

This great influence possessed by Ministers of old was doubtless, in a large measure, due to the selfless spirit in which many of them served the State. Though such Ministers controlled the destinies of large kingdoms and sometimes extensive empires, they, as a rule, led very simple lives,[1] and were renowned for their honesty, integrity, and nobility of character. Numerous examples of devotedness to duty on the part of Ministers, sometimes under very difficult and trying circumstances, are recorded in Indian history and literature.[2]

But it would be a mistake to suppose that Ministers were invariably honest and free from vice. Some of them were greedy. "The Treasurer-general," says Chānakya, "appropriates to himself the money which is paid into the treasury by others; the Collector-general fills his own pockets first, and then gathers revenue for the King, or destroys the revenue collected, and then takes other people's property at his

[1] Chānakya says: "A Minister should never live in luxurious style." Bk. V. ch. 6. In the Mudrā-Rākshasa, Kautilya himself is described as living in an old and dilapidated hut. Act III. With this picture may be compared Plato's ideal picture of Guardians who "were not to have houses or lands or any other property; their pay was to be their food, which they were to receive from other citizens and they were to have no private expenses; for we intended them to preserve their true character of Guardians." Republic, V.

[2] In Bhāsa's Pratimā-Nātaka and Svapna-Vāsavadatta, the Prime Minister is described as a man ready to undertake any risks for the sake of the King. The devotion with which Rākshasa sought to serve a fallen master's family extorted the highest praise even from his bitter enemy Chānakya (Mudrā-Rākshasa, Act II.).

pleasure."[1] Some Ministers were cruel and oppressive, and often gave a wrong advice to the King. In the words of the poet:

> "'Tis thus that evil councillors impel
> The heedless prince into the scorching flames
> Of fierce iniquity and foul disgrace;
> And countless victims perish by the guilt
> Of treacherous ministers, who thus involve
> Both prince and people in promiscuous ruin."[2]

[1] Arthaśāstra, Bk. II.

[2] Mrichchakatikā (Wilson), Act IX.

CHAPTER X

THE SUBORDINATE EXECUTIVE

THE details of executive administration were in the hands of the subordinate officials (yukta and upayukta) [1] working under the control and general supervision of the Ministers. The business of the State was divided into a number of departments, each of them being under a Superintendent. In one passage Chānakya speaks of eighteen departments (ashtādaśa tīrthāḥ),[2] which probably refers only to the more important departments. In his actual treatment of the subject of administration, he mentions about thirty departments.[3]

One of the most important of the Government departments was that of Accounts. It was under a Superintendent who appointed a number of capable accountants (gāṇanika), sub-accountants (saṅkhyāyaka), totalisers (nīvī-grāhaka) and coin-examiners (rūpa-darśaka) to carry on the work. It was the duty

[1] Arthasāstra, Bk. II. ch. 9.

[2] Ibid. Bk. II. ch. 13. Vide also Mahābhārata, Sabhā Parva, V. 38.

[3] Ibid. Bk. II. chs. 1-36.

of the Superintendent to keep the account-books in proper order, and to see to it that no part of the State finances was misappropriated or misapplied. He received accounts from the officials of all departments and had them properly audited.[1]

It was the duty of the Superintendent of the Treasury to admit into the store-house gems and pearls as well as various other articles, whether of superior or inferior value, such as corals, fragrant substances, skins, woollen fabrics, cotton fabrics, and silk fabrics. He also received and kept accounts of agricultural produce, taxes, incomes derived from commercial operations, exchange realisations, presents, arrears of revenue, etc. It was his duty to acquaint himself with the values, qualities, and uses of all kinds of articles, and to take proper steps for the preservation of things kept in the store-house. The Superintendent was expected to regulate the consumption of stores in such a way that one-half might always be kept as a reserve for emergencies. He had also to replace old things by new.

The Superintendent of Mines attended to the actual condition of the mines which were being worked, as well as to exploration work in connection with the discovery of new mines. He had to ascertain the richness and the value of ores. It was also his business

[1] Arthasāstra, Bk. II. ch. 7. The accounts were to be regularly submitted in the month of Āshādha, and if the officials failed to submit them in proper time, they were to be fined.

to attend to the collection of diamonds, precious stones, pearls, corals and conch-shells, and the regulation of the commerce in those commodities.[1]

The Superintendent of Metals and Metallic Manufactures supervised the manufacture of such metals as bell-metal, and sulphate of arsenic, and the production of articles of merchandise from various kinds of metals.

The Superintendent of the Mint supervised the coining of various denominations of silver and copper coins. It was his business to regulate the currency as a medium of exchange for purposes of trade and also as a legal tender.

It was the duty of the Superintendent of Commerce to acquaint himself with the demand for, and supply of, commodities, and the rise and fall of prices. He also made it his business to see to it that articles of merchandise were sent to profitable markets.[2]

The Superintendent of Forests attended to the collection of forest produce by employing suitable men for the work, and fixed the dues that were to be paid by people for making use of forests for various purposes.

The Superintendent of the Armoury looked to the manufacture of weapons and other instruments used

[1] Various kinds of pearls were known in those early times, e.g. tāmraparṇika, pāṇḍyakavāṭaka, pāśikya, kauleya, chaurneya, māhendra, kārdamika, srotaseya, hrādīya, and haimavata. Gems were also of many kinds. Vide Arthaśāstra, Bk. II. ch. 11, and Yukti-Kalpataru.

[2] See post, Ch. XVIII. for further details.

in battle, or in the construction and defence of forts, or in the destruction of the enemy's forts. He had also to ascertain the need for, and the supply of, all kinds of weapons, their application, wear and tear, decay and loss. He had to keep everything in its proper place and always ready for use.

The Superintendent of Weights and Measures had weights and measures of various kinds manufactured,[1] as well as balances of many descriptions. He also took steps to prevent the use of false weights and balances. Another Superintendent looked after the instruments used for measuring space and time.

The Superintendent of Tolls had toll-houses erected near the city gates, and supervised the work of the toll-collectors, who had the duty of entering in their books the names of merchants, the place of origin of their merchandise, the quality and value of their goods, the amount payable as toll on each article, and the presence or absence of seal-marks.

The Superintendent of Shipping looked after navigation on the sea, rivers, and lakes. It was his duty to prevent piracy and to keep the water-ways open and safe for merchant shipping. Irrigation formed the charge of another Superintendent.

The Superintendents of Agriculture and Weaving supervised the work of their respective departments. The Superintendents of elephants, horses, and cows

[1] Weights were made of iron or stone or such other material as does not contract in cold or expand in heat. Vide Arthaśāstra, Bk. II. ch. 19.

attended to the health and breed of those animals. The Superintendent of chariots looked to the construction of these vehicles for military as well as ordinary purposes. The Superintendent of pass-ports issued permits to people desirous of entering or leaving the city. The department of spirituous liquors, the slaughter-house, and some other minor departments were also each under a Superintendent.

The Sukranīti mentions some other supervising officers, such as Superintendents of charities and religious institutions. These officers exercised a sort of general supervision over all institutions established for the promotion of religion and charity, and it was their duty to see to it that the funds provided for such objects were properly applied.

The most important of the civil administrative departments was that of the Police. The duty of the Police was two-fold; to prevent the commission of crimes and to bring the offenders to justice. In pursuance of the first object, they kept an eye on all suspicious characters. When a theft occurred, and the police officers failed to trace and catch the thief, they had to make good the loss. Gautama says: "Having recovered property stolen by thieves, he (the King) shall return it to the owner; or (if the property is not recovered) he (the King) shall pay (its value) out of his treasury."[1] The Agni Purāna says: "The King should pay to the owner the price

[1] Gautama, X. 46-47. Cf. also Āpastamba and Vishnu.

of an article stolen by a thief, and re-imburse himself out of the salaries of police officers."[1] This wise regulation must have contributed in no small measure to the efficiency of the police service.

Allied with the Police Department was the Intelligence Department, which seems to have been under the direct control of one of the Ministers, usually the Collector-general. The 'reporters' helped the police in detecting criminals. They also gave the Ministers information regarding the loyal or disloyal feelings of the people, and kept them acquainted with the conduct of Government officials. They apprised the Ministers of the doings of foreign kings and of their intrigues within the kingdom. They were sometimes sent to foreign countries to win over the disaffected people. The 'reporters' worked under various disguises,—as recluses, ascetics, desperadoes, buffoons, commercial travellers, physicians, musicians, idiots, and lunatics.[2]

It is an astonishing fact that although these 'reporters' performed duties of a mean and despicable nature, they were generally honest and truthful. But Chānakya warns Ministers against putting implicit

[1] Agni Purāna, Ch. CCXXII.

[2] Chānakya says: "Merchant spies inside the forts, saints and ascetics in the suburbs, cultivators and recluses in the country parts; herdsmen near the boundaries of the country; forest-dwellers, śramaṇas, and chiefs of wild tribes in forests shall be stationed to watch the movements of enemies. All such spies must be very quick in the despatch of business." Arthaśāstra, Bk. II. ch. 13. And "Spies set up by foreign kings shall be found out by local spies." Ibid.

faith in their reports. "When the information," says he, "derived from three independent sources is the same, then it shall be held reliable. If the sources differ, the 'reporters' concerned shall be either punished or dismissed."[1]

The 'reporters' were, in fact, the eyes and ears of the executive government. Megasthenes seems to refer to this class of officers when he says, "The sixth consists of overseers, to whom is assigned the duty of watching all that goes on, and making reports secretly to the King. Some are entrusted with the inspection of the city, and others with that of the army. . . . The ablest and most trustworthy men are appointed to fill these offices."[2]

There were clerks (lekhakāḥ), messengers, and other inferior officers in each department. Though there was a Superintendent at the head of each department, the final control of the work of the department was vested in a Committee of three, four, or five men. Chānakya says: "The departments should be under the control of many chiefs (bahu-mukhya)." The Sukranīti offers the following advice: "Each department should be under the control of three persons."[3] Megasthenes tells us that each of the departments was under the charge of a Committee of five men. In addition to these, a class of inspecting officers or

[1] Arthaśāstra, Bk. II. ch. 13.

[2] Megasthenes (McCrindle), Fragment XXVIII.

[3] Ch. II. s. 109.

directors (pradeshṭāraḥ)[1] was sometimes appointed to supervise the work of all departments and to bring the work of each department into line with that of the others.

Some care, it seems, was taken in selecting officers of government. They were usually appointed in view of their general qualifications as well as their fitness for the particular kinds of work they were expected to perform. The Agni Purāna says: "Virtuous men should be employed in work which requires a high degree of moral culture, while men of valour should be appointed in the army. Intelligent men should be employed where the revenue of the State is concerned, while for all kinds of work the King should select men who are above corruption."[2] Officers were at first appointed on probation, and after they had gone through a period of apprenticeship, they were made permanent.[3] Once in the service, they rose step by step as they showed competency in their work, until the ablest and most devoted among them reached the highest rungs of the ladder.[4] This system of a trained bureaucracy for the details of administrative work must have contributed largely to the efficiency of the central government.

The capacities and characters of individual officers, of course, varied. While many officers were devoted

[1] Arthaśāstra, Bk. II. ch. 9.
[2] Agni Purāna, Ch. CCXX.
[3] Sukranīti, Ch. I. sl. 112.
[4] Sukranīti, Ch. I. sl. 115.

to the interests of the State, there were others who had to be kept on the path of duty by a strict system of supervision and control. The subordinate officers of the revenue and financial departments, in particular, did not enjoy much reputation for honesty. Chānakya observes, "Just as it is impossible not to taste the honey or the poison that is below the tongue, so it is impossible for a King's revenue-officer to refrain from tasting even a little of the royal revenue." The fact, however, that the administration was so efficient shows that the State was able to command the services of a large number of competent and honest officers.

The officers of government were remunerated on a liberal scale, so that, being above want and temptation, they might exert themselves in the performance of their duties. Chānakya lays down the following scale of salaries: The Preceptor, the High Priest, the Royal Teacher, the Prime Minister, the Commander-in-Chief, the Crown Prince, the Queen-mother, the Queen-consort,—48,000 panas each (per annum); the Superintendents of the city gates and the palace, the Chief of the Police, the Collector-general, the Treasurer-general,—24,000 each; the princes, the mothers of princes, the chief officer of the city, the judges, the heads of departments, the Members of Council, the prefect of police, the chief officers of boundaries,—12,000 each; the leaders of corporations, the Superintendents of horses and elephants, and inspecting officers,—8,000 each; the Superintendents of infantry, cavalry, chariots, and the forest rangers,—4,000 each, and so on.[1] The salaries were paid either in cash or in kind, or partly in cash and partly in kind. Sometimes grants of lands were made to State officials as a reward for their services. After a long period of service, officials became entitled to pensions,[2] and if they died while in the service of the State, the members of their families received subsistence allowances.[3]

[1] Arthasāstra, Bk. V. ch. 3. These panas were probably silver coins.

[2] Ibid.

[3] "The King incurs a debt if he does not maintain the relations of an officer who has died in the service of the State." Nītivākyāmrita, Ch. XXX.

CHAPTER XI

LEGISLATION

LAW in Ancient India was regarded as higher than society, and it was held the duty of society to conform to Law. Strictly speaking, therefore, there could be no such thing as legislation in the early ages. In fact, if the term 'law' be understood in the limited sense of a command of the sovereign authority, there was no law at all. And yet there were rules of conduct which were binding on all, and violations of which were visited with punishments of some kind or other. Law (Dharma), as understood in the early times, was the entire body of rules by which society was believed to be held together, and which was supposed to conduce to the well-being of the people. Such rules fell into two classes, namely, (1) moral and religious rules, and (2) positive laws. In Ancient India, as in other early societies, these two classes were dealt with together; but though no sharp line of division was drawn between the two, the distinction was more or less clearly understood. People were cognisant of the fact that the sanction for the first kind of rules was religious or social, and that for the second, political; and the recognition of this distinction became more and more clear as society advanced in civilisation. In the course of time a body of rules composing secular law (Vyavahāra) was evolved, which soon acquired as great an authority as the Sacred Law.[1]

The belief prevailed among the ancient Āryans of India, as among other early communities, that all laws, political as well as moral, were of divine origin. And the divine will was assumed to have been manifested in the Sacred Books and in immemorial customs. These, then, were the fountain-heads to which people were to look for their knowledge of law. Thus, Gautama, one of the earliest writers on law, says: "The sources of law are the Vedas, and the tradition and practice of those who know the Vedas."[2] But he adds that the administration of justice should be regulated by the Vedas, the Institutes of the Sacred Law, the Angas, the Purānas, the (special) laws of countries, castes and families (not being opposed to the sacred records), the usages of cultivators, traders, herdsmen, money-lenders, and artisans.[3] Āpastamba mentions the Vedas as the primary source of law, and the agreement among

[1] In later times, although 'dharma' was regarded as the principle underlying law, 'vyavahāra' became what may be called lawyer's law. Thus Abul Fazl, writing in the sixteenth century of the legal system of the Hindus, refers to 'vyavahāra' and not to 'dharma.' According to the Chānakya-sūtra, "'vyavahāra' is more important than 'dharma.'"

[2] Gautama, XI. 19-21.

[3] Gautama, I. 1, 2.

learned men as the secondary source.[1] Bodhāyana's list is slightly different. He says: "The Sacred law is taught in each Veda. (The Sacred law) taught in the Tradition (Smriti, stands) second. The practice of the Sishtas (stands) third."[2] According to Manu, the sources of law are: (1) The Vedas, (2) the Smritis, (3) good customs, and (4) self-satisfaction.[3] Yājnavalkya gives Manu's four sources, but adds ten more as subsidiary sources, thus bringing the total up to fourteen. The secondary sources are (5) deliberation, (6) decisions of Parishads and of persons learned in the Vedas, (7) the Purānas, (8) Nyāya, (9) Mīmāmsā, (10) the Dharmasāstras, (11) temporary needs not inconsistent with one's duties, (12) royal edicts, (13) special usages of corporations, guilds, and communities of heretics, etc., and (14) local customs.[4] Manu also incidentally refers to the primeval laws of countries, of castes, of families, and of heretics and companies (of traders and the like) as rules governing human conduct.[5]

Let us try to examine these sources. The Vedas contain very little of what is called positive law, and they are practically of no importance to us from the juridical standpoint. The Smriti works, on the other hand, are very important. They, in fact, formed the chief basis on which the legal system

[1] Āpastamba (Sacred Book of the East), I. 1, 2, 3.
[2] Bodhāyana, I. 1, 1, 1-5.
[3] Manu, II. 6 and II. 12.
[4] Yājnavalkya, I. 1, 2 and I. 1, 8.
[5] Manu, I. 118.

of the Hindus was built up. The earliest Smriti works were in Sūtra form, and only a few fragments of some of them are now known to us. These were probably composed between the tenth and the fifth centuries B.C. They were gradually superseded by the later works composed in verse and known as the Dharmasāstras. The material of the Dharmasūtras was worked into the Dharmasāstras, but many additions were made at the time of the change of form. The Dharmasāstras themselves underwent many alterations in the course of time.

Yājnavalkya gives the following list of the compilers of Dharmasāstras: Manu, Atri, Vishnu, Hārīta, Yājnavalkya, Usanas, Angiras, Yama, Āpastamba, Samvarta, Kātyāyana, Brihaspati, Parāsara, Vyāsa, Sankha, Likhita, Daksha, Gautama, Sātātapa, and Vasishtha.[1] This list, as Vijnānesvara points out, is only illustrative, and not enumerative, for we know the names of other compilers besides these, the most notable among them being Nārada.

The third, and in some respects the most important source of law, was custom, as it prevailed among Sishtas. Āpastamba says: "It is difficult to learn the sacred law from the Vedas (alone); but by following the indications, it is easily accomplished." These indications are the practices of Sishtas.[2]

[1] Yājnavalkya, I. 4-5.

[2] Āpastamba, II. 11, 29, 13. He further explains the passage thus: The indications for these (doubtful cases are)—"He shall regulate his course of

The 'Sishtas,' according to Bodhāyana, are persons "who are free from envy, free from pride, contented with a store of grain sufficient for ten days, free from covetousness, and free from hypocrisy, arrogance, greed, perplexity, and anger." "(Those are called) Sishtas," adds Bodhāyana, "who, in accordance with the sacred law, have studied the Veda together with its appendages, who know how to draw inferences from that, (and) who are able to adduce proofs perceptible by the senses from revealed texts."[1] Sishtas in Bodhāyana's opinion were to be chiefly found in Āryāvarta, and, therefore, the rule of conduct which prevailed in that country was to be held authoritative. Manu gives a slightly different definition of the term. According to him, the custom handed down in regular succession (since time immemorial) among the (four chief) castes and the mixed races of the country called Brahmāvarta was regarded as the conduct of virtuous men, and the custom of Brāhmanas in the country of Brahmarshi ranked next in importance.

Customs were of various kinds: some were general, that is to say, prevailing among the whole

action according to the conduct which is unanimously recognised in all countries by men of the three twice-born castes, who have been properly obedient (to their teachers), who are aged, of subdued senses, neither given to avarice, nor hypocrites. Acting thus, he will gain both worlds. Some declare that the remaining duties must be learnt from women and men of all castes."

[1] Bodhāyana, I. 1, 1, 5-6.

community; some were tribal, that is, observed by a particular tribe; some appertained to a particular class, such as tradesmen, artisans, or cultivators; and some were confined to single families. There is a dispute among the compilers of the laws as to the extent of the validity of customs. Some, like Bodhāyana, are of opinion that all customs should be recognised;[1] while others hold that no heed should be taken of any practices that are opposed to the tradition of Sishtas. As a matter of fact, the customs of the non-Āryan races who entered the pale of Āryan civilisation were not disturbed, unless they appeared to be grossly immoral. These customs, however, underwent considerable modifications in imitation of the laws of Āryas. When a new country was conquered, its laws were, as a rule, maintained intact. Vishnu says: "On conquering a country, the conqueror should not destroy its laws." So, Yājnavalkya offers the advice: "Whatever custom, law, or family practice exists in a (conquered) country, should be maintained in the form in which it has come down from the past." On the other hand, in Chānakya's opinion, righteous laws were established in a conquered country.

Self-satisfaction was rather a rule of conduct for

[1] "There is a dispute regarding five practices in the south and in the north. . . . For each (of these customs) the (rule of the) country should be considered the authority. But Gautama declares that that is false. And one should not take heed of either (set of practices) because they are opposed to the tradition of the Sishtas." I. 1, 2, 5-8.

the individual in cases giving rise to doubts, than a source of law. It was merely the recognition of the right of a man to act according to the dictates of his own conscience when no definite rule of law was available as a guide. The other subsidiary authorities mentioned by Yājnavalkya, such as Mīmāmsā and Nyāya, were in reality guides for the interpretation of legal rules, and not exactly sources of law.

If direct legislation was impossible in early times, indirect methods were available. Law could not be made, but it could be declared. In the Brihadāranyaka, Law is thus defined: "Law is what is called the true. And if a man declares what is true, they say he declares the law; and if he declares the law, they say he declares what is true."[1] For the declaration of the law in doubtful cases, a duly authorised body of persons was needed. Such a body was a *Parishat* (or parshat) composed of learned Brāhmans. A Parishat was properly constituted when there were present in the assembly ten Brāhmanas, learned in the Vedas, skilled in reasoning, and free from covetousness.[2] Bodhāyana quotes the following verse: "Four men, who each know one of the four Vedas, a Mīmāmsaka, one who knows the Angas, one who recites the sacred law, and three Brāhmanas belonging to (three different) orders, (constitute) an assembly consisting, at least, of ten

[1] Brihadāranyaka, I. 4, 14. [2] Gautama, XVIII. 48.

members."[1] Such an ideal assembly was, however, not always easy to get together, and very often three or four Brāhmanas were held sufficient to constitute an assembly, if they were persons who commanded the respect and confidence of the people. Vasishtha says: "What four or (even) three (Brāhmanas) who have completely studied the Vedas proclaim, that must be distinctly recognised as the sacred law, not (the decision) of a thousand fools."[2] Sometimes, even the opinions of single individuals of pre-eminent virtue and wisdom had the same weight as the decision of Parishats. In regard to the decision of one individual, however, Bodhāyana gives this wise advice: "Narrow and difficult to find is the path of the sacred law, towards which many gates lead. Hence if there is a doubt, it must not be propounded by one man only, however learned he may be."[3]

The Parishats of olden days may, in a sense, be called legislative assemblies. Although their main business was to interpret—not to enact—laws, yet in performing this duty they, not unoften, changed

[1] Bodhāyana, I. 1, 9.

[2] Vasishtha, III. 7. He also says: "Many thousands (of Brāhmanas) cannot form a legal assembly (for declaring the sacred law), if they have not fulfilled their sacred duties, are unacquainted with the Vedas, and subsist only by the name of their caste." III. 5. Vide also Bodhāyana, I. 1, 16. In regard to the number, Bodhāyana says: "There may be five, or there may be three, or there may be one blameless man who decides (questions regarding) the sacred law." I. 1, 9.

[3] Bodhāyana, I. 1, 10.

the laws so as to bring them into greater harmony with the altered circumstances of changed times. The rules of conduct were not inflexible in ancient times, and the Parishats, while maintaining the infallibility of the Vedas and the Smritis, considerably modified the spirit of the laws. The text-book writers, in compiling the old laws of the country, greatly helped the process of change, and, in later times, the commentators also contributed to the same result.

As time went on, these indirect modes of changing the laws of the country must have been found very inconvenient. Originally, the King had no power to legislate for the country, but as society became more complex, it must have been found necessary to entrust the King with some power to issue orders which would be recognised by the law-courts. So some of the law-books mention the King's ordinances as one of the subsidiary sources of law. These edicts, it seems, at first dealt only with particular cases, and did not lay down any general rules. Moreover, they generally related to the work of executive government, and formed something like the *droit administratif* of France.[1] In more modern times, it seems, the King in Council considerably extended the right of issuing ordinances, and the Agni Purāna and the

[1] Vide Manu: "Let no (man), therefore, transgress that law which the King decrees with respect to his favourites, nor (his orders) which inflict pain on those in disfavour." VII. 13.

Sukranīti mention a Law Member of Council as one of the principal Officers-of-State. The advice of the Sukranīti that notices of newly-passed ordinances should be put up at the cross-roads, and that the people should be informed of them by beat of drum suggests that the issue of legislative ordinances was not very infrequent in the later years of the Hindu Period of Indian history.

CHAPTER XII

THE ADMINISTRATION OF JUSTICE

In early Vedic times justice was administered by the tribe and clan assemblies, and the judicial procedure was very simple.[1] But with the extension of the functions of the State and the growth of the royal powers, the King came gradually to be regarded as the fountain of justice,[2] and a more or less elaborate system of judicial administration came into existence.

According to Brihaspati, "judicial assemblies are of four sorts: stationary, not stationary, furnished

[1] Prof. Macdonell says: "(In the early Vedic Age) there is no trace of an organised criminal justice vested either in the King or in the people. There still seems to have prevailed the system of wergeld (Vaira), which indicates that criminal justice seems to have remained in the hands of those who were wronged. In the Sūtras, on the other hand, the King's peace is recognised as infringed, a penalty being paid to him, or according to the Brahminical text-books, to the Brahmins. It may, therefore, reasonably be conjectured that the royal power of jurisdiction steadily increased; the references in the Satapatha-Brāhmana to the King as wielding punishment (Daṇḍa) confirm this supposition." Vedic Index, I. pp. 391-392.

He adds that there is very little recorded as to civil law or procedure in early Vedic literature.

[2] "The King is the fountain-head of justice." Nārada, (Jolly) Legal Procedure, III. 7. But Brihaspati says: "A Brāhmana is the root of the tree of justice; the sovereign prince is its stem and branches; the ministers are its leaves and blossoms; and just government is its fruit." I. 34.

with the King's signet ring, and directed (by the King). The judges are of as many sorts. A stationary court meets in a town or village; one not stationary is called movable; one furnished with (the King's) signet ring is superintended by the Chief Judge; one directed is held in the King's presence."[1] Nārada says: "Family meetings (kula), corporations (śreṇi), village assemblies (gaṇa), one appointed (by the King), and the King (himself) are invested with the power to decide lawsuits; and of these, each succeeding is superior to the one preceding it in order."[2]

At the head of the judicial system stood the King's Court. This Court was held at the capital, and was presided over, sometimes by the King himself, but more often by a learned Brāhmana appointed for the purpose, who was known as the *Adhyaksha* or *Sabhāpati*. The Adhyaksha perhaps originally selected for each particular occasion in course of time became a permanent Officer-of-State, and held the position of the Chief Justice (Prāḍvivāka) of the realm. The King, together with the Prāḍvivāka and three or four other judges (dhārmikāḥ), formed the highest Court of Justice.[3] It was, however, the

[1] Brihaspati, I. 2-3. [2] Legal Procedure (Jolly), 7.

[3] Manu says: "A King desirous of investigating law cases must enter his Court of Justice, preserving a dignified demeanour, together with Brāhmanas and experienced councillors. There, either seated or standing, raising his right arm, without ostentation of his dress or ornaments, let him examine the business of suitors." VIII. 1-2.

Yājnavalkya says: "The King, putting aside wrath and covetousness,

Chief Justice who in reality presided over the King's Court, even when the King was present. Nārada says: "Attending to the dictates of the law-book, and adhering to the opinion of his Chief Justice, let him (i.e. the King) try causes in due order, adhibiting great care."[1] Brihaspati describes the respective duties of the different members of the King's Court in these words: "The Chief Justice decides causes: the King inflicts punishments: the judges investigate the merits of the case."[2] The number of judges varied. According to Manu, three judges, besides the Chief Justice, were enough to form a court, but Chānakya held that the judicial assembly should consist of six persons,—three Officers-of-State, and three other learned persons.[3] According to the Sukranīti, the number of judges was to be uneven,—seven, five, or three.

The jury system, as it now prevails in the European countries, is somewhat different from what prevailed in Ancient India. The three or five members of the judicial assembly acted as jurors as well as judges, but the final decision rested with the Chief Judge.

should decide cases with the assistance of learned Brāhmanas and in accordance with law." II. 1. According to the Sukranīti, the King was never to try cases alone and by himself.

[1] Nārada (Jolly), Legal Procedure, 35.

[2] Brihaspati, I. 6. "He (the Adhyakṣa) should decide cases with the assistance of three members (of the judicial assembly)." Manu, VIII. 10. The Sukranīti also says that the chief judge should sit with the members of the judicial assembly (sabhyaiḥ saha) to decide cases. II. 96.

[3] Arthaśāstra, Bk. III. ch. 1.

There is, however, one point on which we still require more light. It seems that, besides the members of the assembly, other persons present in court were permitted, on certain occasions, to offer their opinions. Nārada says: "Whether authorised or unauthorised, one acquainted with the law shall give his opinion. He passes a divine sentence who acts up to the dictates of law."[1] The Sukranīti quotes this passage with approval, and adds: "Duly qualified merchants should be made hearers."[2] The Sukranīti also quotes another passage from the Smritis, namely, "Either the court-house should not be entered, or the right word should be said. A man who does not speak, or speaks unjustly, incurs sin." The point is not clear, and we wonder how the custom, if it existed at all, worked in practice.

The Chief Justice and the puisne judges were chosen in view of their eminent character and deep learning.[3] They were, as a rule, Brāhmanas, but sometimes a few of them were selected from the other castes.

[1] Nārada, Legal Procedure, III. 2. [2] Sukranīti, IV. 5, 27.

[3] "The King should appoint as judges persons who are well versed in the Vedas and the other branches of learning, who are acquainted with the Sacred Law, and who are truthful and impartial towards friends and foes." Yājnavalkya, II. 2-3. Cf. Brihaspati, I. 29-30, and Sukranīti, IV. 5, 14. Nārada says: "He is called a (Prāḍvivāka or) chief judge who—fully acquainted with the eighteen titles (of law) and with the eight thousand subdivisions thereof, skilled in logic and other branches of science, and thoroughly versed in revealed and traditional lore—investigates the law relative to the case in hand by putting questions (prat) and passing a decision (vivecayati) according to what was heard or understood by him." Quotations from Nārada, I. 1-2. Sacred Books of the East, Vol. XXXIII.

The King's Court, it seems, had two sorts of jurisdiction, namely, original and appellate. As an original court it tried all cases which arose within the boundaries of the capital. On its appellate side it was the highest Court of Appeal for all cases which were triable in the first instance by the inferior courts.[1] The King's Court also exercised a sort of general supervision over the administration of justice throughout the country.

Next in importance to the King's Court were the principal courts held in the important centres[2] and in the larger towns forming the headquarters of districts or sub-districts.[3] The constitution of these courts was very similar to that of the King's Court. Royal officers, assisted by persons learned in the law, administered justice in these courts. They were presided over by Adhyakshas appointed by the Central Government. They had original jurisdiction in respect of all cases arising within the boundaries of the towns in which they sat, and also of the more important civil and criminal cases occurring in the neighbouring villages. And it seems that they had a sort of appellate jurisdiction over the decisions of the lower courts within the districts or sub-districts of which the towns formed the headquarters.

As a rule, the same courts tried both civil and criminal cases. The Smriti works do not draw any

[1] Brihaspati, I. 30. [2] 'Janapada-sandhi,' Arthasāstra, Bk. II. ch. 36.

[3] 'Saṅgraha,' 'droṇamukha,' 'sthānīya,' Arthasāstra, Bk. II. ch. 36.

distinction between civil and criminal courts. But Chānakya mentions, besides the ordinary law courts (dharmasthīya), a class of "courts for the removal of the thorns of the state" (Kaṇṭaka-śodhana). These latter were what may be called administrative courts. They were presided over by three Officers-of-State,[1] and dealt with offences which affected not so much the rights of individuals as the interests of the community, and interfered with the proper government of the realm.[2]

Besides these courts, each village had its local court, which was composed of the headman and the elders of the village.[3] Such courts decided minor criminal cases, such as petty thefts, as well as civil suits of a trifling nature, like disputes relating to the boundaries of lands situate within the village.[4] Their

[1] These officials were to be either ministers (amātyāḥ) or directors (pradeshṭāraḥ). Arthasāstra, Bk. IV. ch. 1.

[2] Arthasāstra, Bk. IV., deals with cases which were triable by these administrative courts.

[3] 'Grāma-vṛddhāḥ,' Arthasāstra, Bk. III. ch. 9.

[4] A flood of light is thrown on the system of administration of justice in Ceylon by the Vevalakatiya Slab-inscription of Mahinda IV. (1026-1042 A.D.). From this inscription we learn that within the Daśagāma justice was administered by means of a Communal Court composed of headmen and responsible householders subject to the authority of the King in Council, and that this Court had the power to try all cases and to inflict even the extreme punishment of death. It runs thus: "... They (the headmen and the householders) shall sit in session and enquire of the inhabitants of the Dasagam (in regard to these crimes). The proceedings of the enquiry having been so recorded that the same may be produced (thereafter), they shall have the murderer punished with death. Out of the property taken by the thieves by violence, they shall have such things as have been identified restored to their respective owners, and have (the thieves) hanged ..." Epigraphia Zeylanica, Vol. I. No. 21.

powers, it seems, were limited to the transfer of the possession of property and the inflicting of small fines. Decisions in these courts were given in accordance with the opinion of the majority of honest persons composing the courts.[1] The idea of a system of local courts for the disposal of cases seems to have been firmly rooted in the minds of the people. The Sukranīti says: "They are the (best) judges of the merits of a case who live in the place where the accused person resides, and where the subject-matter of the dispute has arisen."[2] Brihaspati goes so far as to recommend that "for persons roaming in the forest a court should be held in the forest, for warriors in the camp, and for merchants in the caravan."[3] And it seems that this recommendation was, at least on some occasions, carried into effect for the convenience of suitors. From a Ceylon inscription we learn that itinerant justices from the capital used to visit different parts of the *island for the disposal of* cases and for the purpose of supervising the system of administration of justice.[4] It is very probable that a similar system existed in India also.

The work of the regular courts was greatly lightened by arbitrators. All cases, except those concerning

[1] "Yato bahavaḥ śuchayo 'numatā vā tato niyaccheyuḥ." Arthaśāstra, Bk. III. ch. 9.

[2] IV. 5, 24.

[3] Brihaspati, I. 25.

[4] The passage runs thus: "Should the inhabitants of these Dasagam villages have transgressed any of the rules stated (above) the royal officials who go annually (on circuit) to administer justice (in the country) shall . . ." Epigraphia Zeylanica, Vol. I. No. 21.

violent crimes, could be decided by arbitration by guilds of artisans, assemblies of co-habitants, meetings of religious sects, and by other bodies duly authorised by the King.[1] Nārada is a great believer in the system of arbitration, and he says: "(In disputes) among merchants, artisans, or the like persons, and in (disputes concerning) persons subsisting by agriculture or as dyers, it is impossible for outsiders to pass a sentence; and the passing of the sentence must, therefore, be entrusted to persons acquainted with such matters (in a cause of this sort)." This system had the great merit of giving substantial justice to the disputants and, at the same time, preventing ruinous litigation.

The relations subsisting between the different kinds of courts are thus described by Brihaspati: "When a cause has not been (duly) investigated by (meetings of) kindred, it should be decided after due deliberation by companies (of artisans); when it has not been duly examined by companies (of artisans), it should be decided by assemblies (of co-habitants); and when it has not been (sufficiently) made out by such assemblies (it should be tried) by appointed (judges)."[2] And again, "Judges are superior in authority to (meetings of) kindred and the rest; the chief judge

[1] Brihaspati, I. 28. Vide also Sukranīti, Ch. IV. sec. 5.

[2] I. 30. Brihaspati adds: "(Meetings of) kindred, companies (of artisans), assemblies (of co-habitants), and chief judges are declared to be resorts for the passing of a sentence, to whom he whose cause has been previously tried may appeal in succession." I. 29.

is placed above them; and the King is superior to all, because he passes just sentences." Nārada[1] and Yājnavalkya[2] also describe these relations in terms almost identical with those used by Brihaspati. A verse quoted by Asahāya in his commentary of Nārada runs thus: "A case tried in the village (assembly) goes (on appeal) to the city (court); and one tried in the city (court) goes (on appeal) to the King (i.e. the King's Court); but there is no appeal from the decision of the King, whether the decision be right or wrong."[3] These and other similar passages leave no doubt in our minds that there was a regular mode of appeal from the decisions of the inferior courts to the superior courts. How far this right of appeal was recognised in practice, and to what extent the people actually availed themselves of the right are questions which our present knowledge of the history of Ancient India does not enable us to answer with any degree of satisfaction.

So much about the Courts of Justice. We now pass on to a consideration of judicial procedure as it prevailed in Ancient India. Justice was administered in accordance with legal rules which fell under

[1] "Kulāni śreṇayaś caiva gaṇāś cādhikṛto nṛpaḥ."
Pratiṣṭhā vyavahārāṇām pūrvebhyas tūttarottaram."

Nārada (Jolly's edn.), I. 7.

[2] Yājnavalkya, II. 30.

[3] Jolly, Nārada, footnote to I. 11:
"Grāme dṛṣṭaḥ pure yāti pure dṛṣtas tu rājani
Rajñā dṛṣṭaḥ kudṛṣṭo vā nāsti paunarbhavo vidhiḥ."

one or other of the following four heads: (*a*) Sacred Law (Dharma), (*b*) Secular Law (Vyavahāra), (*c*) Custom (Charitra), and (*d*) Royal Commands (Rāja-śāsana).[1] "Sacred Law," says Chānakya, "is the embodiment of truth; Secular Law depends upon evidence; Custom is decided by the opinion of people; and Royal Edicts constitute administrative law."[2] Some of the Smriti works adopt slightly different orders of classification, and they are often unwilling to admit the validity of Royal Edicts in the administration of justice. Opinion is also divided as to the relative importance of the different sets of legal rules. Chānakya and Nārada agree in holding that "each following one is superior to the one previously named" in the above classification; but the former adds, "When there is disagreement between Sacred Law and Secular Law, or between Sacred Law and Custom, the matter should be decided according to Sacred Law. When, however, there is disagreement between Sacred Law and Morality, Morality shall prevail, for it is likely that the original text (governing such a case) has been

[1] Arthasāstra, Bk. III. ch. 1. The Smriti works adopt slightly different orders of classification.

[2] Arthasāstra, Bk. III. ch. 1. A similar passage occurs in Nārada (Legal Procedure, 10-11); but instead of 'caritraṁ saṁgrahe puṁsām,' we find there the words 'caritraṁ pustakaraṇe.' Prof. Jolly's translation of this passage does not appear to us to be correct.

'Vyavahāra' is defined in the Sukranīti as that "which, by discriminating between good and evil, enables the people to remain on the path of virtue, and promotes their welfare." IV. 5, 4.

lost."[1] According to Nārada, "When it is impossible to act up to the precepts of Sacred Law, it becomes necessary to adopt a method founded on reasoning, because Custom decides everything and overrules the Sacred Law. Divine Law has a subtile nature, and is occult and difficult to understand. Therefore (the King or the judges) must try causes according 'to the visible path.'"[2] Thus, in practice, customs were the most important of the four divisions of law, and Manu[3] and almost all the other law-givers lay it down as the essential principle in the administration of justice that disputes should be decided according to the customs of countries and districts (janapada), of castes (jāti), of guilds (śreṇi), and of families (kula).

The regular courts met once or twice every day, usually in the mornings and evenings. The court-house was looked upon as a sacred place, and it was open to all. Trials were always held in public. The Sukranīti says: "Neither the King nor the members of the judicial assembly should ever try cases in private."[4] Cases were taken up for disposal either in the order of their respective applications, or of their urgency, or of the nature of the injury suffered, or of the relative importance of the castes of suitors. The royal officers were strictly forbidden to take any

[1] Arthaśāstra, Bk. III. ch. 1. Yājnavalkya, comparing Dharmaśāstra and Arthaśāstra, remarks that the former is the more authoritative of the two.

[2] Nārada (Jolly), Legal Procedure, 41.

[3] Manu, VIII. 41.

[4] Sukranīti, IV. 4, 6.

[5] Sukranīti, IV. 5, 161.

part either in the commencement or in the subsequent conduct of a suit. Manu is very emphatic on this point. "Neither the King," says he, "nor any servant of his shall cause a lawsuit to be begun, or hush up one that has been brought (before the court) by (some) other (person)."[1] It is not very clear whether this rule was confined only to civil suits, or applied to criminal cases as well. But it is probable that, in the graver criminal offences, the State took upon itself the duty of conducting the prosecution.[2]

Lawsuits, according to Nārada, have three efficient causes, for they proceed from one or other of three motives, namely, carnal desire, wrath, and greed.[3] "When mortals," says Nārada, "were bent on doing their duty, and were habitually veracious, there existed neither lawsuits, nor hatred, nor selfishness. The practice of duty having died out among mankind, lawsuits have been introduced."[4] The topics which give rise to lawsuits are grouped by the law-givers under eighteen titles, namely, (1) recovery of debts, (2) deposit and pledge, (3) sale without

[1] Manu, VIII. 43. Cf. Nārada (Jolly), Judicial Procedure, 3.

[2] In the Trial Scene in the Sūdraka's Mrichchakatikā, however, we find that in a murder case the court commences its proceedings on the application of a private person (arthī). It is difficult to say whether this was or was not the usual practice.

[3] Nārada (Jolly), I. 26.

[4] Nārada (Jolly's edn.), I. 1-2. This is an illustration of the fact that men in all ages have looked back upon the remote past as the Golden Age of the World.

ownership, (4) concerns among partners, (5) resumption of gifts, (6) non-payment of wages, (7) non-performance of agreements, (8) rescission of sale and purchase, (9) disputes between owners of cattle and herdsmen, (10) disputes regarding boundaries, (11) assault, (12) defamation, (13) theft, (14) robbery and violence, (15) adultery, (16) duties of man and wife, (17) inheritance and partition, and (18) gambling and betting.[1] It is evident that the list includes both civil and criminal cases. Although it was not found necessary to draw a line of separation between the two classes, the distinction, it appears, was fully understood. This becomes clear from the following passage which occurs in Brihaspati Smriti: "Law-suits are of two kinds, according as they originate in (demands regarding) wealth or in injuries. Law-suits originating in wealth are (divided again) into fourteen sorts, those originating in injuries into four sorts."[2] Most of these titles had sub-divisions, which, taken together, amounted to one hundred and thirty-two.[3]

[1] Manu, VIII. 4-7. The titles given in some of the other law books are slightly different.

[2] Brihaspati, II. 5.

[3] Nārada gives the following list: "'Recovery of debt' has twenty-five divisions; 'deposits' has six; 'partnership' has three; 'resumption of gifts' has four; 'breach of service' consists of nine divisions; 'wages' has four divisions; there are two divisions of 'sales effected by another than the rightful owner'; 'non-delivery of a sold chattel' has a single division only; 'rescission of purchase' has four divisions; 'transgression of compact' is one-fold; 'boundary disputes' is twelve-fold; there are twenty divisions in 'mutual duties of husband and wife'; 'the law of

The judicial proceedings in a case consisted of four stages, namely, (1) the statement of the plaintiff (pūrva-paksha), (2) the reply of the defendant (uttara-paksha), (3) the actual trial, consisting of the evidence to establish the case and the arguments on both sides (kriyā), and (4) the decision (nirṇaya).[1]

Proceedings at law, according to Nārada, were of two kinds: "attended by a wager, or not attended by a wager. A lawsuit attended by a wager is where (either of the two parties) stakes in writing a certain sum which has to be paid besides the sum in dispute (in case of defeat)."[2] This system of wager, however, is not to be found in other works, and probably in Nārada's time only the remembrance existed of a custom which had died out long ago. It is interesting to note that the system of wagers in India was analogous to a similar custom in Rome in the earlier stages of the development of Roman legal procedure.

All civil actions as well as criminal cases were commenced by written petitions or verbal complaints made before the Court by the aggrieved party. The date and the place of occurrence, the nature of the

---

inheritance' consists of nineteen divisions; 'heinous offences' of twelve; of both 'abuse' and 'assault' there are three divisions; 'gambling with dice and betting on animals' has a single division; 'miscellaneous' has six divisions." I. 20-25.

[1] Brihaspati, III. 1-2. Vide also Sukranīti, IV. 5, 153. A good description of the actual proceedings in a criminal case is to be found in Sūdraka's Mrichchakatikā. Probably, this portion of the drama, like the rest, was based upon a much earlier work entitled 'Chārudatta' by Bhāsa; but, unfortunately, the whole of this latter book has not yet been discovered.

[2] Nārada (Jolly), Legal Procedure, 4.

wrong done or of the claim made, and the names of the plaintiff (arthī) and the defendant (pratyarthī) were entered in the books of the court.[1] An important point for the Court to determine at this stage was the capacity of the parties. If one of the parties was incapable of suing or defending, the suit could not be proceeded with.

The first important step in the trial was the statement of the case by the plaintiff.[2] He had to cause the plaint to be put in writing, either by the officer of the court or by his legal adviser. A great deal of care, it seems, had to be taken in the preparation of the plaint, for Nārada mentions the following as the defects of a plaint, namely, "(1) if it relates to a different subject, (2) if it is unmeaning, (3) if the amount claimed has not been properly stated, (4) if it is wanting in propriety, (5) if the writing is deficient, or (6) redundant, (7) if it has been damaged."[3] A small verbal error, however, did not vitiate the plaint.[4] On the other hand, a plaint, though otherwise faultless, was held as incorrect if it was contrary to established law and usage.[5]

[1] Arthaśāstra, Bk. IV. ch. 1. Yājnavalkya says that the representation, as made by the plaintiff, is to be put in writing in the presence of the defendant—the year, month, fortnight, and day, together with the names, caste, etc., being given.

[2] "The accusation," says Nārada, "is called the plaint; the answer is called the declaration of the defendant." Legal Procedure, 28. There were, according to Nārada, two modes of plaint, "because a plaint may be either founded on suspicion or a fact." Ibid. 27.

[3] Nārada, Legal Procedure, II. 8.

[4] Ibid. II. 25.

[5] Ibid. II. 15.

The next step was the issue of summons for the attendance of the defendant. It was the duty of the defendant to attend the court on receipt of the summons; and if he attempted to abscond, the plaintiff might arrest him, to secure his presence in court. Such arrest might be one or other of four kinds, namely, local arrest, temporary arrest, inhibition from travelling, and arrest relating to his work.[1]

The defendant, after having become acquainted with the tenor of the plaint, had to give a written reply.[2] A reply might be one or other of four sorts, namely, a denial (mithyā), a confession (sampratipatti), a special plea (pratyavaskandana), a plea of former judgment (prāṅnyāya).[3] Before the answer to the plaint was tendered, the plaintiff was at liberty to amend his plaint in any way he liked,[4] but after the delivery of the reply, no amendment was permitted. The plaintiff was entitled to submit a rejoinder to the defendant's reply.

If the case was a simple one, it was decided then and there. But if it was one which involved any important questions of fact or of law, and was not

[1] Nārada, Legal Procedure, 47. The following classes of persons, according to Nārada, might not be arrested, namely, "one about to marry; one tormented by illness; one about to offer a sacrifice; one afflicted by a calamity; one accused by another; one employed in the King's service; cowherds engaged in tending cattle; cultivators in the act of cultivation; artisans while engaged in their own occupations; a minor; a messenger; one about to give alms; one fulfilling a vow; one harassed by difficulties."

[2] The reply, according to Nārada, was to correspond with the tenor of the plaint. Legal Procedure, II. 2.

[3] Nārada (Jolly), II. 4. [4] Ibid II. 7.

a matter of any urgency, the parties were given time to prepare their respective sides of the case.[1] Where the defendant denied the charge or claim, the plaintiff had to prove his accusation or demand. Under certain circumstances, however, the burden of proof might be shifted from the plaintiff to the defendant.[2] If the plaintiff failed to produce witnesses, or did not appear within three fortnights, he was non-suited. And if it was proved that the plaintiff had no just cause for bringing the suit, he was ordered to pay a fine. Counter-charges, were not, as a rule, permitted. "One accused," says Nārada, "of an offence must not lodge a plaint himself, unless he have refuted the charge raised by the other party."[3] But in certain classes of civil actions, such as disputes between members of a trade guild or between merchants, or in quarrels leading to duels, counter-suits were allowed.[4] When two persons brought suits against each other, he was admitted as plaintiff whose grievance was the greater, or whose affair was the more important of the two, and not the person

[1] Gautama says: "If (the defendant) is unable to answer (the plaint) at once (the judge) may wait for a year. But (in an action) covering kine, draught-oxen, women, or the procreation (of offspring) the defendant (shall answer) immediately; likewise in a case that will suffer by delay." XIII. 28-30. Nārada also advises the King to give time to the defendant except in urgent affairs, heinous offences, etc. I. 44-45.

[2] For instance, "when the defendant has evaded the plaint by means of a special plea, it becomes incumbent on him to prove his assertion, and he is placed in the position of a claimant." Nārada (Judicial Procedure), II. 31.

[3] Nārada, Legal Procedure, 55.

[4] Arthaśāstra, Bk. III. ch. 1.

who was the first to go to law.[1] A person who had already been accused by another person could not be accused by a different party of the same offence, "for it is wrong to strike one again who has been struck (by another)."[2]

Facts in a case were proved by evidence,[3] which was either oral, or documentary, or real.[4] In cases relating to property, possession was regarded as some evidence of ownership.[5] Although all the forms of evidence were equally admissible, the oral evidence of witnesses was the commonest mode of proving a fact. Direct evidence was generally regarded as

[1] Quotations from Nārada (Jolly), I. 8. [2] Nārada, I. 55.

[3] In six cases, witnesses were held unnecessary, and indications of the crime committed were regarded as sufficient. "It should be known," says Nārada, "that one carrying a firebrand in his hand is an incendiary; that one taken with a weapon in his hand is a murderer; and that where a man and the wife of another man seize one another by the hair, the man must be an adulterer. One who goes about with a hatchet in his hand and makes his approach may be recognised as a destroyer of bridges (and embankments); one carrying an axe is a destroyer of trees. One whose looks are suspicious is likely to have committed an assault. In all these cases, witnesses may be dispensed with; in the case of assault, careful investigation is required." I. 175. The indications may be regarded as constituting what is called 'real' and 'circumstantial' evidence.

[4] "Evidence of guilt against a suspected person shall consist in the instruments used, his advisers and abettors, the article stolen, and any intermediaries." Arthasāstra, Bk. IV. ch. 8. Vasishtha says: "It is declared in the Smriti that there are three kinds of proof which give title to (property, viz.), documents, witnesses, and possession; (thereby) an owner may recover property which formerly belonged to him (but was lost)." He adds: In a dispute about a house or a field, reliance (may be placed on the depositions) of neighbours. If the statements of the neighbours disagree, documents (are) proof. If conflicting documents are produced, reliance (may be placed) on (the statements of) aged (inhabitants) of the village or town, and on (those of) guilds and corporations (of artisans and trades).

[5] Cf. the English legal proverb, "Possession is nine points of the law."

superior to circumstantial evidence, but in certain cases, e.g. theft and housebreaking, the latter was often the only kind of evidence available, and was held sufficient.[1] It seems that hearsay evidence was not always excluded.[2]

The eligibility of witnesses was an important question. Householders, men with male issue, and natives of the country belonging to any of the four castes were regarded as eligible witnesses.[3] Persons who had an interest in the suit, familiar friends and companions, enemies of the parties, persons formerly convicted of perjury, persons suffering from some severe illness, and those tainted by mortal sin, were ineligible as witnesses.[4] And no person belonging to any of the following classes could be called as a witness, except under special circumstances: the King, mechanics, and actors, a student of the Veda, an ascetic, one wholly dependent, a person of ill repute, a dasyu, a person who followed forbidden occupations, an aged man, an infant, a man of the lowest castes, one extremely grieved or intoxicated, one oppressed by hunger, thirst, or fatigue, a mad man, one tormented by desire, a wrathful man, and

[1] Arthaśāstra, Bk. IV. ch. 8.

[2] Manu says: "Evidence in accordance with what has actually been seen or heard is admissible." VIII. 74.

[3] Manu, VIII. 62. Cf. Nārada (I. 177-190), who gives a longer list.

[4] According to Vishnu, the proper witnesses are those born of a high family, possessing good qualifications or wealth, devoted to religious practices and sacrifices, those who have sons, who are versed in the law, who are truthful, who are devoted to study. Ch. 8 (Jolly's Sanskrit text).

a thief.[1] The reasons why such persons were excluded from the witness box are thus indicated by Nārada:[2] "A child would speak falsely from ignorance, a woman from want of veracity, an impostor from habitual depravity, a relative from affection, and an enemy from desire of revenge." The ground on which some of the other classes were excluded appears to have been the desire on the part of the State to prevent, as far as possible, any interference with the ordinary avocations of the people. On failure of competent witnesses, however, the evidence of an infant, an aged person, a woman, a student, a relative, or a servant, might be offered.[3]

Uncorroborated evidence of a single witness was regarded as insufficient for the decision of a case, unless the witness happened to be a person possessed of exceptional qualifications and was agreeable to both the parties.[4]

Before the deposition of a witness was taken, it was the duty of the judge to impress on the witness the necessity of telling the truth, and the consequences, legal and moral, of telling a

[1] Manu, VIII. 65-68. [2] I. 191.

[3] Manu, 69-70. "But," adds Manu, "the judge should consider the evidence of infants, aged and diseased persons as untrustworthy, likewise that of disordered minds." VIII. 71. The competence of witnesses, in the opinion of Manu, should not be strictly examined in certain classes of criminal cases, e.g. violence, theft, adultery, defamation, and assault. VIII. 72.

[4] Nārada, I. 192; Manu, VIII. 77; Yājnavalkya, II. 72; Vishnu, VIII. 9.

falsehood.[1] Witnesses were also charged on oath to speak the truth. According to Gautama, in the case of persons other than Brāhmanas the oath was to be taken in the presence of the gods, of the King, or of the Brāhmanas.[2] Perjury was regarded as a dire sin as well as a serious offence, and a witness who perjured himself was liable to be fined from one hundred to one thousand paṇas, the exact amount of the fine depending upon the motive which induced him to give false evidence.[3]

Documentary evidence (lekhya) was frequently resorted to in Ancient India, specially in civil actions. Vishnu mentions three kinds of documents, namely, (1) attested by the King's officers, (2) attested by private witnesses, and (3) unattested.[4] According to Nārada, a document, to be valid, " should be signed by witnesses, the (natural) order of ideas and syllables should not be interrupted, local customs and general rules should be observed in it, and it should be complete in every respect." [5]

[1] Manu says that the judge should exhort the witnesses as follows: " A witness who speaks the truth in his evidence gains (after death) the most excellent regions (of bliss) and here (below) unsurpassable fame." " Such testimony is revered by Brahman himself." And so on. Manu, VIII. 81-86. According to Gautama, Vasishtha, and Bodhāyana also, by giving false evidence a person incurs sin in varying degrees.

[2] Gautama, XIII. 12-13.

[3] Manu, VIII. 120-121. Megasthenes says: " A person convicted of bearing false witness suffers mutilation of his extremities." Fragment XXVII.

[4] Vishnu (Jolly's Sanskrit text), Ch. V. Brihaspati says: " Writings are declared to be tenfold." V. 18.

[5] Quotations from Nārada, IV. 1.

For the purpose of drawing conclusions from the evidence offered in court, it was the duty of the judge to weigh such evidence, and not merely to count the number of witnesses and documents on each side.[1] Nārada says: "There are some who give false evidence from covetousness, there are other villainous wretches who resort to forging documentary evidence. Therefore, both sorts of evidence must be tested by the King with great care: documents according to the rules regarding writings, witnesses according to the law of witnesses."[2] The means of arriving at the truth were regarded as four-fold, namely, (1) visible indications (pratyksha), reasoning (yukti), inference (anumāna), and analogy (upamāna).[3] If the witnesses disagreed with one another as to time, age, matter, quantity, shape, and species, such testimony was to be held as worthless. The judges were advised to note the demeanour of a witness in court, and to draw an inference as to his veracity therefrom.[4] But

[1] Manu, however, says: "On a conflict of witnesses the King shall accept (as true) the (evidence of the) majority; if (the conflicting parties are) equal in number, (that of) those distinguished by good qualities; on a difference between (equally) distinguished (witnesses, that of) the best among the twice-born." VIII. 73.

[2] Nārada, Legal Procedure, 70.

[3] Sukranīti, II. 93.

[4] "If a man being questioned does not uphold a statement duly made by himself (at a former stage of the trial); or if he ends by admitting what had been previously negatived by himself; or if he is unable to produce any witnesses after having declared that they are in existence, and having been asked to produce them; by all such signs as these, persons devoid of virtue may be known." Nārada, Legal Procedure, 61.

Abul Fazl, describing the Hindu system of administration of justice, says: "The Judge will derive collateral proof by the physiognomy and prevarication of the party." Ayeen-i-Akbery (Gladwin), p. 496.

Nārada, very wisely, cautions judges against accepting indications too readily. "Liars," says he, "may have the appearance of veracious men, and veracious men may resemble liars. There are many different characters. Therefore, it is necessary to examine (everything)." Proper safeguards were provided against the miscarriage of justice through belief in false evidence. And whenever it was found that the decision in a case was based upon false or insufficient evidence, the judgment was reversed, and all the proceedings in the case were declared null and void.[1]

The other modes of arriving at the truth, besides evidence, were the oath and the ordeal (divya).[2] These methods, it seems, were resorted to only when evidence failed to establish the case one way or the other. As to the oath, Manu says, "let the judge cause a Brāhmana to swear by his veracity, a Kshatriya by his chariot or the animal he rides on and by his weapons, a Vaisya by his kine, grain, and gold, and a Sūdra by (imprecating on his own head the guilt) of all grievous offences."[3] The ordeal was a divine test. It was used in criminal cases, and was of various kinds, such as (i) by the balance, (ii) by fire, (iii) by water, and (iv) by poison.[4] If the accused

[1] Manu, VIII. 117.

[2] 'Divya' is a term not found in early Vedic literature.

[3] Manu, VIII. 113.

[4] Manu, VIII. 114. Vishnu and Nārada give detailed descriptions of the different kinds of ordeal. Hiuen Tsiang, who was perhaps an eye-witness of ordeals, thus describes them: "When the ordeal is by water, then the

person was unhurt, or did not meet with any speedy misfortune, he was held to be innocent.[1] Resort was had to the expedient of the ordeal when both the parties failed to bring witnesses, or to produce documentary evidence, and the merit of the case was so doubtful that the judges felt disinclined to take upon themselves the responsibility to give a decision.[2] These methods were thus used only on rare occasions, and they became obsolete in course of time, leaving evidence as practically the sole method by which the court arrived at the right decision as to the guilt or innocence of an accused person.

Sometimes judicial investigation supplemented the information obtained by evidence offered in court. But great care was taken against an abuse of this method. Hiuen Tsiang emphatically states that "in

accused is placed in a sack connected with a stone vessel and thrown into deep water. They then judge of his innocence or guilt in this way—if the man sinks, and the stone floats, he is guilty; but if the man floats and the stone sinks, then he is pronounced innocent. Secondly, by fire: They heat a plate of iron, and make the accused sit on it, and again place his feet on it, and apply it to the palms of his hands; moreover, he is made to pass his tongue over it; if no scars result, he is innocent; if there are scars, guilt is proved. In case of weak or timid persons who cannot endure such ordeal, they take a flower-bud and cast it towards the fire; if it opens, he is innocent; if the flower is burnt, he is guilty. Ordeal by weight is this: A man and a stone are placed in a balance evenly; then they judge according to lightness or weight. If the accused is innocent, then the man weighs down the stone, which rises in the balance; if he is guilty, the man rises, and the stone falls. Ordeal by poison is this: They take a ram, and make an incision in the thigh (of the animal); if the man is guilty, then the poison takes effect and the creature dies; if he is innocent, then the poison has no effect, and he survives. By these four modes of trial, the way of crime is stopped." Beal, Buddhist Records, Bk. II.

[1] Manu, VIII. 115. [2] Vide Abul Fazl's Ayeen-i-Akbery, p. 495.

the investigation of criminal cases there is no use of rod or staff to obtain proofs." [1]

The next stage of the trial was the argument on both sides. When the parties themselves were persons unacquainted with the law, they were sometimes represented for the purpose of arguing the case by their relatives, or friends, or professional lawyers (pratinidhi).[2] Such representation, it seems, was usual in the civil suits and in the less serious criminal cases, but no representation was permitted in the graver criminal offences, such as murder, adultery, abduction, forgery, sedition, robbery, and theft.[3]

Judgment was delivered at the end of the hearing of a case. In applying the law to a particular case, the judges were expected to take into consideration all the circumstances. "No sentence," says Brihaspati. "should be passed merely in accordance with the letter of the law. If a decision is arrived at without considering the circumstances of the case, violation of justice will be the result." [4] The judgment was embodied in a document, a copy of which was furnished to the victorious party.[5]

[1] Buddhist Records (Beal), Bk. II.

[2] Sukranīti, IV. 5, 110. According to Sukra the lawyer's fee was to be one-sixteenth of the value of the suit. IV. 5, 114.

Nārada says: "He deserves punishment who speaks in behalf of another, without being either the brother, the father, the son, or the appointed agent." Nārada (Judicial Procedure), II. 23.

[3] Sukranīti, IV. 5, 120.

[4] Brihaspati, II. 12.

[5] Nārada says: "The victorious party shall receive a document recording his victory, and couched in appropriate language." Legal Procedure, II. 43.

The remedies given by the courts depended upon the character and circumstances of each case. In civil actions, the usual remedies were restoration of property and fines. The courts had also power to declare agreements as invalid. Thus, for instance, contracts entered into under provocation, compulsion, or intoxication, or by dependents, infants, aged persons, and lunatics, were often held as void.[1] In an action for the recovery of debts the court had the power to modify the whole transaction, and to grant only a reasonable rate of interest. In criminal cases, the punishments were:[2] (i) fine, (ii) imprisonment, (iii) whipping, (iv) physical torture, (v) banishment, (vi) condemnation to work in the mines, and (vii) death.

The punishment awarded in criminal cases corresponded to the nature of the offence.[3] The extreme penalty of death was rarely inflicted,[4] and any other kind of corporal punishment was uncommon. "The

Brihaspati says: "Whatever has been transacted in a suit, the plaint, answer, and so forth, as well as the gist of the trial, should be noted completely in the document recording the success (of the claimant or defendant)."

[1] Arthaśāstra, Bk. III. ch. 1.

[2] Nārada says: "Punishment is pronounced to be two-fold: bodily punishment and fines. Bodily punishment is declared to be of ten sorts, fines are also of more than one kind. Fines begin with a *kākaṇi*, and the highest amount is one's entire property. Bodily punishment begins with confinement, and ends with capital punishment." Jolly, Appendices, 53-54.

[3] Brihaspati, VI. 2.

[4] Sung Yun, speaking of the Kingdom of Udyāna (Kasmir), says: "Supposing a man has committed murder, they do not suffer him to be killed, but banish him to the desert mountains." Buddhist Records, p. 188.

King," says Fa Hian, "in the administration of justice inflicts no corporal punishment, but each culprit is fined in money according to the gravity of his offence, and even in cases where the culprit has been guilty of repeated attempts to excite rebellion, they restrict themselves to the cutting off of his right hand."[1] This statement is confirmed by Hiuen Tsiang and Sung Yun. Hiuen Tsiang says: "There is no infliction of corporal punishment; they are simply left to live or die, and are not counted among men."[2] Megasthenes mentions cropping of the hair as a punishment. "If one is guilty," says he, "of a heinous offence, the King orders his hair to be cropped, this being a punishment in the last degree infamous."[3]

Sureties (pratibhū)[4] for good behaviour were also sometimes taken from persons found guilty of criminal offences. Abettors of a crime were punished in a manner similar to the punishment provided for the principal offender.

The extra-judicial remedy of self-help was also recognised by the courts within reasonable limits. Manu, for instance, says: "By moral suasion, by suit of law, by artful management, or by the customary proceeding, a creditor may recover property lent; and fifthly, by force. A creditor who himself recovers his property from his debtor must not be

[1] Fa Hian (Beal), Ch. XVI.

[2] Buddhist Records (Beal), Bk. II.

[3] Fragment XXVII. D.

[4] Sukranīti, IV. 5, 125.

blamed by the King for retaking what is his own."[1]

If any person was dissatisfied with the judgment, and thought that the case had been decided in a way contrary to justice, he might have it re-tried on payment of a fine. Nārada says: "When a lawsuit has been judged without any previous examination of witnesses (or other evidence), or when it has been decided in an improper manner, or when it has been judged by unauthorised persons, the trial has to be renewed."[2] An appeal also lay from the decision of an inferior court to a higher tribunal, where the whole case was re-tried.[3]

We now pass on to a consideration of some of the important features of the administration of justice in Ancient India. The first characteristic that strikes the enquirer is the responsibility of the judges and their independence. The judges had to perform their duties in accordance with the law, and it was their duty to deal out equal justice to all.[4] If they transgressed the laws, or acted improperly in the discharge of their duties, they not only incurred sin,[5] but were

[1] Manu, VIII. 49-50.

[2] Quotations from Nārada (Jolly), I. 14.

[3] Brihaspati, I. 29-30.

[4] Manu, VIII. 13-14.

[5] Manu says: "When any injustice is done, one-fourth of the sin attaches to the wrong-doer, one-fourth to the witness, one-fourth to the judges, and the remaining fourth to the King." VIII. 18. Abul Fazl, speaking of the administration of justice in Hindu India, says, "He (the judge) must consider it a religious obligation to discharge the duties of his office with impartiality and justice." Ayeen-i-Akbery (Gladwin), p. 495.

liable to be punished. Chānakya prescribes punishment for any unrighteous behaviour on the part of the judges. "If a judge," says he, "chides or threatens or sends out or unjustly silences a litigant, he shall be liable to the first amercement. If he defames any litigant, his punishment shall be double the amount. If he does not ask any questions which ought to be asked, or asks questions which ought not to be asked, or having asked a question, leaves it out, or tutors a witness, or reminds him what he said before, he shall be liable to the second amercement. If he does not enquire into relevant matters or enquires into irrelevant matters, or unnecessarily delays the trial, or maliciously postpones business, or makes one of the parties leave the court disgusted and tired, or leaves out statements which may lead to a right decision, or lends assistance to the witnesses, or takes up a case already decided, he shall be liable to the first amercement. On a repetition of the offence, his punishment shall be double, and he shall be removed from office."[1] So also, Yājnavalkya says: "If the members of the judicial assembly give any decisions contrary to law and custom, through affection, temptation, or fear, each of them would be liable to double the punishment provided

[1] Arthasāstra, Bk. IV. ch. 9. Kautilya says further: "If the judge, or the director, unjustly fines anybody, he shall be fined twice the amount. If he condemns any person unjustly to bodily punishment, he shall himself suffer the same punishment, or be fined twice the amount of the ransom payable."

for the case."[1] But if the responsibility of the judges was great, so was their independence. The law was their only master and guide, and they had power to deal equally with the high and the low. The administration of justice was kept separate from the executive functions of the State, and no interference with judicial business by the executive was permitted.

Another feature of the judicial system was that every person resident in the country, whatever his position might be, and whether he was a native or a foreigner,[2] received the protection of the courts. Such protection was, of course, specially appreciated by the weaker members of society. If a Dāsa, for instance, was ill-treated, he was permitted by the courts to leave his master, and the courts inflicted a punishment on the master if he failed to liberate his Dāsa on receipt of a ransom.[3] So also, servants were protected from ill-treatment at the hands of their masters. A servant could, with the help of the courts, enforce the payment of his wages, and any agreement made between master and servant to the prejudice of the latter was liable to be set aside by the courts.[4]

The third feature of the legal system is not one which is very pleasing to note. Although every

[1] II. 4. Some of the other Smriti works also prescribe punishments for judges who transgress the law.

[2] Vide Arthaśāstra, Bk. IV. ch. 2.

[3] Arthaśāstra, Bk. III. ch. 13.

[4] Arthaśāstra, Bk. III. ch. 14.

member of the society had a locus standi in the courts, the idea of equality before the law was not fully developed in Ancient India. A modified form of privilege ran through the whole system of Hindu Jurisprudence. The law was not the same for all, but depended upon the status of the person concerned. If a man belonging to one of the higher castes committed an offence, his punishment was lighter than what would be inflicted on a man of a lower grade for a similar offence. As an instance may be mentioned the fact that the Brāhmanas, as a rule, enjoyed immunity from the more degrading kinds of punishment provided for criminal offences.[1]

From the records preserved in Indian literature as well as from the accounts left by foreign travellers, it seems quite clear that the administration of justice was very efficient in Ancient India. This must have been the result of three factors, namely, the uprightness of the judges, the efficiency of the police, and the general honesty and probity of the people. Judges were recruited from the class of learned Brāhmanas

[1] Gautama says: "A learned Brāhmana (i.e. one deeply versed in the Vedas and other branches of learning) must be allowed by the King immunity from (the following) six (kinds of opprobrious treatment): he must not be subjected to corporal punishment, he must not be imprisoned, he must not be fined, he must not be exiled, he must not be reviled, nor be excluded." VIII. 12-13. But Kautilya says: "When a Brāhmana has committed a crime, he should be branded, his crime should be proclaimed in public, his property should be confiscated, and he should be condemned to work in the mines." Arthasāstra, Bk. IV. ch. 18. In the Mrichchakatikā we read that the sentence of death passed on a Brāhmana becomes the immediate cause of a revolution.

who were noted for their high character and purity of life. Adequate measures were taken to secure the efficiency of the police force. As for the last factor, the testimony of the most eminent foreign observers is conclusive. "Theft," says Megasthenes, "is of very rare occurrence . . . The simplicity of their laws and their contracts is proved by the fact that they seldom go to law. They have no suits about pledges or deposits, nor do they require either seals or witnesses, but make their deposits, and confide in each other. Their houses and property they generally leave unguarded. These things indicate that they possess good, sober sense."[1] This statement is confirmed by Hiuen Tsiang, the great Chinese monk, who travelled in India a thousand years after Megasthenes. His words are: "With respect to the ordinary people, although they are naturally light-minded, they are upright and honourable. In money matters they are without craft, and in administering justice they are considerate. They dread the retribution of another state of existence, and make light of things of this world. They are not deceitful or treacherous in their conduct, and are faithful to their oaths and promises. In their rules of government there is remarkable rectitude, while in their behaviour there is much gentleness and sweetness."[2]

[1] Fragment XXVII.

[2] Hiuen Tsiang's Travels, Buddhist Records (Beal), Bk. II.

CHAPTER XIII

PUBLIC FINANCE

In the earliest period of Indian history the State perhaps depended for its own support on the voluntary contributions of the people. But some method of compulsory contribution must have been found necessary in India as soon as a more improved form of government had come into existence. The early tax-system, however, was a very simple one, and the evolution of a complex system of Public Finance was doubtless a slow and gradual process. By the fourth century B.C. the system of Public Finance had reached a very advanced stage of development, as is evidenced by Chānakya's Arthasāstra and the Brahmanical and Buddhistic religious works.

The income of the State was derived from various sources. In very early times, the burden of taxation was extremely light. But as the duties of the State increased, the burden became progressively heavier. Gautama, one of the early law-givers, says: "Cultivators must pay to the King a tax (amounting to) one-tenth, one-eighth, or one-sixth (of the produce).[1] Some declare that (there is a tax) also on cattle and gold, (viz.) one-fiftieth. In the case of merchandise one-twentieth was the duty, and of roots, fruits, flowers, medicinal herbs, honey, meat, grass, and firewood, one-sixtieth."[2] In the time of Vishnu, who perhaps wrote about two centuries later, the rates of taxation were appreciably higher,—namely, a sixth part of every kind of crops and of meat, fruits, and flowers, a duty of 2 per cent. levied on cattle, gold, and cloths, of 10 per cent. on goods locally manufactured, and of 5 per cent. on articles imported from abroad.[3] Manu mentions even higher rates, except as regards the land, and also gives a longer list of articles on which taxes were to be levied. He says: "A fiftieth part of the (increments on) cattle and gold may be taken by the King, and the eighth, sixth, or twelfth part of the crops. He may also take the sixth part of trees, meat, honey, clarified butter, perfumes, (medicinal) herbs, substances used for flavouring food, flowers, roots, and fruits; of leaves, pot-herbs, grass, (objects) made of cane, skins, of earthen vessels, and all (articles) made of stone."[4] The Mahābhārata describes the tax-system in very general terms. It says: "With a sixth part, upon a fair calculation, of the yield of the soil, with fines

[1] It seems that the rate varied according to the quality of the soil. Rich soils were more highly taxed than poor lands.

[2] Gautama, X. 24-27.

[3] Vishnu (Jolly's Sanskrit text), Ch. 3.

[4] Manu, VII. 130-132.

and forfeitures from offenders, with the imposts levied according to the Sāstras upon merchants and trades in return for the protection granted to them, a King should fill his treasury." [1]

We are indebted to Chānakya for a detailed description of the financial system as it existed in Chandragupta's time. He gives two distinct classifications of the revenues of the State. According to the first, the income is classified under seven heads, in view of the sources from which they are derived, namely, (1) the capital, (2) the country parts, (3) mines, (4) public works, (5) forests, (6) pasture-lands, and (7) trade-routes.[2]

The various kinds of income from the capital were: excise duties levied on certain articles locally produced, such as cotton goods, oils, salt, liquors, and metallic manufactures; taxes on warehouses, guilds of artisans, and temples; duties collected at the city gates; and fines on gambling and betting. The rates of duties were fixed in view of the nature of a particular commodity and also of its place of origin.[3]

[1] Mahābhārata, Sānti Parva, Sec. 71, sl. 10.

[2] Arthasāstra, Bk. II. ch. 6.

[3] Arthasāstra, Bk. II. ch. 21. So, Manu says: "Having well considered (the rates of) purchase and (of) sale, the length of the road, (the expenses for) food and condiments, the charges of insuring the goods, let the King make the traders pay duty." VII. 127. Duties were remitted in the case of merchants who sold goods at a loss. Vide Arthasāstra, Bk. II. The Sukranīti says: "The King should not realise any duties from a merchant who sells his goods at a price which is less than, or equal to, the cost of production; but he may realise the duty from the buyer if he has made a bargain."

The duties varied from one-tenth to one-twentieth.[1] If it was a harmful commodity, a fine was imposed in addition to the usual duty. But goods which were calculated to be of special benefit to the community, such as valuable seeds, were allowed to enter toll-free, as also were articles required for marriage ceremonies and the worship of gods. In order that the duties might not be evaded, the sale of goods at the place of production was prohibited.[2]

The income from country places consisted of the produce of the State lands, a share of the produce of each plot of land cultivated by private individuals, minor taxes assessed on lands, tolls paid at the ferries, and road cesses.

The mines formed a very important source of revenue to the State. The receipts from mines consisted of the yield of the State-mines and also a share of the produce of mines privately owned, whether the produce consisted of precious metals or of ordinary minerals. The nine kinds of income derived from mines were: (i) output of minerals, (ii) a share of the output, (iii) a duty of 5 per cent., (iv) assaying charges, (v) fines, (vi) tolls, (vii) compensations for the loss of the King's revenues, (viii) coining charges, and (ix) a premium of 8 per cent.[3]

[1] Megasthenes also speaks of this duty of one-tenth. The Agni Purāna, however, puts it at one-twentieth.

[2] Arthasāstra, Bk. II. ch. 22. The duties were collected either on the roads or at the market-places. Sukranīti, IV. 2.

[3] Arthasāstra, Bk. II. ch. 12.

The receipts from public works were: fruits of trees, vegetables grown in the public gardens, the yield of fisheries, and so forth. The forest revenue was derived from the lease of forest lands for hunting, and for the sale of elephants and other animals. The income from pastures consisted in dues paid to the State for grazing cattle on public lands. The tolls payable on land-routes and water-ways formed another important source of State income.

The other classification of the revenues given by Chānakya is also important. This we may slightly modify and put in modern form. The income of the State, according to this classification, would fall into two parts, namely, (1) tax-revenue and (2) non-tax-revenue. The first head would comprise (i) fixed taxes (piṇḍa-kara), (ii) one-sixth share of the produce (shaḍbhāga), (iii) supply of provisions for the army (senā-bhakta), (iv) religious taxes (bali), (v) tributes from subordinate rulers (kara), (vi) forced benevolences (utsanga), (vii) royalties (pārśva), (viii) compensations (pārihīṇika), (ix) presents (aupāyanika), and rents of public buildings (kaushṭheyaka). Under the second head fall (i) the agricultural produce of crown lands, (ii) sale proceeds of grains, (iii) grains obtained by special request, (iv) incidental gains from trade and commerce, (v) interest on capital, and (vi) profits of manufactures undertaken by the State. Besides these, there were certain minor sources of income, such as escheats, fines, confiscations, and forfeitures of the property of rebels.[1]

Taxes were paid either in cash or in kind, or partly in cash and partly in kind. Kautilya expresses himself strongly in favour of the collection of taxes in cash. Industrialists, Sūdras, and all other persons who lived by their labour (karma-jīvinaḥ) gave their labour free to the State for one day in every month in lieu of taxes.[2] But no forced labour was exacted.[3] Brāhmanas were exempt from the payment of taxes on the ground that they paid taxes to the State in the shape of their religious services.[4] The other classes of persons who were exempt were women, minors, students, blind, deaf, dumb, and diseased persons, and those to whom the acquisition of property was forbidden.[5]

In times of financial stress, a ruler was held justified in raising money by means other than those laid down in the Sāstras. For instance, he might demand

[1] Arthasāstra, Bk. II. ch. 15. The Sukranīti treats of the various sources of income in Ch. II. sls. 335, etc.

[2] Vishnu (Jolly's Sanskrit text), Ch. III. So, Manu says: "Mechanics and artisans, as well as Sūdras who subsist by manual labour, he may cause to work (for the State) one (day) in each month." VII. 138.

[3] Hiuen Tsiang says: "The families are not entered on registers, and the people are not subjected to forced labour." Buddhist Records, Bk. II. And again, "When the public services require it, labour is exacted but paid for. The payment is in strict proportion to the work done." Buddhist Records, Bk. II.

[4] It was, however, only the learned Brāhmanas who were exempt. Those Brāhmanas who were engaged in occupations proper to the inferior castes had to pay taxes.

[5] Āpastamba, II. 10, 26, 14-17. Vasishtha, Vishnu, Manu, and Kautilya also express similar opinions.

one-fourth or even one-third of the share of the produce of the soil, as well as a higher percentage of the other kinds of produce. The King's officers might also compel the people to grow additional crops in the interests of the public treasury. In case such measures failed to bring in enough money, the Collector-general asked the people for benevolences in view of the needs of the State, and those who offered handsome amounts received precedence in rank, robes of honour, and decorations. Religious institutions were also compelled to contribute to the funds of the State. On occasions of grave financial difficulty, various other devices were adopted, but, in order that these might not lead to trouble, Chānakya utters the voice of warning in these words: "Such expedients should be resorted to only once, and never more than once."[1]

It should be noted that the land-tax was the most important of all the sources of the State revenue. The King, however, was never regarded as the owner of the land, and he never claimed a right to the unearned increment of the land. His claim was limited to a fixed share of the produce.[2] In later

[1] But Kautilya adds: "He should not make such demands of persons who cultivate soils of a middling or inferior quality, nor of those who are of great assistance to the State in the construction of forts, irrigation works, trade routes, colonisation of waste lands, exploitation of mines, preservation of forests, nor of border tribes, nor of those who had no means of subsistence." Bk. V. ch. 2. Also, Sukranīti, IV. 2, 10.

[2] The King's share of the produce of the land was regarded as his pay for the services he rendered to the State. Vide Bodhāyana's Dharma-sūtra, and cf. ante, Ch. VII.

times, kings came to possess private landed properties of their own, and the income derived from such crown lands, as Hiuen Tsiang observed, helped considerably to lighten the incidence of taxation on the people.

The principles on which the tax-system was based were sound and reasonable. To use the language of modern Economics, ability and least sacrifice were the guiding principles of the framers of the financial regulations of ancient times. "The King," says the Mahābhārata, "should act in such a way (in collecting his revenues) that his subjects should not feel the pressure of want."[1] Arbitrary exactions were strongly condemned by law-givers as well as by political teachers. Vasishtha, one of the early law-givers, for instance, says: "Let him not take property for his own use from (the inhabitants of) his realm."[2] "Never desire to fill thy treasury by acting unrighteously or from covetousness" is the advice given in the Mahābhārata to the King. And, again, the King is thus admonished in the Great Epic against indulging in exactions: "That avaricious King who through folly oppresses his subjects by levying taxes not mentioned in the Sāstras brings ruin upon himself."[3] Kautilya condemns the conduct of over-zealous revenue officials in these words: "When an officer realises double the usual amount

[1] Sānti Parva, Sec. 71, sl. 13. [2] Vasishtha, X. 14.

[3] Cf. Āpastamba, "Dharmyaṁ śulkam avahārayet." II. 10, 26, 9.

of revenue, he drinks the life-blood of the people. The King should prevent such exactions."

These were the principles. In practice, while there were many rulers who followed a righteous and wise policy in their collection of taxes, there were others whose love of luxury and ostentation prompted them to fill their empty treasuries by despoiling their subjects. Under weak governments, royal officials often enriched themselves at the expense of both the State and the people.

Public welfare was—in theory at least—the guiding principle in the expenditure of the public revenues. Kālidāsa, the greatest of Indian poets, says: "Just as the Sun takes moisture from the earth to give it back a thousandfold, so the King gathers taxes from the people only to provide for their welfare."[1]

The main heads of expenditure, according to Kautilya, were: sacrifices, worship of ancestors, charity, expenses of the royal household, charges of the civil departments, expenses in connection with the maintenance of foreign missions, the expenses of the army and the army supply services, public works expenditure, and the expenses for the preservation of forests.[2]

The allocation of funds to the various items of expenditure depended upon the respective needs of

[1] "Prajānām eva bhūtyartham sa tābhyo balim agrahīt: Sahasraguṇam utsraṣṭum ādatte hi rasaṁ raviḥ." Raghuvamsa.

[2] Bk. II. ch. 6.

the departments. In order to provide against contingencies, wise financiers of old always considered it prudent to budget for a surplus after meeting all expenditure. Some of them, perhaps, were over-cautious in this respect. The views of such financiers are expounded in the Sukranīti, according to which only one-half of the State revenue was to be spent for the six purposes of administration in the following proportions: (1) the salaries of headmen,—one-twelfth; (2) the army,—three-twelfths; (3) charities, —one-twenty-fourth; (4) expenses incurred for works of public utility,—one-twenty-fourth; (5) salaries of officials,—one-twenty-fourth; (6) personal expenses of the King and of the royal household,—one-twenty-fourth.[1] According to the Sukranīti, there was to be enough money in the treasury to cover public expenses for twenty years.[2]

The prosperity of the State finances was regarded as a matter of the greatest importance,[3] and Kautilya's views in this regard seem to have been very sound. Circumstances which, in his opinion, tended to keep the treasury full were: prosperity of the people, rewarding of officers for meritorious work, punishment of thieves, prevention of corruption among government officers, abundance of crops,

[1] Sukranīti, Ch. I. sls. 316-317. [2] Sukranīti, IV. 2, 13.

[3] According to Kautilya, the best treasury is that "which is justly acquired by either inheritance or self-acquisition, which is full of gold, silver, pearls and gems of various kinds, which is capable of withstanding calamities for a long time." Bk. II. ch. 1.

prosperity of commerce and trade, freedom from troubles and calamities, non-remission of taxes, and receipt of revenue in gold. Matters which led to the depletion of the treasury were the following: obstruction (to the realisation of revenue), giving of loans, litigation, falsification of accounts, loss of revenue, gains made by officials, adverse exchange, and defalcation.

The control of the department of Public Finance was vested in two officials, namely, the Collector-general (Samāhartā) and the Treasurer-general (Sannidhātā). The former was in charge of the collection of the revenues, while the latter was the custodian of the finances and was responsible for their proper disbursement. It was the duty of the Collector-general to divide the country into several districts for revenue purposes, and to classify the villages, according as they (i) were exempt from the payment of taxes, (ii) supplied soldiers for the defence of the country in lieu of taxes, (iii) paid their taxes in gold, (iv) paid taxes in kind, that is to say, in grains, cattle, raw products, or dairy produce, or (v) supplied free labour.[2] The Treasurer-general, as the custodian of the funds of the State, was expected to acquaint himself with the income and expenditure of the State over the period of a century, so that he might be able to frame accurate budgets

[1] Arthaśāstra, Bk. II. ch. 7.

[2] Ibid.

and to show a good balance at the end of each year.

For the proper control and administration of the finances of the realm it was considered necessary to have a good system of keeping accounts, and this important department was placed under the control of one of the Chief Superintendents. It was the duty of this official so to arrange the business of his department that everything relating to the finances was entered in the books. He was required not only to show the net revenue that remained at the end of a year, but to cause to be entered in the books all details of expenditure, mentioning whether an item was incurred for a purpose, internal or external, public or private, important or unimportant. The account officers had also to enter in their books the names of departments; the description of the work carried on and the results obtained in the several manufactories; the amounts of profit, loss, expenditure, and interest of each factory; the number of labourers engaged, and their wages; the values of different kinds of gems, and of other commodities; presents made to the King's officers and courtiers; remissions of taxes granted; allowances, pensions, and gifts of lands or money to the King's wife and children; and receipts from or payments to foreign Kings. The annual accounts of every department were regularly submitted to the Accounts Department, and after they had been examined by the

Superintendent they were audited by competent auditors. They were then submitted to the Ministers in charge of the different departments, and considered by them sitting together as a cabinet.[1]

[1] Arthasāstra, Bk. II. ch. 7.

CHAPTER XIV

FOREIGN RELATIONS

As we saw in a previous chapter, the normal state of affairs in India was for the country to be divided into a large number of Kingdoms and Principalities. The maintenance of foreign relations thus formed a very important department of the public activity of every State, and, naturally, foreign policy was regarded as an extremely useful art.

Some of the more powerful monarchs, besides maintaining friendly relations with the rulers of the other parts of India, kept up friendly intercourse with the kings of countries outside India. Seleukos Nikator, for instance, sent Megasthenes as ambassador to the Court of Chandragupta, and Deimachos and Dionysios were attached to the Court of Bindusāra Amitraghāta as ambassadors from Antiochus Soter, King of Syria, and Ptolemy Philadelphos, King of Egypt. Asoka's edicts show that that great monarch maintained friendly relations not only with Ceylon [1]

[1] In the Mahāvamsa, Devānampiya Tissa is described as an "ally" of Asoka. There is no doubt that frequent communications took place between the two Kings. Vide Mahāvamsa, Ch. XI.

and other neighbouring countries, but also with many kings of distant countries, such as Antiochos Theos of Syria, Ptolemy Philadelphos of Egypt, Antigonos Gonatas of Macedon, Magas of Cyrene, and Alexander II. of Epirus. The names of ambassadors mentioned above are, as Prof. Rapson points out, "no doubt typical of a class." It is in every way probable that constant relations were maintained between India and the west during the period of the Maurya Empire.[1] Kings of other parts of India also, besides Magadha, kept up more or less frequent communications with foreign kings. We know that so late as the seventh century A.D., Pulakesi, King of Mahārāshtra, had friendly relations with Khosrū Parwīz, King of Persia, and Harshavardhana of Thānesvar maintained diplomatic relations with China.

In order to determine the kind of policy to be adopted in each case, foreign rulers are classified by Kautilya under four heads, namely, enemies (Ari), friends (Mitra), mediators (Madhyama), and neutrals (Udāsīna).[2] Inimical and friendly rulers, again, are each divided into two kinds, natural and artificial. A king and his immediate neighbour are, according to Kautilya, natural enemies to each other.[3] A

[1] Rapson, Ancient India.

[2] Arthasāstra, Bk. VI. ch. 2.

[3] Abul Fazl, describing the Hindu system of public administration, says: "The Prince whose territory adjoins to his, although he may be friendly in appearance, yet ought not to be trusted; he should always be prepared to oppose any sudden attack from that quarter. With him whose country

king who attempts to give trouble to another without reasonable cause is an artificial enemy of that other. The ruler whose territory is separated from that of another ruler by the territory of an enemy, and whose friendship has come down from father and grandfather is a natural friend.[1] A ruler whose friendship is courted for the sake of the protection of life and property is an acquired friend. The ruler whose territory is situated close to that of a king and his fro-ward enemy, and who is capable of helping both the kings or of resisting either of them, is a mediatory king. The ruler whose territory is situated between the territories of two rival kings, and who is powerful enough to help or resist either of them or a mediatory king, is a neutral.[2] "The third and fifth States from a Madhyama," says Chānakya, "are likely to be friendly, and the second, fourth, and sixth States are likely to be inimical to him. If the Madhyama king be on good terms with both these classes of States, a ruler should be friendly with him; otherwise he should ally himself with the second class of States."[3]

---

lies next beyond the one last mentioned, he should enter into alliance; but no connection should be formed with those who are more remote." Ayeen-i-Akbery (Gladwin), p. 495.

[1] The best kind of friend, according to Kautilya, is he who is "constant, easy to be roused, noble, straightforward, and whose friendship has been inherited from father and grandfather." Arthaśāstra, Bk. VIII. ch. 9.

[2] The distinction between a neutral and a mediatory King is not at all clear. Perhaps, the term 'Udāsīna' (neutral) was applied to a King who remained passive in regard to both the contending parties, while the 'Madhyama' King was one who exerted his influence to bring about a reconciliation.

[3] Arthaśāstra, Bk. VII. ch. 18.

The neighbouring kings belong to one or other of four classes, namely, rearward enemy (pārshṇigrāha), rearward friend (ākranda), ally of a rearward enemy (pārshṇigrāhāsāra), and ally of a rearward friend (ākrandāsāra).[1]

We read a great deal about Circles of States (maṇḍala) in the literature of Ancient India. A Circle consists of three kings,—a ruler, his friend, and his friend's friend. As each of these kings is supposed to possess six elements of sovereignty, a Circle consists of eighteen elements. Foreign rulers being of four kinds, there are thus four primary Circles of States, twelve kings, sixty elements of sovereignty, and seventy-two elements of States.[2] A powerful and wise king would always try to make himself the centre (nābhi) of the Circle and to make the friendly powers the spokes of the wheel (nemi).[3]

The attitude of a ruler towards foreign rulers depended upon the special circumstances of each case. He was supposed to adopt one or other of six sorts of policy, namely, peace (sandhi), war (vigraha), neutrality (āsana), preparedness for war (yāna), alliance (saṁśraya), and double dealing (dvaidhībhāva).[4]

[1] Arthasāstra, Bk. VI. ch. 2. Vide also Nitivākyāmrita, Ch. 28, and Agni Purāna, CCXXXIII.

[2] Arthasāstra, Bk. VI. ch. 2. A State is supposed to have seven elements. See ante, Ch. VII., and Arthasāstra.

[3] Arthasāstra, Bk. VII. ch. 2.

[4] Ibid. Bk. VII. ch. 1. In the opinion of Vātavyādhi, foreign policy is only two-fold, namely, war and peace; but Chānakya refuses to accept this view.

In Chānakya's view expediency was to be the main consideration in foreign policy. "If a king," says Chānakya, "is weaker than his neighbour, he should adopt a peaceful policy; but if he is superior in strength to his rival he should make war.[1] When neither of the two is the superior of the other, both should be neutral. When one king is endowed with an excess of quality, he should prepare for war; but if he is powerless, he should make an alliance. If the circumstances be such that it is desirable to crush a rival, but this can only be done with the assistance of some other Power, then the king should adopt a policy of double-dealing."[2]

The measures that were to be adopted by kings to carry into effect their foreign policy were four, namely: (i) conciliation (sāma); (ii) making of gifts (dāna); (iii) sowing of dissensions (bheda); and (iv) punishment (daṇḍa).[3]

In view of the peculiar position of affairs in India in ancient times, alliances were regarded as a great necessity by most of the Powers. The purposes,

[1] That this policy actually governed the actions of statesmen for long ages is shown by the fact that Abul Fazl, writing in the sixteenth century, speaks of the foreign policy of the Hindus in the following terms: "With those princes who are his equals in power, he takes care to maintain peace and friendship, and from those who are weaker than himself he exacts tribute. If any monarch is more powerful than himself, he continually strives to sow dissension among his troops; and if he is not able to do this, prudently purchases his friendship." Ayeen-i-Akbery (Gladwin), p. 495.

[2] Arthasāstra, Bk. VII. ch. 1.

[3] Arthasāstra. Vide also Nītivākyāmrita (Ch. 28), the Sukranīti, and Kāmandaki.

however, for which alliances were made were various. Sometimes, the object of an alliance was the joint acquisition of territory, or the colonisation of uninhabited tracts of country. More often, kings combined to crush a powerful rival. But in a large majority of cases, alliances were made for the purpose of defence against other Powers.[1]

Alliances were made either on equal terms (samasandhi) or on unequal terms (hīnasandhi). The first kind was an alliance properly so called, because in this the positions of the two parties were equal, and the benefit was mutual. The second was a subordinate alliance, and from it one of the parties often derived more benefit than the other. The duties of a subordinate ally, according to the Agni Purāna, were to appease public feeling, to collect allies and auxiliaries, to help the paramount sovereign in other ways, and to enable him to distinguish friends from disguised enemies.

From the Harshacharita [2] as well as from Hiuen Tsiang's account [3] we learn that the King of Kāmarūpa entered into a sort of subordinate alliance with Harshavardhana of Kanauj. Fifteen different kinds of subordinate alliances are described in the Arthasāstra.[4]

[1] Arthasāstra, Bk. VII. ch. 1.

[2] The Harshacharita gives a description of the alliance which the King of Kāmarūpa entered into with Harsha. Harsha is made to say: "Stout-armed himself, with me a devotee of the bow, for his friend, to whom save Siva need he pay homage?" Ch. VII.

[3] Beal, Buddhist Records.

[4] See post, Ch. XVI.

Alliances were made by means of treaties. A treaty is defined by Chānakya as "that which binds kings in mutual faith."[1] The observance of a treaty either depended upon the plighted word (satya, śapatha) or was enforced by means of sureties (pratibhū) and hostages (pratigraha). Very often, the word of honour was held sufficient; but sometimes ascetics and men who were considered powerful enough to influence the action of the government stood sureties for the fulfilment of treaty obligations. In case of an apprehension of a breach of faith, one party often required the other to swear by fire, water, gold, etc., and to send as hostages his relatives and children. According to the older teachers, a treaty made by word of honour was regarded as impermanent (cala), while that supported by sureties or hostages was considered permanent (sthāvara). But Chānakya dissents from this view and says: "A treaty dependent upon the plighted word is permanent, not only in this world, but also in the next, while a treaty depending upon a hostage or a surety is good only for this world. Truthful kings of old made treaties only with the words 'we enter into agreement.'"[2] In spite of this theory, the maintenance of a treaty was often found very difficult, and when there was any deviation from the terms on the part of one of the parties, it taxed to the full the ingenuity and resourcefulness of the statesman, whether they

[1] Arthaśāstra, Bk. VII. ch. 17. [2] Ibid. Bk. VII. ch. 17.

tried to restore the treaty or to break off friendly relations.

Communications were kept up between the Courts of the different Powers through diplomatic agents. Even as early as the time of the Rig-Veda,[1] we hear of envoys, but the practice of attaching diplomatic agents to foreign Courts could not have been established until much later times. There were various kinds of such agents, and their powers and responsibilities differed a great deal. Some were Plenipotentiaries (Nisṛishtārtha), some Ambassadors (Dūta), some Chargés-d'affaires (Parimitārtha), while the rest were mere conveyors of royal messages (Śāsanahara).[2] Plenipotentiaries had power to demand the observance of treaties, to declare war or conclude peace, and to issue ultimatums in emergent cases.[3] Krishna, for example, was a plenipotentiary when he was sent by the Pāndavas to the Kuru Court with full powers just before the Great War.[4] The ambassadors kept their own governments fully informed of the activities of the Court to which they were attached. They lived on terms of friendship with the great Officers-of-State, and acquainted themselves

[1] Rig-Veda, II. 127, 9.

[2] Arthasāstra, Bk. I. ch 16. The Agni Purāna (Ch. 241), the Nitivākyāmrita (Ch. XIII.), and the Yukti-Kalpataru mention envoys of three kinds, nihśṛishṭārtha, mitārtha, and śāsanaharaka.

[3] Arthasāstra, Bk. I. ch. 16. "In urgent cases the ambassadors have to act like ministers."

[4] The Nītivākyāmrita gives this illustration. Ch. XIII.

with all the affairs of the country. In particular, they made it their business to ascertain the number, size, and positions of the forts and military stations, the strength of the army, and the strong and weak points of the State.[1] A Parimitārtha was sent to a foreign court on a particular mission and possessed limited authority. The diplomatic agents of the inferior type took note of intrigues against the ruler, and supervised the work of the spies[2] engaged in collecting information.

As the representative of a Foreign Power, an envoy enjoyed great privileges and immunities. A sort of sanctity was believed to attach to his person. The Nītivākyāmrita says: "An envoy should never be killed, even if he is a Chandāla, not to speak of a Brāhmana."[3] The envoys were always courteously treated. In Bhāsa's Pratimā-Nātaka, King Udayana is made to stand up when he receives a message from Mahasena Pradyota. As the responsibilities of an envoy were great, some care had to be taken in selecting the proper person. The Nītivākyāmrita mentions the following qualifications as essential in an ambassador: "Loyalty to the King, freedom

[1] Arthasāstra, Bk. I. ch. 16.

[2] The Agni Purāna has a very low opinion of the work of an ambassador. "An ambassador is but an open spy, and a spy is but an envoy travelling in the enemy's country in the guise of a trader, a mendicant, or a strolling physician." CCXLI. sl. 12.

[3] So also the Nītiprakāsikā says: "Even if an ambassador is guilty of a grievous wrong, he cannot be put to death." VII. 64.

from vices, capacity, honesty, strength of character, eloquence, brilliance, forgiveness, ability to divine other people's thoughts, and high birth."[1] Great stress used to be laid on the conduct of an ambassador at a foreign Court. He was expected to behave with dignity and courtesy, and to preserve the good name of the State which he represented. When on a mission to an enemy State it was the duty of the emissary to act with courage and resolution, and at the same time show moderation and tact.[2]

The maintenance of a balance of power was one of the problems in Foreign Politics which engaged the attention of the diplomats in ancient days. Chānakya insists that a monarch should always take care that none of the other Powers grow either too strong or become too weak. The Agni Purāna says: "A King should always contemplate the balance of power among the twelve monarchs constituting the circle of foreign monarchs having dealings with his own government."[3]

[1] Nītivākyāmrita, Ch. 13. The Agni Purāna says: "The ambassador sent to represent the King at a foreign court, should be a man of a very sharp intellect, sweet-voiced, possessing eloquence of speech, and well versed in the arts of diplomacy." Ch. CCXX.

[2] Arthasāstra, Bk. I. ch. 16.

[3] Ch. CCXL. sl. 1.

CHAPTER XV

THE MILITARY ORGANISATION

As wars were rather frequent in ancient days, each State in India found it necessary to maintain a large military force.[1] At the battle of the Hydaspes, which was fought between Alexander and Poros, the latter had with him a cavalry 4,000 strong, 300 chariots, 200 elephants, and an efficient infantry force of 30,000 soldiers.[2] The King of Magadha had about this time a large and powerful army consisting of 600,000 foot-soldiers, 30,000 horses, and 8,000 elephants. The Gangaridae (perhaps the people of Bengal) possessed 1,000 horse, 700 elephants, and 60,000 foot-soldiers. Pliny further mentions, on the authority of Megasthenes, that the Āndhra Kingdom had 100,000 foot-soldiers, 2,000 cavalry, and 1,000 elephants, while Kalinga kept in arms 60,000 foot, 10,000 horse, and 700 elephants, and the King of the Saurāshtras maintained an army of 1,600

[1] Megasthenes says: "In fact no one invested with kingly power ever keeps on foot a military force without a very great number of elephants and foot and cavalry." Fragment LVI. B.

[2] Alexander's Invasion (McCrindle), p. 65.

elephants, 150,000 foot, and 5,000 cavalry.[1] From Hiuen Tsiang we learn that when Harshavardhana ascended the throne of Kanauj, that Kingdom possessed an army of 5,000 elephants, 2,000 cavalry, and 50,000 foot-soldiers, and after Harshavardhana had succeeded in bringing the greater part of Northern India under his imperial sway, he found it necessary to increase his army to 60,000 war elephants and 100,000 cavalry.[2]

The military organisation seems to have been very efficient. The army was divided into four sections, namely, infantry, cavalry, chariots, and elephants. The relative usefulness of the different sections depended upon the seasons and the nature of the operations in which the army was engaged. Thus, according to the Mahābhārata, an army in which chariots and horsemen predominated was regarded as very effective in battle in fine weather, while one which had a large number of foot-soldiers was held as better in the rainy season.[3]

Foot-soldiers were of various classes. Chānakya classified them as regulars (maula), hired soldiers (bhṛita), those supplied by fighting corporations (śreṇi), those recruited from the enemies' country, those recruited from the country of an ally, and

[1] Megasthenes, Fragments LVI. and LVI. B. Megasthenes also mentions that the Pāndyans had a cavalry 4,000 strong, and an army of 150,000 foot-soldiers and 500 elephants. LVI.

[2] Buddhist Records, Bk. V.

[3] Mahābhārata, Sānti Parva, Sec. 160, sls. 24, 25.

lastly, those recruited from amongst wild tribes.[1] The best army, in the opinion of Chānakya, is that which has come down from father and grandfather, which is constant, obedient, contented, not averse from making long sojourns, everywhere invincible and possessed of the power of endurance, which has received a training in all kinds of warfare and has fought in many battles, which is ready to follow the fortunes of the monarch whether in weal or in woe, and which consists mainly of Kshatriyas.[2]

The main body of the soldiers of the country was selected from the bravest of the people; and as sons followed the profession of their fathers, they soon became very proficient in the art of war. On the battle-field the hereditary soldiers were placed in front and in positions of importance, while the mercenary troops were usually stationed in the rear.[3] The comparative values of mercenaries and thorough-bred soldiers are described in the Ājañña-Jātaka in these words:

> "No matter when or where,
> In weal or woe,
> The thorough-bred fights on;
> The hack gives in." [4]

[1] Arthasāstra, Bk. IX. ch. 1. The Sukranīti divides soldiers into two classes, namely, maula (regulars) and sadyaska (recent recruits), and sub-divides each of these into various sub-classes. Ch. IV. sec. 7.

[2] Arthasāstra, Bk. VI. ch. 1. [3] Hiuen Tsiang, Buddhist Records, Bk. II.

[4] The Jātaka (Cowell), I. 24.

So the Sukranīti says: "The King should go to battle with his main army. Such an army never desires to forsake their master even at the point of death." IV. 7, 184.

The cavalry formed a very important part of the army. Its great value lay in its quick movement, and it was regarded as specially useful for occupying advanced positions, for protecting the treasury and commissariat, for cutting off the enemy's supply, for delivering attacks against the enemy's forces, and for pursuing a retreating foe.[1] A large cavalry force was held essential in order to keep an extensive kingdom under control, and we know that Chandragupta's military strength depended very largely upon the superiority of his cavalry.

Chariots were of various kinds. They were of special use in protecting the army against the enemy's attacks, seizing the enemy's positions and breaking the compact array of the enemy's army.[2]

Elephants were regarded as very useful in warfare. The destruction of the enemy's army was believed mainly to depend upon elephants.[3] Megasthenes speaks of the Gangaridae as a nation which possessed a vast force of the largest sized elephants, and remarks: "Owing to this, their country has never been conquered by any foreign King; for all other nations dread the overwhelming number and strength of these animals."[4] Even as late as the seventh century A.D., we are told by Hiuen Tsiang that the defeat of Harshavardhana at the hands of Pulakesi, King of Mahārāshtra, was due to the fact that the

[1] Arthaśāstra, Bk. X. ch. 4.

[2] Ibid.

[3] Arthaśāstra, Bk. VII. ch. 11.

[4] Fragment I.

latter possessed a large number of savage elephants.[1] But they were sometimes more a hindrance than a help, as was found in the battle of the Hydaspes, where, maddened by the wounds received from the enemy's missiles, they "attacked friend and foe indiscriminately, pushed them, trampled them down, and killed them in all manner of ways," and, being at last spent with wounds, "spread havoc among their own ranks." [2]

Some of the more powerful rulers had, besides the four-fold armies, naval departments. Megasthenes mentions the naval department as one of the six military departments of the State, and Chānakya speaks of warships which were to be under the control of the Superintendent of Navigation. According to Hiuen Tsiang, the King of Assam possessed a fleet of 30,000 ships.

Each section of the army was divided into various divisions, which were named Patti, Senāmukha, Gulma, Gaṇa, Vāhinī, Pratna, Chamū, Anīkinī, and Akshauhiṇī. These would correspond roughly with the modern divisions of the army, such as sections, platoons, brigades, companies, battalions, regiments, divisions, and army corps. It is said that in the

[1] Life of Hiuen Tsiang, Bk. IV. In this book we are further told: "When these (elephants) are drawn up in battle array, they give them intoxicating spirits to drink, till they are overpowered with it, and then at a given signal, when in this condition, they excite them to rush against the enemy. The foes are thus without fail put to flight." Bk. IV.

[2] Alexander's Invasion (McCrindle), p. 106.

Mahābhārata War eighteen Akshauhiṇīs, or army corps, were engaged in battle. This is an enormous number, making a total of 3,936,600 in the whole of the forces engaged, and is doubtless a great exaggeration.

Besides the fighting forces, there were the transport and supply services. According to the Sukranīti, the smallest unit of the army (including the transport and supply services) was to consist of 300 foot-soldiers, 80 horses, 1 chariot, 2 cannons (bṛihannālika), 10 camels, 2 elephants, 2 carts, and 16 bulls.[1] The Sukranīti considers it desirable to have the infantry four times the cavalry; bulls, one-fifth of the horse, and camels, one-eighth; elephants, one-fourth of the camels; chariots, half of elephants; and cannons, twice the number of chariots. The various divisions of the army were commanded by officers (bala-mukhyāḥ) whose ranks depended upon the number of soldiers serving under them.[2]

The different regiments were designated by distinguishing flags and badges. They had also different kinds of trumpets, kettle-drums, and conch-shells.[3] Signalling was a very important part of the army organisation, and communications were made by means of homing pigeons and various other devices. The different divisions of the army were given a

[1] IV. 7, 22-23. [2] IV. 7, 21.

[3] "Tūrya-dhvaja-patākābhir vyūha-saṁjñāḥ prakalpayet." Arthaśāstra, Bk. II. ch. 33.

regular training in the art of war. In times of peace they had their daily exercises, at which the King sometimes used to be present.

The Commander-in-Chief (Pradhāna Senāpati) was the head of the military department of the State. Usually he was a man well trained in all the arts of warfare, and familiar with use of all kinds of weapons. It was his duty to attend to the training and efficient organisation of the army and the enforcement of proper discipline among the soldiers. The Harsha-charita gives a poetic description of the appearance and character of the Commander-in-Chief of the Kingdom of Sthānvesvara from which we make the following extract: "... a man foremost in every fight, in person yellow as the hill of orpiment, stately as a great full-grown Sāl tree's stem, and tall as if ripened by valour's exceeding heat ... So stubborn was his frame that even old age laid but a trembling hand, timidly as it were, upon his stiff hair. He seemed while still alive to have been born anew into a lion's nature ... In spite of age his broad chest was rough with great gashes of wounds ... and all across it ran in lines the writings of many great scars graven by the axe-edge of sharp swords, as though he were making a calculation of the hour of victory in every battle." [1]

Under the Commander-in-Chief were the Chief Commandants (adhyakshāḥ) of the four great divisions,

[1] Harshacharita, Ch. VI. (Cowell and Thomas).

namely, the infantry, the cavalry, the elephant force, and the chariots. Subordinate to the Chief Commandants were other officers of various grades. According to Chānakya, for every ten units of each of the constituents of the army, there was to be an officer called Padika, ten Padikas were to be under a Senāpati (commander), and ten Senāpatis under a Nāyaka (general).[1] The Sukranīti also mentions such officers as Śatānīkas (officers commanding one hundred soldiers) and Sāhasrikas (officers commanding one thousand soldiers).

The direction of military affairs was, at the time of Megasthenes's visit, in the hands of a governing body of thirty members. This body was grouped into six committees of five members each, they being in charge of the four divisions of the army, and the commissariat and the naval department. "One division is appointed," says Strabo, "to co-operate with the admiral of the fleet, another with the superintendent of the bullock-trains which are used in transporting engines of war, food for the soldiers, provender for the cattle, and other military requisites. They supply servants who beat the drum, and others who carry gongs; grooms also for the horses, and mechanists and their assistants. To the sound of the gong they send out foragers to bring in grass, and by a system of rewards and punishments ensure the work being done with despatch and safety. The

[1] Arthaśāstra, Bk. X. ch. 6.

third division has charge of the foot-soldiers, the fourth of the horses, the fifth of the war chariots, and the sixth of the elephants. There are royal stables for the horses and elephants, and also a royal magazine for the arms, because the soldier has to return his arms to the magazine, and his horse and elephant to the stables ... In addition to the charioteer there are two fighting men who sit up in the chariot beside him. The war-elephant carries four men—three who shoot arrows, and the driver." [1]

Various kinds of weapons were used in the ancient times for offensive and defensive purposes. In the Rig-Veda we read of bows, arrows, armours, and coats-of-mail.[2] Chānakya classifies weapons as immovable machines (sthita-yantra), movable machines (chala-yantra), bows, arrows, swords, weapons with pointed edges like ploughshares, and miscellaneous weapons.[3] Each of these classes is again subdivided into many kinds. In the Mahābhārata we find mention of many kinds of weapons, of which those most often used were the mace, the battle-axe, the

[1] Megasthenes, Fragment XXIV.

[2] "Little is known of Vedic warfare, but it seems to have been simple. A body of foot-soldiers with charioteers composed every army, the two going together, and the foot-soldiers being often overthrown by the charioteers, who were doubtless the Kshatriyas and their foremost retainers. Probably the foot-soldiers bore little armour, and used only the bow for offence ... The nobles, on the other hand, may have had cuirass (varman), helmet (sipra), and hand-guard (hastaghna). On the car was the charioteer, and on his left the warrior ... The offensive weapon was practically the bow; spear and sword and axe were seldom used." Vedic Index, II. p. 417.

[3] Arthasāstra, Bk. II. ch. 28.

discus, the bow, the arrow, and the vajra (thunderbolt). The Agni Purāna[1] arranges weapons in five classes, namely, (i) those thrown by machines (yantra-mukta), (ii) those thrown by the hand (pāṇi-mukta), (iii) those thrown and drawn back (mukta-sandhṛita), (iv) those not thrown (amukta), and (v) weapons used in hand-to-hand fights (bāhu-yuddha). The Sukranīti mentions the following chief weapons: iśu (arrow), gadā (mace), paṭṭiśa, ekadhāra, kshura-prānta, khaḍga, chakra, supāśaka, and karaja.[2] From the Nītiprakāsikā,[3] we get a full list of the instruments used in warfare.

I. Mukta (which are thrown): dhanu (bow), iśu (arrow), bhiṇḍipala, śakti (spear), drughaṇa (hatchet), tomara (tomahawk), nālika (musket), laguḍa (light club), pāśa (lasso), chakra (discus), danta-kaṇṭaka (tooth-thorn), masuṇḍi (octagon-headed club).

II. Amukta (which are not thrown): vajra (thunderbolt), īlī (hand-sword), paraśu (axe), gośira (cow-horn spear), asidhenu (stiletto), lavitra (scythe), āstara (scatterer), kunta (lance), sthūṇā (anvil), prāsa (spear), pināka or triśūla (trident), gadā (heavy club), mudgara (hammer), śirā (ploughshare), musala (pestle), paṭṭiśa (battle-axe), maushṭika (dagger), mayūkhī (pole), śataghnī (hundred-killer), and 44 other varieties.

[1] Agni Purāna, Ch. 148, 2. [2] Ch. IV. sec. 7.

[3] Although the Nītiprakāsikā is a comparatively modern book, it is based on older works, and most of the instruments mentioned in it were probably in use from early times.

III. Mantra-mukta (thrown by mantras or spells).

These were mythical weapons, and were supposed to be so powerful that nothing could frustrate them. These were: Vishṇu-chakra (discus of Vishnu), vajrāstra (thunderbolt), Brahmāstra (missile of Brahmā), Kāla-prāsaka (noose of death), Nārāyanāstra (missile of Nārāyana), and Pāśupatāstra (missile of Siva).[1]

The chief defensive weapons consisted of shields and bucklers. Warriors were also clad in armour made of iron or skin.[2] The Greek writers tell us that Poros's person was rendered shot-proof by his coat-of-mail which was "remarkable for its strength and the closeness with which it fitted his person."[3] All instruments of war were kept in the armoury, stamped with the royal seal, and could not be moved except under sealed orders.[4]

The question whether the use of fire-arms was known in India in ancient times has not yet been settled. There are a few terms to be found in the Rāmāyana and the Mahābhārata, such as 'vajra,' 'nālika,' and 'āgneyāstra,' which may be interpreted as pointing to the use of fire-arms. Chānakya gives recipes for the preparation of inflammable powders (agni-dhāraṇa and agni-yoga) which were to be hurled against the enemy.[5] The Sukranīti treats of the

[1] Ch. II. [2] Arthasāstra, Bk. II. ch. 18.

[3] Alexander's Invasion (McCrindle), p. 108.

[4] Arthasāstra, Bk. V. ch. 2.

[5] "Small balls prepared from the mixture of sarala (pinus longifolia), deva-dāru (deodar), pūtitriṇa (stinking grass), guggula (bdellium), śrīveshṭaka

preparation of gun-powder, and also of the use of cannons and muskets, but these passages are evidently a later addition. The Nītiprakāsikā, which is doubtless a recent work, mentions burning and explosive oil, and injurious and irritating compounds which were thrown at the enemy. From these and other similar passages Mr. Gustav Oppert concludes that gunpowder was first invented in India, and that fire-arms were used by Indians long before they were known in any other country. We do not find, however, any mention of fire-arms in the writings of foreign travellers, and in the absence of fuller proof the question must be regarded as unsettled.

Of the equipment of the soldiers at the time of Alexander's invasion Arrian says: "The foot-soldiers carry a bow made of equal length with the man who bears it. This they rest upon the ground, and pressing against it with their left foot, thus discharge the arrow, having drawn the string far backwards; for the shaft they use is little short of being three yards long, and there is nothing which can resist an Indian

(turpentine), the juice of saraja (vatica robusta), and lākshā (lac) combined with dungs of an ass, camel, sheep and goat are inflammable (agnidhāraṇa, i.e. such as keep fire). The mixture of the powder of priyāla (chironjia sapida), the charcoal of valguja (canyza, serratula, anthelmintea), madhūchchhishta (wax), and the dung of a horse, ass, camel, and cow is an inflammable powder to be hurled against the enemy. The powder of all the metals as red as fire, or the mixture of the powder of kumbh (gemelia arborea), sīsa (lead), trapu (zinc), mixed with the charcoal powder of the flowers of pāribhadraka (deodar), palāśa (butea frondosa), and hair and with oil, wax, and turpentine, is also an inflammable powder." Arthasāstra, Bk. XIII. ch. 4 (Shama Shastri's trans.).

archer's shot, neither shield nor breast-plate, nor any stronger defence, if such there be. In their left hand they carry bucklers made of undressed ox-hide, which are not so broad as those who carry them, but are about as long. Some are equipped with javelins instead of bows, but wear a sword which is broad in the blade, but not longer than three cubits; and this when they engage in close fight (which they do with reluctance), they wield with both hands to fetch down a lustier blow. The horsemen are equipped with two lances like the lances called saunia, and with a shorter buckler than that carried by foot-soldiers."[1]

Hiuen Tsiang, writing in the seventh century, describes in the following words the weapons used and the method of fighting adopted by each of the four divisions of the army. "The elephants are covered with strong armour, and their tusks are provided with sharp spurs. A leader in a car gives the command, whilst two attendants on the right and left drive his chariot, which is drawn by four horses abreast. The general of the soldiers remains in his chariot, he is surrounded by a file of guards, who keep close to his chariot wheels.

"The cavalry spread themselves in front to resist an attack, and in case of defeat they carry orders hither and thither. The infantry by their quick movements contribute to the defence. These men

[1] Arrian (McCrindle), XVI.

are chosen for their courage and strength. They carry a long spear and a great shield; sometimes they hold a sword or sabre, advance to the front with impetuosity. All their weapons are sharp and pointed. Some of them are these—spears, shields, bows, arrows, swords, sabres, battle-axes, lances, halberds, long javelins, and various kinds of slings. All these they have used for ages."[1]

Before the commencement of a battle it was thought necessary to select a proper site for pitching camps. According to the Mahābhārata, a region lying near the woods was to be regarded as suited for encampment. "In choosing the field of battle," says the Mahābhārata, "men conversant with war approve of a region that is not miry, not watery, not uneven, not abounding with bricks and stones, as well suited to the operations of cavalry; a field that is free from mire and holes is fit for car-warriors; a region that is overgrown with bushes and trees and is under water is fitted for elephant warriors; and a ground that contains many inaccessible spots, and has large trees and topes of cane bushes, as also a mountainous or woody tract, is well fitted for the operations of infantry."[2] Chānakya also enters into a similar discussion of the suitability of a field, but gives the general advice: "The conqueror should choose such a place as may be suitable for the

[1] Buddhist Records (Beal), Bk. II.

[2] Mahābhārata, Sānti Parva, Sec. 100, sls. 21-23.

manœuvre of his army and (at the same time) inconvenient for that of his enemy."[1]

Sometimes it was necessary to occupy particular positions for a considerable length of time. On such occasions, a more permanent sort of camp was constructed. With regard to such a camp, Chānakya says: "On a site well-suited for the construction of buildings, the general, the carpenters, and the astrologers should measure a circular, rectangular, or square plot of land (according to the shape of the available land) for the camp which should contain four gates, six roads, and nine divisions, and should be provided with ditches, parapets, walls, means of exit, watch towers, temporary residence of the King, etc."[2]

Much care, evidently, was bestowed on the arrangement of troops in battle. Veterans and soldiers noted for their strength and courage were stationed in the van and in positions of danger, while the weaker combatants formed the rear of the army.[3] Various kinds of array are described in the Mahābhārata. In the Great War, the Pāndavas drew up their armies in different kinds of array on different days. The most important form adopted by the Kauravas was a Maze (chakra-vyūha), the object of which was

[1] Mahābhārata, Bk. IX. ch. 1. Vide also Sukranīti, Ch. IV. sec. 7.

[2] Arthasāstra, Bk. V. ch. 2.

[3] Sukranīti, Ch. IV. sec. 7. The Nītiprakāsikā says: "The strength of the army should be concentrated at the point where there is any danger from the enemy." VII. 53.

especially to protect the great heroes in the centre.[1] Chānakya mentions the daṇḍa, bhoga, maṇḍala, and asaṁhata as the four principal kinds of array. Each of these, again, has several varieties, which he describes thus: "The arrangement of the army in transverse sections is called a daṇḍa (staff) array. An array in which the lines (of troops) follow one another is called a bhoga (snake). Stationing the army so as to face all directions is called a maṇḍala (circle) array. An arrangement of the army in separate and detached portions is called an asaṁhata (detached) array. A daṇḍa array is of equal strength on its wings, flanks, and front. This array is called pradara (breaking the enemy's array) when its flanks are made to project in front. It is known as dṛiḍhaka (firm) when its wings and flanks are stretched back. It is called asahya (irresistible) when its wings are lengthened. When, after the formation of the wings, the front is made to bulge out, it is called a śyena (eagle) array. These four varieties are called chāpa (a bow), chāpa-kukshi (the centre of a bow), pratishṭha (a hold), and supratishṭha (stronghold) respectively when they are arranged in the reverse orders.

"That array in which the wings are arranged like a bow is called a sañjaya (victory). The same with a projected front is called vijaya (victory). The

[1] In the Journal of India Art and Industry (ed. by Col. T. H. Hendley), Vol. VII., a picture of the Maze has been reproduced from the Razmnāmah (temp. Akbar).

array which has its flanks and wings thick is called sthūlakarṇa (big ear); the array with its front made twice as strong as the vijaya is called viśāla-vijaya (great victory); that which has its wings stretched forward is called chamū-mukha (face of an army); and the same is called jhashāsya (face of a fish) when it is arrayed in the reverse form. That variety of daṇḍa array in which one (constituent of the army) is made to stand higher than the others is called the sūchī (needle). When this array consists of two such lines, it is called valaya (aggregate), and when of four lines, durjaya (invincible). These are the varieties of the daṇḍa array.

"That variety of the bhoga array in which the wings, flanks, and front are of unequal depth is called sarpasāri (which has a serpentine movement), or gomūtrika. When it consists of two lines in front and has its wings arranged in a daṇḍa array, it is called a śakaṭa (cart); the reverse of this is called makara (crocodile); the śakaṭa array which consists of elephants, horses, and chariots is called vāripatantaka (water-fall). These are the varieties of the bhoga array.

"That variety of maṇḍala array in which the distinction of wings, flanks, and front is lost is called sarvatomukha (facing all directions) or sarvatobhadra (all auspicious), ashṭānīka (consisting of eight divisions), or durjaya (invincible). These are the varieties of the maṇḍala array.

"The arrangement in which the wings, flanks, and front are stationed separate from one another is called an asaṁhata (detached) array. When five divisions of the array are arranged in detached order, it is called vajra (diamond) or godhā (alligator); when four divisions, it is called udyānaka (park) or kākapadī (crow's foot); when three divisions, it is called ardhachandrikā (half-moon) or karkaṭaka-śriṅgī (the horn of a crab). These are the varieties of the asaṁhata array.

"The array in which chariots form the front, elephants the wings, and horses the rear is called arishṭa (desirable); that in which infantry, cavalry, chariots, and elephants stand one behind the other is called acala (immovable); that in which elephants, horses, chariots, and infantry stand in order, one behind the other, is known as apratihata (irresistible)." [1]

The method of attacking the enemy, when both the armies have been arranged in battle order is, according to Chānakya, this: "He (i.e. Commander-in-Chief) should assail the pradara by means of the dṛiḍhaka; the dṛiḍhaka by means of the asahya; the śyena by means of the chāpa; a pratishṭha by means of a supratishṭha; sañjaya by means of a vijaya; sthūlakarṇa by means of a viśālavijaya, vāripatantaka by means of sarvatobhadra. He may assail all kinds of arrays by means of the durjaya.

[1] Arthaśāstra, Bk. X. ch. 6.

Of the infantry, cavalry, chariots, and the elephants, the Commander-in-Chief should strike the one previously mentioned by means of that which follows it. He should attack a small contingent with a large one."[1]

Poros's distribution of the army at the battle of the Hydaspes, as described by Greek writers, is very interesting in this connection. Poros distributed his cavalry on the wings, and placed his elephants in his front line at equi-distances, so arranged as to strike the enemy with terror. In the intervals between the animals he stationed the rest of his soldiers, instructing them to succour the elephants and protect them from being assailed in flank by the enemy's missiles. The whole disposition of the army gave it very much the appearance of a city—the elephants as they stood resembling its towers, and the men-at-arms placed between them resembling the lines of wall intervening between tower and tower.[2]

Trench (khātaka) warfare and mining (khanaka) were known in ancient times. Chānakya praises these kinds of fighting, because under these systems the soldiers are in a very favourable position. Another method was that of fighting from heights (ākāśayuddha).[3] The system of siege-warfare was

[1] Arthaśāstra, Bk. X. ch. 6.

[2] Vide Alexander's Invasion (McCrindle) and V. A. Smith's Early History of India.

[3] Arthaśāstra, Bk. VII. ch. 10.

also practised in Ancient India. Chānakya describes in detail the suitable time for commencing a siege, and for storming a besieged place.

Forts began to be constructed in India from very early times. Even the pre-Āryan races of India had forts. In Hymn 20, Bk. II. of the Rig-Veda we read the following:

"When in his arms they laid the bolt,
He slaughtered the Dasyus and cast down their forts of iron."[1]

And again in Hymn 12, Bk. III.:

"Indra and Agni have cast down the ninety forts which Dasas held,
Together with one mighty deed."[2]

The Vishnu Smriti[3] mentions forts of many kinds. Manu points out the necessity for possessing forts in the following passage: "One bowman placed on a rampart is a match in battle for one hundred (foes), one hundred for ten thousand; hence it is prescribed (in the Sāstras that a King shall possess) a fortress."[4] He mentions desert-forts, forts built of stone and earth, forts protected by water or trees, forts protected by armed men, and hill-forts, of which hill-

[1] Rig-Veda (Griffith's trans.). [2] Rig-Veda (Griffith's trans.).

[3] Vishnu Smriti (Jolly's Sanskrit text), Ch. 3.

"Dhanva-nṛ-mahī-vṛkṣa-giri-durgāṇi." The Agni Purāna and the Sukranīti also mention these kinds of forts. The Mānasāra mentions 'śivira,' 'vāhinīmukha,' 'sthānīya,' 'droṇaka,' 'saṁsiddhi,' 'kolaka,' 'nigama,' 'skandhāvāra,' as the eight varieties of forts. Ch. XI.

[4] Manu, VII. 74.

forts are the best. The Mahābhārata also mentions various kinds of forts, and offers the King the following advice in regard to the arrangements of the fortress: "When the King takes refuge in a fortress against a powerful invader, he should raise outer ramparts round his forts, fill the trenches with water, driving pointed stakes at the bottom and filling them with crocodiles and sharks. Over all the gates he should place destructive engines. He should store food, fuel, and all other requisites, and ensure the supply of water by constructing wells. He should construct depots, arsenals, camps, and quarters for soldiers, stabling for horses and elephants, supply himself with wealth, and collect stores of all sorts, such as food, oil, fat, honey, clarified butter, medicines, grass, arrows, fuel, swords, lances, fruits, etc."[1]

According to Chānakya, forts were to be constructed in all the four quarters of the territory of the State. There were to be island forts, forts in the plains, forts in low-lying places, forts protected by water, forts built of stone, cave-forts, hill-forts, desert forts, and forts constructed in forests. A Sthānīya fort was to be built in the centre of eight hundred villages, a Droṇamukha, of four hundred, a Khārvaṭika, of two hundred, and a Saṅgrahaṇa, of ten.[2] In the opinion of Sukrāchārya, forts were

[1] Mahābhārata, Sānti Parva, Sec. 69, sls. 33-41.

[2] Arthasāstra, Bk. II. ch. 1.

to be constructed in accordance with a definite system so that each might be helpful to the others in case of need.

Some of these forts were very strong. Alexander the Great found the greatest difficulty in capturing some of the forts of the Punjab and Sindh.[1] Of the fortifications of Mazaga, the chief fort of the Kshudrakas, Curtius says: "An army of 38,000 infantry defended the city, which was strongly fortified both by nature and art. For on the east an impetuous mountain stream with steep banks on both sides barred approach to the city, while to the south and west, nature, as if designing to form a rampart, had piled up gigantic rocks, at the base of which lay sloughs and yawning chasms hollowed in the course of ages to vast depths, while a ditch of mighty labour drawn from their extremity continued the line of defence. The city was, besides, surrounded by a wall 35 stadia in circumference, which had a basis of stonework supporting a superstructure of unburnt, sun-dried bricks. The brickwork was bound into a solid fabric by means of stones."[2]

Recent excavations in Mandor have brought to light the remains of the old hill-fort, Mandavya-durga, built about the sixth century A.D. These remains give us some idea of the structure of a hill-fort of

[1] The chief stronghold of the Malloi (Mālavas) was captured by Alexander only by showing a desperate personal courage and after he had been dangerously wounded.

[2] Alexander's Invasion (McCrindle), p. 195.

ancient times. The walls rise to a considerable height. They were constructed of massive blocks of stone, their width averaging some 24 or 25 feet, and originally they were further strengthened and protected by bastions on the outside, of which several are still preserved on the north and west sides. Along the curtain of the walls these bastions are either square or rectangular in plan; but the one at the north-west angle is circular, and it is possible that those at the other three corners were of the same form. The gateways are hidden under the fallen debris, but can be recognised. The main approach to the castle as well as to the city is a broad paved causeway, which ascends the plateau from the plains and runs alongside the moat.[1]

[1] Vide Archaeological Survey of India, 1909-10.

CHAPTER XVI

CONQUEST AND DEFENCE

When the Āryas, after their settlement in the Punjab, began to spread themselves in different directions, every step of their advance was opposed by the non-Āryan tribes. The Rig-Veda is replete with allusions to these conflicts between Āryas and Dasyus. Hymn VIII, Mandala I. of the Rig-Veda, for instance, runs thus :

"Indra, bring wealth that gives delight, the victor's ever-conquering wealth,
Most excellent to our aid ;
By means of which we may repel our foes in battle hand to hand,
By thee assisted with the car.
Aided by thee, the thunder-armed, may we lift up the bolt,
And conquer all our foes in fight.
And thee, O Indra, for ally with missile-darting heroes, may
We conquer our embattled foes." [1]

Again, in Hymn 11, Mandala II., we read :

"Hero, assume the might wherewith thou clavest Vṛitra piecemeal, the Dānava Aurṇavābha,

[1] Rig Veda (Griffith's trans.).

Thou hast disclosed the light to light the Ārya ; on thy left,
O Indra, sank the Dasyu,
May we gain wealth, subduing with thy succour and with
the Ārya, all our foes, the Dasyus." [1]

In the heroic age of Indian history of which accounts are preserved in the Rāmāyana and the Mahābhārata, the fame of a great warrior was much coveted by powerful monarchs, and their ambition was to be acknowledged paramount sovereign by the neighbouring rulers. Jarāsandha, King of Magadha, is described in the Mahābhārata as having, with the assistance of Sisupāla, King of Chedi, who acted as his generalissimo, subjugated almost all the Kings of Middle India. He was a wicked man, and so when he was preparing to declare himself Emperor, the Pāndavas were persuaded by the other Kings to declare war against him in which Jarāsandha was killed.[2] Then King Yudhishthira's brothers set out, each at the head of a large army, on a Digvijaya, or conquest of the four quarters. They succeeded in defeating all the brave monarchs of Northern India, and compelled them to acknowledge Yudhishthira as their paramount sovereign and to pay tribute to him. But the acquisition of territory was not that great King's object. As the poet Bāna Bhatta puts it:

[1] Rig Veda (Griffith's trans.). In the Mahābhārata we come across the following passage: "War was invented by Indra for the destruction of Dasyus, and bows, weapons, and armour were created for the same purpose. Therefore, merit is acquired by the destruction of Dasyus." Udyoga Parva, Sec. 29, sls. 30-31.

[2] Mahābhārata, Sabhā Parva, Sec. XV.

"Not too ambitious, surely, of conquest were the ancients, seeing that in a small part of the earth there were numerous monarchs, such as Bhagadatta, Dantavakra, Krātha, Karṇa, Kaurava, Śiśupāla, Śālva, Jārasandha, and Sindhurāja. King Yudhisthira was easily content, since he endured quite near at hand the Kingdom of the Kimpurushas, when the conquests of Dhananjaya had made the earth to shake."[1]

Although righteous warfare was supported and even extolled in olden times, the ancient teachers did not regard war in general as a profitable business. They seem to have clearly realised the fact that war inflicts heavy losses on both parties, and that even the victorious party does not derive much advantage from it. So the Mahābhārata advises Kings not to engage in wars until all peaceful means of settling disputes have failed.[2] In spite of such advice, however, aggressive wars became gradually more and more frequent. Thus we find Manu offering the King a different sort of advice: "When," says Manu, "he is thus engaged in conquest, let him subdue all the opponents whom he may find by the (four) expedients, conciliation and the rest. If they cannot be stopped by the first three expedients, then let him, overcoming

[1] Harshacharita, Ch. VII. The translation given here is that of Cowell and Thomas.

[2] "Sāntvena tu pradānena bhedena ca narādhipa
Yam arthaṁ śaknuyāt prāptuṁ tena tuṣyeta paṇḍitaḥ."
Sānti Parva, Sec. 69, sl. 24.

them by force alone, gradually bring them to subjection." [1]

Chānakya was the great champion of a universal monarchy in India, and as such he regarded the acquisition of territory by means of conquest as a very desirable object. " A conqueror, well versed in the science of Politics," says Chānakya, " who acquires territory from enemies gains superiority " ; and in his opinion any ruler who opposes such an attempt was to be crushed, whatever might be the cost of the undertaking.[2]

Chānakya's disciple, Chandragupta, was the first great conqueror of historical times who subdued all the countries of Northern India. His son and grandson were also renowned for their conquering arms. Asoka, however, repented of his sins after the conquest of Kalinga, and turned his eyes to conquests of a different kind. In the fourth century A.D. we hear of the achievements of Samudragupta, who has been called by a well-known historian " the Indian Napoleon." The Allahābād inscription speaks of him as one " who was skilful in engaging in a hundred battles of different kinds ; whose only Ally was the prowess of the strength of his own arm ;—who was noted for his prowess ;—whose most charming body

[1] Manu, VII. 107-108. He adds : " Among the four expedients conciliation and the rest, the learned always recommend conciliation and (the employment of) force for the prosperity of Kingdoms." VII. 109.

[2] Vide Arthasāstra, Bk. VII. chs. 10 and 12.

was covered with all the beauty of the marks of a hundred confused wounds, caused by the blows of battle-axes, arrows, spears, pikes, barbed darts, swords, lances, javelins and whose great good fortune was mixed with so as to be increased by the favour shown in capturing and then liberating Mahendra of Kosala Vyāghrarāja of Mahākāntāra,—and all other Kings of the South,—whose imperious commands were fully gratified by giving all taxes and obeying orders and coming to perform obeisance by the frontier Kings . . . whose tranquil fame, pervading the whole world, was generated by establishing (again) many royal families fallen and deprived of sovereignty . . . who had no antagonist of equal power in the world." [1]

King Yasodharman describes himself in his inscriptions as one who conquered countries not enjoyed by the Guptas, "before whose chieftains bow down Kings from the neighbourhood of Lauhitya (Brahmaputra) to Mahendra, and from Himālaya to the Western Ocean." [2] Harshavardhana was also a great conqueror who, according to the Chinese traveller Hiuen Tsiang, went from East to West subduing all the Kings of Northern India, and whose victorious armies reposed only after thirty years of incessant fighting. [3]

[1] Vide Corpus Inscriptionum Indicarum, Vol. III. Vide also the Eran stone Inscription of Samudragupta and the Mathurā and Sānchī Inscriptions of Chandragupta II.

[2] Mandasor Pillar Inscription of Yasodharman, Corp. Ins. Ind. Vol. III.

[3] Buddhist Records, Bk. V.

It ought to be noted that the Kings of India, as a rule, confined their military activities within the borders of India, and Indian history does not record many invasions of foreign countries. In the opinion of Megasthenes, it was a sense of justice which "prevented any Indian King from attempting conquest beyond the limits of India." The conquests of Ceylon, Siam, Cambodia, Java, and Sumatra seem to have been exceptions to this rule; but, really, they were in part military achievements and in part colonising enterprises.

In Chānakya's military philosophy warfare was of three kinds, namely, open (prakāśa), treacherous (kūṭa), and silent (tūshṇīm). "Open warfare consists of threatening, assault, creating confusion in the enemy's ranks, and divert attack. Treacherous warfare consists in keeping up good relations by gifts, etc., and attacking at the same time. Silent warfare is the attempt to win over the officers of the enemy." [1] Enthusiasm, superiority in strength, and skilful diplomacy were regarded as the three great requisites for success in war, and of these, the second was held better than the first and the third the best of all. "The arrow shot by an archer," says Chānakya, "may or may not kill one person; but the skilful diplomacy of a wise man kills even those who are not yet born." [2] Chānakya advises a would-be conqueror to ascertain, before marching to battle, the

[1] Arthaśāstra, Bk. VII. ch. 6. [2] Ibid. Bk. X. ch. 6.

comparative strength and weakness of his own army and that of his enemy, and to carefully consider the advantages and disadvantages likely to result from the undertaking, the possibility of the recruitment of new soldiers, the expenditure both in men and money, the dangers of the undertaking, and the probable consequences. The conqueror is also advised to commence his march during a favourable season of the year,[1] and to leave one-third or one-fourth of the army in the capital for protection against rearward enemies and wild tribes.[2] If the enemy offered battle, he was to be vanquished on the battle-field, but should he take shelter in a fort, he was to be besieged. The five means of capturing an enemy's fort, in the opinion of Kautilya, were: intrigue (upajāpa), employment of spies (upasarpa), winning over the people (vamana), siege (paryupāsana), and carrying by assault (avamarda).[3]

Before the commencement of a battle it seems to have been the practice for the King or the Commander-in-Chief to address words of encouragement to the soldiers. The Mahābhārata gives a specimen of

[1] According to Vishnu, Agrahāyana and Chaitra were the proper months for marching against an enemy. Ch. 3. Vide also Manu, VII. 182-185, and Mahābhārata, Sānti Parva, Sec. 100, sl. 11. According to Kautilya, a march in the month of Mārga-sirsha (November-December) was the best, but marches might be commenced during other months, such as Chaitra and Jyaishtha. "A conqueror may march against an enemy at any time when the latter is in trouble." Bk. IX. ch. 1.

[2] Arthasāstra, Bk. IX. ch. 1.

[3] Vide Arthasāstra, Bk. XIII. ch. 4. The proper times for commencing and for storming a siege were fully discussed in this chapter.

such a speech, from which we extract the following lines:

"Let us swear to conquer and never to desert one another. Let those who are overcome with fear stay behind. Let those also stay behind who would cause their chiefs to be slain by themselves neglecting to act heroically in battle. Let only such men come who would never turn back from battle, or cause their comrades to be slain. . . . The consequences of fleeing away from battle are loss of wealth, infamy and reproach. . . . Those that flee from battle are wretches among men. They only swell the number of human beings on earth, but, for true manhood, they are neither here nor hereafter. Victorious foes proceed cheerfully in pursuit of retreating combatants, while their praises are sung by bards. When enemies coming to battle tarnish the fame of a person, the misery which he feels is more poignant than the pangs of death. Know that victory is the root of religious merit and of every kind of happiness. . . . Resolved upon acquiring heaven, we should fight, regardless of life or death; and with this determination to conquer or die, attain a blessed end in heaven." [1]

Chānakya also advises that before the commencement of a battle, the Prime Minister and the Royal Priest should encourage the soldiers with words like the following:

"It is declared in the Vedas that the goal which

[1] Mahābhārata, Sānti Parva, Sec. 100. sls. 32-41.

is reached by sacrificers after the performance of sacrifices is the very goal which brave men are destined to attain."[1] In regard to this there are two verses:

"Beyond those places which Brāhmanas, seeking heaven, attain by performing a number of sacrifices or by practising penances, are the places which brave men, giving up their lives in righteous battles, reach immediately."

"Let not a new vessel filled with water, consecrated, and covered with darbha grass, be the acquisition of that man who does not fight in return for the subsistence received by him from his master, and who is destined to go to hell."[2]

This last verse is also to be found in Bhāsa's Pratimā-Nātaka, where it is used in encouraging the soldiers on the battle-field.[3] As a matter of fact, the people of Ancient India were very brave, and an appeal to their sense of honour was never made in vain. Courage was highly extolled and cowardice was strongly condemned in society. The historians of Alexander's invasion bear ample testimony to this fact. The biographers of Hiuen Tsiang, alluding to the customs of the Mahārāshtra country, say: "He (the King) is fond of military affairs, and boasts of

[1] The same is to be found in Parāsara-Smriti. "Two classes of persons ascend to heaven after passing through the region of the sun. They are ascetics who devote themselves to meditation and warriors who die on the field of battle."

[2] Arthasāstra, Bk. X. ch. 3.

[3] Pratijnā-Yaugandharāyana, Act IV.

his arms. In this country, the troops and cavalry are well equipped and the rules of warfare thoroughly understood and observed. Whenever a general is despatched on a warlike expedition, although he is defeated and his army destroyed, he is not himself subjected to bodily punishment, only he has to exchange his soldier's dress for that of a woman, much to his shame and chagrin. So, many times, those men put themselves to death to avoid such disgrace." [1]

The laws of war were humane and honourable. The Mahābhārata says: "A King should never desire to subjugate countries by unrighteous means, even if such subjugation would make him the sovereign of the world." [2] And again: "A Kshatriya who destroys righteousness and transgresses all wholesome barriers, does not deserve to be reckoned a Kshatriya, and should be driven from society." [3] The Mahābhārata further lays down the following rules:

"A warrior whose armour has fallen off, or who begs for quarter, saying 'I am thine,' or who has laid aside his weapon, may simply be seized, but may not be slain. Nor should those be killed who are asleep, or thirsty, or fatigued, or whose accoutrements have fallen away, nor any person who has set his heart on final emancipation, or is fleeing, or is walking

[1] Life of Hiuen Tsiang, Bk. IV.

[2] Sānti Parva, Sec. 96, sl. 2.

[3] Sānti Parva, Sec. 96, sl. 10.

along a road, or is engaged in eating or drinking, or is mad, or has been wounded mortally, or is exceedingly weak with wounds, or is staying trustfully, or has a task in hand unfinished, or is skilled in a special art, or is in grief, or goes out of the camp for forage and fodder, nor those who are camp followers or who wait at the gates of the King and the ministers, or who do menial services." [1]

The ancient law-givers also lay down similar rules.[2] Manu says: "When he fights with his foes in battle, let him not strike with weapons concealed, nor with (such as are) barbed, poisoned, or the points of which are blazing with fire. Let him not strike one who (in flight) has climbed on an eminence, nor a eunuch, nor one who joins the palms of his hands (in supplication), nor one who (flees) with flying hair, nor one who sits down, nor one who says, 'I am thine,' nor one who is asleep, nor one who has lost his coat-of-mail, nor one who is naked, nor one who is disarmed, nor one who looks on without taking part in the flight, nor one who is fighting with another foe; nor one whose weapons are broken, nor one afflicted (with sorrow), nor one who has been grievously wounded, nor one who is in fear, nor one who has

[1] Sānti Parva, Sec. 96, sls. 27-29.

[2] According to Gautama, the following persons should not be killed in war: those who have lost their horses, charioteers, or arms; those who join their hands (in supplication); those who flee with flying hair; those that sit down with averted faces; those who have climbed (in flight) on eminences or trees; those who act as messengers, and those who declare themselves cows and Brāhmanas. X. 18.

turned to flight; (but in all these cases let him) remember the duty (of honourable warriors). . . . Thus has been declared the blameless primeval law for warriors, from this law a Kshatriya must not depart, when he strikes his foes in battle."[1]

Such laws were, as a rule, observed in practice; but we find on occasions of exceptional difficulty even righteous men like Yudhishthira, Bhīma, and Arjuna thought it prudent to depart from the rules of righteous warfare.

One thing is worthy of notice in this connection, namely, the abstention on the part of the fighters from inflicting harm on non-combatants. The invading soldiers never destroyed the crops, nor devastated the enemy's country. So far as practicable, battle-fields were selected in remote and uninhabited parts of the enemy's territory.[2] To this fact Megasthenes bears eloquent testimony. Says he: "Whereas among other nations it is usual, in the contests of war, to ravage the soil, and then to reduce it to an uncultivated waste, among the Indians, on the contrary, by whom husbandmen are regarded as a class that is sacred and inviolable, the tillers of the soil, even when battle is raging in their neighbourhood, are undisturbed by any sense of danger for the combatants on either side in waging the conflict make

[1] Manu, VII. 90-98. The translation is that given by G. Bühler.

[2] Arthasāstra, Bk. XIII. ch. 4. But Kautilya adds: "If, however, the people be hostile, the conqueror may destroy their crops, stores, granaries, and trade."

carnage of each other, but allow those engaged in husbandry to remain quite unmolested. Besides, they neither ravage an enemy's land with fire nor cut down its trees."[1]

After the conquest of a territory the defeated monarch was usually allowed to continue as ruler, subject to the suzerain authority of the conqueror: but if he refused to submit or was killed in battle, another prince of the royal family was placed on the throne. The conqueror, as a rule, adopted a policy of conciliation towards the people of the conquered country.[2] Vishnu gives the following advice to a conqueror: "having conquered the country of his foe, let him not abolish (or disregard) the laws of that country. . . . A King having conquered the capital of his foe, should invest there a prince of the royal race of that country with the royal dignity. Let him not extirpate the royal race, unless the royal race be of ignoble descent."

Chānakya goes into much greater detail in regard to this matter. "A conquered country," says he, "should be given complete security so that the people may sleep without fear. If the people rise in rebellion, they should be pacified by rewards and

[1] Megasthenes, Fragment I.

[2] "When he has gained victory, let him duly worship the gods and honour righteous Brāhmanas, let him grant exemptions, and let him cause promises of safety to be proclaimed. But having fully ascertained the wishes of all the (conquered), let him place there a relative of the (vanquished ruler on the throne), and let him impose his conditions." VII. 201-202.

remissions of taxes." And further: "He (the King) should cover up the faults of the enemy by his own virtues, and exceed the enemy's virtues by himself showing double the amount. He should please the people by properly observing his own duties, by remitting taxes, and by bestowing on them rewards and honours. He should undertake measures which contribute to the general welfare and prosperity. . . . He should adopt the manners, customs, dress and language of the conquered people; and show respect to their national, religious, and social ceremonies, and festivals. . . . He should hold the sages of the country in high esteem, and honour the learned men, the renowned orators, the religious leaders, and the heroes by gifts of land and wealth, and by remissions of taxes. He should release all prisoners,[1] and help the needy, the friendless, and the afflicted. . . . After prohibiting customs which may appear as unrighteous or as injurious to the state revenue or to an efficient system of administration, he should establish righteous laws and customs."

The policy pursued by the weaker Kings when they were attacked by their more powerful neighbours varied with the circumstances of each case. Some-

[1] The custom prevailed in India of liberating all prisoners on happy occasions, like the birth of a son to the King, or the coronation of a new King, or the inauguration of the Crown Prince, or the conquest of a new territory. In the Mudrā-Rākshasa we read of the liberation of all prisoners by order of Kautilya after Chandragupta's consolidation of his conquests. In the Mrichchakatikā also we find a reference to this custom. Arthasāstra, Bk. XIII. ch. 5.

times they sought the protection of another strong ruler; at other times, they took refuge in forts. Not unoften they had to surrender themselves to the invaders.[1] Kautilya divides invaders into three kinds, viz. virtuous conquerors, demon-like invaders, and greedy invaders, and lays down the following lines of policy to be pursued in different cases: "A virtuous conqueror is satisfied with mere submission; so a weak King should submit to him. A greedy invader, fearing his own enemies, is satisfied with what he can safely get in land or money; therefore, a weak King should satisfy such an invader with the gift of wealth. A demon-like invader not only covets the territory and wealth of the weak King, but also tries to destroy him; such an invader should be kept at a distance by the offer of land and wealth."[2]

When a weak King found himself obliged to sue for peace, he entered into an agreement with the conqueror. Such an agreement might be one or other of twelve different forms. These different forms of agreement are thus described by Kautilya:

"An Agreement made on the condition that the King should (personally) attend with the whole or a

[1] The ancient teachers were divided in their opinion in regard to the justice and expediency of the policy of surrender. Bharadvāja says, he who surrenders himself to the strong, bows down before Indra. But in Viśālāksha's opinion a weak should fight with all his resources, because bravery overcomes all difficulties, and because this (fighting) is the natural duty of a Kshatriya, no matter whether he gains a victory or sustains a defeat in battle. Vide Arthaśāstra, Bk. XII. ch. 1.

[2] Arthaśāstra, Bk. XII. ch. 1.

part of his army is called an ātmāmisha (one's own flesh) agreement.

"When the condition is that the Commander-in-Chief and the Crown Prince should attend, it is called purushāntara-sandhi (peace by offering the services of another person); such an agreement is conducive to self-preservation, for it does not require the personal attendance of the King.

"When the condition is that either the King himself or somebody else at the head of the army should be present at a particular place, the agreement is termed adṛishṭapuruṣa (peace with no specified person as hostage). This conduces to the safety of the King as well as of the chiefs.

"These are the varieties of the daṇḍopanata agreement (*i.e.* one made by offering the army). When by the offer of money, the other elements of sovereignty are left free, that peace is called parikraya (purchase). When peace is concluded by offering such a sum of money as has to be carried on shoulders, it is called an upagraha (tribute). When mutual trustfulness leads to a union of hearts, it is called suvarṇa-sandhi (golden peace). The reverse of such an agreement is kapāla (beggar's bowl) which is concluded on payment of a large sum of money.

"These are the different varieties of Koshopanata agreement.

"When by ceding a part of the territory the rest of the Kingdom is saved, it is called ādishṭa (ceded).

"When that part of the territory (not being the central part) is ceded which is devoid of all resources, it is called uchchhinna-sandhi (agreement involving ruin).

"When on condition of payment of the produce, the lands are set free, the agreement is called apakraya (payment of rent). The agreement which is concluded by the promise of paying more than the produce of land is called paribhūshaṇa (abundant supply). These are the varieties of deśopanata (agreement made on condition of ceding territory)." [1]

While the rulers of different parts of India fought with one another for supremacy, the country remained constantly exposed to the danger of foreign invasions. The history of these invasions shows us in a clear light the weak points of the political system of Ancient India. The most important of the early invasions—if it was not the earliest—was that of Alexander the Great in 327 B.C. He remained in the country not more than twenty months all told, and although every step of his advance was stubbornly resisted, he succeeded in reducing the greater part of the Punjab and the whole of Sindh. Such an achievement appears to us all the more surprising when we remember that the people were of a martial temperament and were well inured to arms. The people, indeed, who then inhabited the Indus valley were, according to Greek writers, "of so great a stature that they were amongst the tallest men in Asia,

[1] Arthasāstra, Bk. VII. ch. 3.

being five cubits in height, or nearly so," and "in the art of war they were far superior to the other nations by which Asia was at that time inhabited." But neither their martial spirit nor their efficient military organisation was of any avail for the preservation of their national independence, for the political condition of the country was eminently favourable to Alexander's designs. The Punjab was then divided into a number of separate States, and instead of presenting a united front to the invader, these States, in most instances, fought him singly, with the result that they were overcome with comparative ease. Whenever some sort of concerted opposition was offered to Alexander's advance, as was done by the Malloi and the Kshudrakas,[1] he found it extremely difficult to overpower the resistance. As Mr. McCrindle rightly remarks, "if Alexander had found India united in arms to withstand his aggression, the star of his good fortune would have culminated with his passage of the Indus." [2]

But the States were prevented by their mutual jealousies and feuds from acting in concert against the common enemy, and each of them fell a prey to the attack of the Macedonian invader.[3]

[1] These two races were composed of widely different elements, and they were seldom at peace with each other; but their mutual hostility was suspended in view of the common danger which threatened their independence.

[2] McCrindle, Ancient India, p. 4.

[3] Some of the rulers even assisted the Conqueror. Thus, for instance, he was hospitably received by Āmbhi, King of Taxilā, who was at enmity with Poros, and Sasiguptas, a deserter, became one of Alexander's generals.

Although the force of circumstances compelled the Indians to submit for a time to Alexander, they did not brook for long the burden and reproach of foreign thraldom. Even before the Conqueror's departure from India, the standard of revolt had been raised in many parts of the country, and within a few years of his death, the whole of the Punjab threw off the foreign yoke. In this work of liberation, the Brāhmanas played an important part,[1] and it was the Brāhmana politician, Chānakya, who not only perceived the necessity for the establishment of a centralised administration in India, but actually helped Chandragupta to bring the whole of Northern India under his imperial sway. The beneficial result of this political change became manifest when only a few years later, Chandragupta was able to inflict a severe defeat on Seleukos, and compelled the Conqueror to sue for peace by offering to cede all the Greek provinces on the frontier of India, including Gedrosia and Arachosia.

But the imperial system of the Mauryas did not last very long, and other invaders appeared on the scene. The Sakas established themselves in Sindh, and gradually made themselves masters of that

[1] "The philosophers gave him no less trouble than the mercenaries, because they reviled the princes who declared for him and encouraged the free states to revolt from his authority. On this account he hanged many of them." A story is also told by Plutarch which is interesting. When one of the philosophers was asked for what reason he had induced Sambhu (Sabbas) to revolt, he answered, "Because I wish him to live with honour or die with honour." Plutarch, p. 314.

province and of Gujrat. In the beginning of the second century A.D. the Parthians succeeded the Sakas as rulers in Sindh, and gradually extended their sway as far as Mathurā. The Yue-chi and the Kushāns followed, and founded powerful Kingdoms near the north-western frontier and in Kashmir. All these invaders settled down in the country, adopted the religion and customs and manners of the Āryans, and became for all practical purposes the natives of the country. Very different from these invasions was that of the Huing-nu or Huns, who devastated the country wherever they went. They broke up the Gupta empire, and although they were several times defeated, they succeeded in finding settlements in North-western Punjab.

In the seventh century there were several expeditions led by the Arabs to the west coast of India, but no real attempt to conquer the country was made until Mahammad Kāsim marched with an army along the Persian coast through Mekrān into Sindh. This invasion, however, proved a failure. Two centuries later came the invasions of Sabuktagin and of his son Sultān Māhmūd, and finally, in the closing years of the twelfth century, Muhammad Ghorī defeated Prithvirāj and Jayachandra, and firmly established Mahomedan Rule in Northern India.

The political condition of India which made possible the foundation of the Mahomedan Empire is thus described by Stanley Lane-Poole: "The country was split up into numerous Kingdoms, many of which were at feud with one another. There were the Brāhmana Kings of Gandhāra on the Indus, the Tomaras of Delhi and Kanauj, the Buddhist Pālas of Magadha, the survivors of the Guptas in Mālwā, the Kālachuris on the Nerbudda, the Chandillas of Mahoba, and many more, who united might have stemmed any invasion, but whose jealousies wrought their ruin." How true is the remark: "Internal division has proved the undoing of India again and again, and has sapped the power of mere numbers which alone could enable the men of warm plains to stand against the hardy mountain tribes!"[1]

[1] Stanley Lane-Poole, Mediaeval India.

CHAPTER XVII

PUBLIC WORKS

THE construction and preservation of works of public utility engaged the attention of the State in India from very early times. The chief kinds of such public works were cities, public buildings, works of art, roads, and canals.

At the time of Alexander's invasion, an appreciable proportion of the population lived in cities. Greek writers inform us that Alexander conquered more than 2,000 cities in the Punjab. In the extensive empire of Chandragupta there was at least one city in every district.[1] Most of these cities, however, were small, and, as might be expected, it was the capital city—the seat of sovereign authority—that received the greatest amount of attention.[2] The Rāmāyana gives a beautiful description of the city of Ayodhyā.[3] In the Mahābhārata we are told that

[1] Arthasāstra, Bk. II. ch. 1.

[2] Rāmāyana, Bālakānda.

[3] The Mānasāra says: "In the centre of the kingdom should be the capital (rāja-nagarī) situated on the bank of a river, and inhabited by a large number of honest citizens"; and then goes on to describe in detail the structure of the city. Ch. XI.

Maya, the Dānava, who was an expert in architecture, constructed a beautiful palace for the Pāndavas at Khāndavaprastha. This city, it is said, was protected by a wide moat encircling it all round, above which rose a rampart many feet high, intersected by gates which were adorned with lofty towers. Within the city were fine buildings beautified by lovely flower and fruit gardens, artificial lakes, and tanks.[1] Arrian, speaking of the Indian cities, says: "It is said that the number is so great that it cannot be stated with precision, but that such cities as are situated on the banks of rivers or on the sea-coast are built of wood, for were they built of brick, they would not last long—so destructive are the rains; those cities, however, which stand on commanding situations and lofty eminences are built of brick and mud. The greatest city in India is that which is called Palimbothra in the dominions of the Prasians, where the streams of Erannoboas and Ganges unite. Megasthenes says further of this city that the inhabited part of it stretched on either side to an extreme length of eighty stadia (10 miles), and that its breadth was fifteen stadia (2 miles), and that a ditch compassed it all round, which was six plethra (600 ft.) in breadth and thirty cubits in depth, and that the wall was crowned with five hundred and seventy towers and had four and sixty gates."[2] When Fa Hian and

[1] Vide Ādi Parva, Sec. 207, sls. 27-51, and Sabhā Parva.

[2] Vide Arrian (McCrindle), Indica, 10, and Megasthenes, Fragment XXVI.

Hiuen Tsiang visited Pātaliputra the town itself was in ruins, but the parapets of the walls were still standing.[1]

The greater writer, Bāna, gives a poetic description of the town of Ujjayinī as it existed in the seventh century A.D., from which we extract the following sentences: "There is a town by name Ujjayinī, the proudest gem of the three worlds . . . It is encompassed by a moat deep as hell . . . and surrounded by fences and walls, white with plaster like Kailāsa . . . It is adorned with large bazaars, like the oceans when their waters were drunk by Agastya, stretching far with gold-dust for sand, with conch and oyster pearls, corals and emeralds laid bare. The painted halls that deck it are filled with gods . . . Its crossways shine with temples like Mandara whitened by the milk raised up by the churning stick . . . Commons grey with Ketakī pollen, dark with green gardens, watered by buckets constantly at work, and having wells adorned with brick seats, lend their charm. Its groves are darkened by bees vocal with honey draughts, its breeze is laden with sweetness of creeper flowers, all trembling . . . It resounds with the cry of peacocks . . . It glitters with lakes, fair with open blue water-lilies . . . It is whitened

[1] Fa Hian, Ch. XXVII., and Life of Hiuen Tsiang, p. 101. The Buddhist books speak of Vaisālī as an opulent, prosperous town, populous, crowded with people, abundant with food; there were 7,707 storeyed buildings, 7,707 pinnacled buildings, and 7,707 pleasure grounds (aramas), and 7,707 lotus ponds. Vinaya Texts (Sacred Books of the East), VIII. 1.

with ivory turrets on all sides, endowed with plantain groves, white as flasks of ambrosial foam . . . It is girt with the river Siprā, which seems to purify the sky with its waves forming a ceaseless frown . . . The city seems possessed of rocks with its palaces; it stretches like a suburb with its long houses; it is like the tree that grants desires with its good citizens; it bears in its painted halls the mirror of all forms."[1] Stripped of poetical embellishments, this seems to be a correct description of a capital city of the ancient times. And we are confirmed in this opinion by the fact that Bāna's description agrees in the main with that given by Hiuen Tsiang. The Chinese traveller says: "The City (Kanyākubja or Kanauj) has a ditch round it, with strong and lofty towers facing one another. The flowers and woods, the lakes and ponds, bright and pure, and shining like mirrors (are seen on every side). Valuable merchandise is collected here in great quantities. The people are well-off and contented, the houses are rich and well formed. Flowers and fruits abound in every place."[2]

In Hiuen Tsiang's time the city of Kanauj was three miles and a half long, and three-quarters of a mile broad. At the time of the invasion of Māhmūd of Ghaznī, its magnificence had greatly increased, it being then described as a city "which raised its head

[1] Bāna's Kādambāri (Ridding's trans.), pp. 210-212.

[2] Buddhist Records, Bk. V.

to the skies, and which in strength and structure might justly boast to have no equal."

The most imposing structure in a capital city was, of course, the Royal Palace. It was usually built on an eminence, and was well protected by walls and bastions, and consisted of numerous apartments.[1] Near the Royal Palace stood the Assembly Hall, and on different sides of it were the Royal Courts of Justice—the Government offices, the places of public worship, the School of Industries and Arts, the houses of the Ministers and other high officials, the armoury, and the soldiers' quarters. Beyond these were the houses of the citizens.

The arrangements of other towns were similar to those of the capital city, but on a smaller scale. From the treatment of the subject in some of the ancient books, such as Chānakya's Arthasāstra, the Agni Purāna, and the Sukranīti, it appears that towns, and even villages, were constructed on definite plans.[2] The building of cities, mansions, and works of art formed the subject of a science known as Silpa Sāstra. There are many treatises which deal with this subject, the most well known of these being the Mānasāra. This work speaks of seven sorts of towns, namely, rājadhānī, nagara, pura, kheṭa, kharvaṭa, kubjaka, and pattana. It also mentions

[1] Vide Arthasāstra, and Sukranīti, Ch. I. sls. 216-217.

[2] Vide Arthasāstra, Bk. II. chs. 1-3; Agni Purāna, Ch. CCXXVII. and Sukranīti, Ch. IV.

eight kinds of villages, namely, Daṇḍaka (that which resembles a staff), Sarvato-bhadra (which is good in every respect), Nandyāvārtta (the abode of happiness), Padmaka (that which has the form of a lotus), Svastika (that which resembles a svastika), Prastara (built of stone), Kārmuka (that which resembles a bow), and Chaturmukha (that which has four faces).[1] Hiuen Tsiang, however, does not evidently think much of the ordinary towns and villages. He says: "The towns and villages have inner gates, the walls are wide and high; the streets and lanes are tortuous, and the roads winding, the thoroughfares are dirty . . . The towers on the walls are constructed of wood or bamboos; the houses have balconies and belvederes."[2]

Not only public buildings but even private dwelling-houses in the cities and villages were usually constructed in accordance with definite rules. A comparatively modern work on architecture says: "Woe

[1] Mānasāra, Ch. XI. Vide also Rām Rāz, Essay on the Architecture of the Hindus. Rām Rāz mentions many other books on Hindu Architecture besides the Mānasāra. The Mānasāra consists of about seventy chapters, and in it are described the measures used in architecture, sculpture, etc.; the different sites to be selected for building temples and houses; their mode of determining the different points of the compass; the several sorts of villages, towns, and cities, with directions for building them; the different parts of an edifice, its ornaments, pedestals, bases, pillars, entablatures; the various sorts of temples consisting of from one to twelve storeys high; the construction of mantapas, porticoes, gates, doorways, palaces, etc. Several MS. copies of this important work have been found, and a Bengali scholar has now undertaken the work of editing and translating the book.

[2] Buddhist Records (Beal), Bk. II. p. 73.

to them who dwell in a house not built according to the proportions of symmetry. In building an edifice, therefore, let all its parts, from the basement to the roof, be fully considered."[1] The builders were often men well trained in the scientific principles of architecture. They were of four descriptions, namely, sthapatis (architects), sūtragrāhīs (those who studied the measurements and were skilled in Mathematics), takshakas (those who prepared the rough wood), and vardhakis (skilled carpenters).

Architecture began to attract the attention of the Hindus from very early times. As Fergusson points out, the Hindus "possessed palaces and halls of assembly, perhaps even temples, of great magnificence and splendour, long anterior to Asoka's accession."[2] But as these ancient structures were usually constructed of wood, stone being employed only for the foundations of buildings or in engineering works, no examples of such buildings have survived the depredations of time. Stone architecture began to be common only from the time of Asoka; most of the ancient monuments, therefore, that are known to us, are Buddhistic. Fa Hian, speaking of Asoka's palace at Pātaliputra, says: "In the middle of the city is the royal palace, the different parts of

[1] Manushyālaya Chandrikā, quoted by Rām Rāz in his Essay on the Architecture of the Hindus, p. 15. In regard to mansions, the Sukranīti says: "A building with one thousand pillars is good, others are middling or inferior." Ch. IV. sec. 4, sl. 1.

[2] Indian and Eastern Architecture.

which he commissioned the genii to construct. The massive stones of which the walls are made are no human work. The ruins of the palace still exist."[1] Asoka spent enormous sums of money for the erection of buildings in aid of Buddhism. He built a great temple at Bodh-Gayā, and enlarged and beautified the famous topes at Sanchi. He is also said to have erected eighty-four thousand stūpas in different parts of his vast empire, besides many pillars and columns on which his edicts were inscribed. As Mr. Vincent Smith remarks: "The arts in the age of Asoka undoubtedly had attained to a high standard of excellence." "The royal engineers and architects," adds Mr. Smith, "were capable of designing and executing spacious and lofty edifices in brick, wood, and stone, of constructing massive embankments equipped with convenient sluices and other appliances, of extracting, chiselling and handling enormous monoliths, and of excavating commodious chambers with burnished interiors in the most refractory rock. Sculpture was the handmaid of architecture, and all buildings of importance were lavishly decorated with a profusion of ornamental patterns, an infinite variety of spirited bas-reliefs, and meritorious statues of men and animals."[2] Asoka's great work was continued by his successors and by other Buddhist rulers.

[1] Fa Hian (Buddhist Records), Ch. XXVII.

[2] V. A. Smith, Asoka, p. 135.

The objects of the Buddhist art, according to Mr. Fergusson, fall under the following five heads: (1) Stambhas or Lāts, which were always among[1] the most original, and frequently the most elegant, productions of Indian art; (2) Stūpas, containing either the relics of Buddha or of some Buddhist saint, or erected to commemorate some event or mark some sacred spot dear to the followers of Buddhism; (3) Rails, which were works of exquisite beauty; (4) Chaityas or Assembly Halls were the Buddhist temples of religion, corresponding to the Churches of the Christians; (5) Vihāras and Saṅghārāmas, or monasteries, which were the residences of monks and centres of educational and charitable establishments.

The most extensive, and perhaps the most interesting, group of topes is that known as the Bhilsa topes. Of this group the most magnificent is the great tope at Sānchī, which has a base 14 ft. high and a dome 42 ft. high and 106 ft. in diameter. But it is believed that there once existed stūpas which were far more magnificent than these. Fergusson says: "If we could now see the topes that once adorned any of the great Buddhist sites in the Doāb, or in Behār, the Bhīlsā group might sink into insignificance."[2] Of

[1] With the Buddhists they were employed to bear inscriptions on their shafts; with the Jainas they are generally dip-danas, or lamp-bearing pillars, but sometimes supporting figures of Jinas; with the Vaishnavas or Saivas, they bore statues or flag-staffs.

[1] Fergusson and Burgess, Indian and Eastern Architecture (1910), Vol. I. p. 66.

Chaityas, some thirty are known still to exist. But the most famous, and architecturally the most wonderful, are the rock-cut caves in Western India, of which not less than twelve hundred are to be found. Three hundred of these are of Brahmanical or Jaina origin, and the remaining nine hundred are Buddhistic. The Kārlī, the Ajantā, and the Ellora caves are the finest specimens of this kind of architecture. As Mrs. Manning points out, this form of architecture "has the signal advantage of protecting the work of architect and sculptor from the threefold destruction caused by insects, rain and vegetation." [1]

Sanghārāmas were innumerable and found in every part of India during the Buddhist period. Hiuen Tsiang described them in these words: "The Sanghārāmas are constructed with extraordinary skill. A three-storeyed tower is erected at each of the four angles. The beams and the projecting heads are carved with great skill in different shapes. The doors, windows, and the low walls are painted profusely; the monks' cells are ornamental on the inside and plain on the outside. In the very middle of the building is the hall, high and wide. There are various storeyed chambers and turrets of different height and shape, without any fixed rule. The doors open towards the east; the royal throne also faces the east." [2]

[1] Ancient and Mediaeval India, p. 396.

[2] Buddhist Records, Bk. II. pp. 73-74.

The Jainas and Hindus also, like the Buddhists, excavated cave-dwellings (Bhikshu-gṛihas) for their recluses. Later on, Hindu temples began to be constructed in large numbers, many of which are still standing. Some of them, specially those of Orissa and of South India, possess splendour and magnificence in an eminent degree.

The more important public buildings, as a rule, were constructed by order of the monarchs, but very often guilds of merchants and, occasionally, rich individuals also constructed works of public utility. In the inscriptions we often read of temples and alms-houses being constructed by order of guilds.[1]

After the time of Asoka, the most flourishing period of Indian architecture was that of the Guptas. As Mr. V. A. Smith points out, "in India the establishment of a vigorous dynasty ruling over wide dominions has invariably resulted in the application of a strong stimulus to the development of man's intellectual and artistic powers. Such a dynasty, exercising its administrative duties effectively, fostering commerce, maintaining active intercourse, commercial and diplomatic, with foreign states, displaying the pomp of a magnificent court, both encourages the desire to do great things and provides the material patronage without which authors and artists cannot live."[2]

[1] Cf. for instance, the Mandasor Inscription of Kumāragupta and Bandhuvarman, Corpus Inscriptionum Indicarum, Vol. III.

[2] Ostasiatische Zeitschrift, 1914, Vol. I.

According to Mr. E. B. Havell, the eighth century saw the complete artistic realisation of both the Buddhist and the Hindu ideals, and it was also about this epoch that the ideals of Indian art and the highest culture expressed in that art found their widest geographical expansion.[1]

The means of communication received considerable attention from the rulers. Roads were constructed in all towns and villages. Chānakya says that each city should have six main roads—three running from east to west, and three from north to south. Besides these principal roads, which were to be 32 cubits wide, there were many other roads which were less broad. There were also roads which connected the different parts of the country with the capital and with one another. The main roads were called King's ways (Rāja-mārga), and the other roads were known as mārgas, vīthīs, or padyas.[2] Pillars were set up on the main roads to mark distances and to show the by-roads.[3] Trees were planted along the roads and, for convenience of travellers, rest houses (pāntha-śālās) were erected at suitable places.[4]

[1] Ostasiatische Zeitschrift, 1912, Vol. I.

[2] Sukranīti, Ch. I. Strabo, on the authority of Megasthenes, says: "They construct roads and at every ten stadia set up a pillar to show the by-roads and distances." Fragment XXXIV. The Sukranīti says that these roads should be like the back of a tortoise, and there should be drains on both sides of a road. The Mānasāra mentions maṇḍala-vīthī, rājapatha, sandhi-patha, and mahā-kāla as the four kinds of roads in a town or village. In the Rig-Veda we find mention of 'mahā-patha' (highway).

[3] Megasthenes, Fragment XXXIV.

[4] Vide Edicts of Asoka and Sukranīti, Ch. IV. sec. 4.

Permanent masonry or wooden bridges were constructed over rivulets and small streams, while bridges of boats were placed for the crossing of large rivers.[1]

Irrigation was practised in India from very early times. In the Rig-Veda we find mention of canals. In the Mahābhārata, Nārada, enquiring about the state of the kingdom, is made to ask Yudhishthira: "Are large tanks and lakes established all over the kingdom at proper distances, in order that agriculture may not be entirely dependent on the showers of heaven?"[2] So Manu advises the King to build tanks, wells, cisterns, and fountains.[3] The larger irrigational works were undertaken by the State, while the smaller ones were often constructed by private enterprise. In order to encourage private enterprise in this direction, rents and taxes were remitted for a certain number of years for the construction of new tanks and for the repair of old works. The village communities, and sometimes private individuals, were held responsible for the keeping of irrigational works in repair, and punishments were inflicted on people who destroyed them or neglected to maintain them.[4] In the Purānas, the construction of irrigation works is regarded as an act of great merit.

[1] The Sukranīti says: "Bridges should be constructed over rivers of various sorts and of beautiful structure. There should be boats and other conveyances for crossing the rivers." Ch. IV. sec. 4, sl. 61.

[2] Sabhā Parva, Sec. V.

[3] VIII. 248.

[4] Arthasāstra.

According to the Agni Purāna, the merit acquired by the gift of water is equal to that acquired by all other gifts combined.[1]

There was an important department of government which controlled the construction and maintenance of canals, lakes and tanks. Megasthenes says: "Some Officers-of-State superintend the rivers, measure the lands, as is done in Egypt, and inspect the sluices by which water is let out from the main canals into their branches, so that everyone may have an equal supply of it."[2] The Irrigation Officers of Chandragupta built a dam at Girnār, and thus formed the great Sudarsana lake. And in Asoka's reign, his governor of Surāshtra constructed canals to utilise the waters of this lake. In 150 A.D. this dam was rebuilt by Rudradāman, and in the fifth century it was repaired by Chakrapālita, Skandagupta's governor.[3] Sung Yun, speaking of irrigation in Kasmir, says: "At the proper time they let the streams overflow the land by which the soil is rendered soft and fertile."[4] In the Rājataranginī we find a detailed account of the irrigational achievements of

[1] Agni Purāna, Ch. 64. [2] Fragment XXXIV.

[3] "Having done honour to the Kings, he laboriously built up with a great masonry work, properly constructed, the lake Sudarsana, which is renowned as not being evil by nature, so that it would last for all eternity." Vide Fleet, Gupta Inscriptions.

[4] The Sukraniti says: "Wells, canals, tanks, and lakes should be constructed in abundance so that there may not be any scarcity of water in the country. Their breadth should be twice or thrice their depth." Ch. IV. sec. 4.

Suyya, the Minister of Avantivarman, King of Kasmir (855-883 A.D.). Some parts of Kasmir were liable to be inundated by disastrous floods, and to remain submerged during a great part of the year. Suyya built dykes to prevent the floods, and drained the marshes. He also constructed canals to divert the water of the rivers, and thus procured a supply of artificial water for villages which had so long been dependent on the rainfall. He further arranged on a permanent basis for the size and distribution of the watercourse for each village, and by this method of using the streams for irrigation, embellished all regions with an abundance of irrigated fields yielding the most excellent produce. Suyya, in the words of the Rājataranginī, "made the different streams (i.e. Sindhu and Vitastā) with their waves which are (like) the quivering tongues of snakes, move about according to his will, just as a conjurer (does with) the snakes."[1]

It is worthy of note that Hindu architecture and art and works of public utility were not confined to India. Some wonderful examples of Buddhist as well as Brahmanical architecture are still to be found

[1] Rājataranginī (Stein), Bk. V. Referring to Suyya's engineering work, Sir Aurel Stein remarks: "It shows alike the large scale and the systematic technical basis of Suyya's regulation. The result of the latter was a great increase of land available for cultivation, and increased protection against disastrous floods which in Kasmīr have been the main causes of famine." Introduction, p. 98. "The facilities secured for cultivation produced a remarkable reduction in the price of rice, the cost of a Khārī being alleged to have fallen from 200 Dīnnāras to 36 Dīnnāras in consequence."

in countries where the Hindus founded settlements, such as Ceylon, Cambodia, Siam, Java, Bali and Sumatra. The Kings of Ceylon paid great attention to the construction of works of public utility. Parākrama Bāhu, for instance, erected innumerable religious edifices and public buildings, and planted beautiful parks and gardens. He built a stone wall and stopped the course of the Kāra-ganga, and turned the wide flow of the waters thereof by means of the great channel Ākāsa-gangā. He also built that famous lake known as the Sea of Parākrama, and constructed the celebrated Jayagangā canal. It is said that the many thousands of lakes, tanks, and canals were constructed and repaired by this great monarch.[1]

Speaking of the ancient public works of Cambodia, Mr. Fergusson remarks : " Wonderful as these temples and palaces are, the circumstance that, perhaps, after all gives the highest idea of the civilisation of these ancient Cambodian is the perfection of their roads and bridges. One great trunk road seems to have stretched for 300 miles across the country from Korat, in a south-easterly direction, to the Mekong river. It was a raised causeway, paved throughout like a Roman road, and every stream that crossed was spanned by a bridge, many of which remain perfect to the present day. Dr. Bastian describes two of them : One 400 feet in length and 50 feet in breadth,

[1] Mahāvamsa, Ch. LXXIX.

richly ornamented by balustrades and cornices, and representations of snakes and the snake-king."[1] In Java and Sumatra "for nearly nine centuries (A.D. 603 to 1477) foreign (i.e. Indian) colonists had persevered in adorning the island with edifices, almost unrivalled elsewhere of their class."[2]

[1] Fergusson, History of Indian and Eastern Architecture, Vol. II. p. 402.

[2] Ibid.

CHAPTER XVIII

INDUSTRY AND COMMERCE

AGRICULTURE was in ancient days—as it still is—the most important industry of the people of India. And, naturally, it received encouragement at the hands of the State in a variety of ways. Credit has always been an essential condition of agriculture in India, as in all other agricultural countries, and the practice of granting loans to needy cultivators began from very early times. In the Mahābhārata, Nārada is made to ask Yudhishthira: "Grantest thou with kindness loans unto the tillers, taking only a fourth in excess?"[1]

The Agricultural Department of the government served as a sort of information bureau for the cultivators. It was presided over by a Superintendent, whose duty it was to study the conditions of cultivation in the different parts of the country and to introduce improved methods, wherever possible. He collected improved varieties of seeds and distributed

[1] Sabhā Parva, Sec. V.

them among the agriculturists.[1] He was also expected to possess a knowledge of the science of meteorology so as to be able to make forecasts of weather conditions and of agricultural outlook.[2] It was under the supervision of this department of the government that uncultivated tracts were brought into cultivation. The Agricultural Department supervised cultivation on State lands and assessed the irrigation rate. It was also responsible for making suitable provision for pasturage.

Associated with this department was that of dairy-farming. In Kautilya's time, dairy-farming was undertaken by the State in one of two ways. Either the State farms were directly worked by the government department with the help of herdsmen employed for wages, or they were leased to herdsmen for a share of the produce. Cattle-breeding also engaged the attention of the State.

Another important activity of the State was that which related to arboriculture. Forests were mostly under government control. The beneficial influence

[1] Arthasāstra, Bk. II. ch. 24. In the Mahābhārata, one of Nārada's questions to Yudhishthira when he enquires into the condition of the kingdom is: "Do not agriculturists in thy kingdom want either seed or food?"

[2] Meteorological forecasts used to be made by observing the position and motion of the planets. "Rainfall," says Chānakya, "is said to be well-distributed, when one-third falls during the first and third months and two-thirds in the second month of the rainy season." The local distribution of rain was considered normal in different parts of the country when the quantity was as follows: Asmaka (Mahārāshtra),—13½ droṇas; forest tracts,—16; Avantī,—23; more moist parts,—24; and immense quantities on the Bombay coast and in the Himālayan regions. Arthasāstra, Bk. III. ch. 24.

of forests in respect of rainfall and the general economic condition of the country was fully appreciated, and proper steps were taken for the preservation of forests.[1] It was the duty of the forest rangers to see that no damage was done to forests. One reason why forests received such care at the hands of the State was that they yielded considerable incomes to the State in the shape of rents, which were largely augmented by the profits of productive works established in many parts of the forest area.[2] Proper measures were also taken for the preservation of beasts and birds, and severe penalties were inflicted on persons who were found guilty of violating the game laws.

Mining was an industry to which great attention was paid in ancient days. The mines supplied a large part of the wealth of India, and were the chief attractions to foreign merchants. Mining was not confined merely to surface diggings, but followed the lodes of metalliferous ores to considerable depths. It was the duty of the mining department to exploit

[1] Hunters were engaged to guard the forests against robbers and hostile persons. These hunters also sent information to the headquarters regarding the movements of wild tribes by means of carrier pigeons. Vide Arthasāstra. Megasthenes also refers to them when he says: "The same persons have charge also of huntsmen, and are entrusted with the power of rewarding or punishing them according to their deserts. They collect the taxes and superintend the occupations connected with the land, as those of the wood-cutters, carpenters, the blacksmiths, and the miners." Fragment XXXIV.

[2] The different kinds of things obtained from forests were in Kautilya's time: timber, bamboo, cane, fibrous plants, rope-materials, leaves, flowers, roots, fruits, medicinal herbs, metals, clay, firewood, fodder, and wild animals. Arthasāstra, Bk. II. ch. 17.

the resources of existing mines in the most economical manner, and to carry on exploring operations which might lead to the discovery of new mines. The principal kinds of ores obtained from mines were gold, silver, copper, lead, tin, and trapu.[1] Gold was also obtained from rivers. "Gold," says Curtius, "is carried down by several rivers, whose loitering waters glide with slow and gentle currents."[2] Curtius refers to precious stones and pearls, and remarks: "Nor has anything contributed more to the opulence of the natives, especially since they spread the community of evil to foreign nations." Pliny, in the latter part of his 37th book, treats of the various kinds of precious stones found in India, and his ninth book is full of details about pearls. In his 15th book, Strabo states that India produced precious stones, carbuncles, and pearls of various kinds. In Ptolemy's Geography and in the Periplus of the Erythraean Sea, mention is made of the diamond, beryl, onyx, cornelian, hyacinth, and sapphire as precious stones obtained in India. The Arthasāstra and the Yuktikalpataru give full and detailed descriptions of the various kinds of gems found in India.[3]

Mines were, as a rule, leased to private persons for a certain proportion of the output or for a fixed

[1] Arthasāstra, Bk. II. ch. 12.

[2] McCrindle, Ancient India.

[3] Arthasāstra, Bk. VII. ch. 12. The Sukranīti also describes in detail the various kinds of gems and precious stones. VI. 2, 40, etc.

rent. But such mines as could be worked with small capital and properly managed by a government department were worked direct by the State.[1] Chānakya complains that the older teachers paid too much attention to the mines which yielded valuable minerals, to the neglect of the inferior metals, and says that, in his opinion, the latter are quite as important as the former.[2]

Associated with mining, but under a separate head, was the department of metallurgy. The treatment and manufacture of metals was centralised and conducted under the supervision of the State. There was a special officer, under the Superintendent, whose duty it was to control the manufacture of articles of jewellery by goldsmiths. Another officer was in charge of the manufacture of the inferior metals.

The working of the mines, as Mr. Hewitt points out, "required practical mechanical skill as well as the scientific aptitude and perseverance necessary to discover the proper method of treating the ores so as to extract the precious metals."[3] In fact, in metallurgical skill the ancient Hindus attained to a very high state of efficiency. Ample evidence of this is to be found in ancient works of industrial art. With reference to the iron pillar near the Kutb Mīnār of Delhi, which is 24 feet in height and which was perhaps erected in the fifth century A.D., Fergusson says:

[1] Arthaśāstra, Bk. II. ch. 12. [2] Arthaśāstra, Bk. VII. ch. 12.
[3] Journal of the Royal Asiatic Society, Vol. 18.

"It opens our eyes to an unsuspected state of affairs to find the Hindus at that age forging a bar of iron larger than any that have been forged even in Europe to a very late date, and not frequently even now." [1]

The manufacture of salt and the brewing of liquors [2] were industries under the direct control of the State. Both of them were government monopolies. There were many other industrial pursuits which, although undertaken by private enterprise, were supervised by the State. Of these, weaving was perhaps the most important. The State encouraged, by offering rewards, spinning and the associated industries, as well as the weaving of the better kinds of cotton cloths, and the manufacture of woollen and silken garments.[3] That there was a great demand for such clothes in early times is proved by the testimony of the Greek writers.[4] In comparatively modern times, Hiuen Tsiang says: "Their garments are made of kausheya and of cotton. Kausheya is the product

[1] Fergusson, Eastern Architecture.

[2] According to Chānakya, it was the duty of the Superintendent of Liquors to prevent such excessive drinking as might lead to the commission of crimes. The intimate relation between alcohol and crime was thus not unknown in ancient times.

[3] Arthaśāstra, Bk. II. ch. 23.

[4] Of the dress of Indians in olden times Curtius says: "They cover their persons down to the feet with fine muslin, are shod with sandals, and coil round their heads cloths of linen. They hang precious stones as pendants from their ears, and persons of high social rank or of great wealth deck their wrists and upper arm with bracelets of gold." Arrian quotes a passage from Nearchos and says that the Indians "wear an undergarment of cotton which reaches below the knee half way down and also an upper garment. They wear shoes made of white leather." Ancient India (McCrindle).

of the wild silk-worm. They have garments also of Kshauma which is a sort of hemp; garments also made of kambala which is woven from fine goat-hair; garments also made from karala."[1] The important reason for controlling the weaving industry seems to have been the necessity for giving employment to widows and partially disabled persons.

The State also regulated the production of goods by bringing under its control the guilds of producers. There were many such guilds, and according to Prof. Rhys Davids, in the early Buddhist times they included the following:

(1) Workers in metal who made iron implements, including those of husbandry and war, but they also did finer work, and gold and silver work of great delicacy and beauty; (2) workers in stone, who did rough as well as fine work, e.g. crystal bowl, or stone coffer; (3) weavers, who not only made ordinary clothes, but manufactured muslins and costly and dainty fabrics; (4) ivory-workers, who made articles for ordinary use and also costly ornaments; (5) jewellers, who made beautiful ornaments of various kinds; (6) leather workers; (7) potters; (8) dyers; (9) fishermen; (10) butchers; (11) hunters and trappers; (12) cooks and confectioners; (13) garland makers and flower sellers; (14) sailors; (15) rush-workers and basket-makers; and (16) painters.[2]

[1] Buddhist Records, Bk. II.

[2] Rhys Davids, Buddhist India, pp. 90-95.

These guilds (śreṇi, pūga) were very useful institutions in olden times, and it was through them that the King summoned the people on important occasions. They settled disputes between members by arbitration, and maintained high standards in production. Their business was conducted in assembly, and their Presidents (Nāyakas, or Mukhyas) [1] occupied high positions in society.

Even more important than the Industry Department was the Commerce Department of the State. The country owed its prosperity largely to trade and commerce; and as these produced large revenues to the State, they received tender care at the hands of the government officials. The chief business of the Superintendent of Commerce was to facilitate the growth of the internal trade as well as of the foreign commerce of the country. And with that view his first duty was to secure the safety and convenience of the mercantile traffic. As different parts of the country produced different sorts of goods, there was an active internal trade, and merchants conveyed their goods either up and down the rivers or right across the country in carts travelling in caravans.[2] Chānakya discusses the comparative merits and defects of land and water routes. According to older writers, the water routes were regarded

[1] Inscriptions from Belgaum (1204 A.D), ed. by L. D. Barnett.

[2] From the Jātaka stories we learn that caravans of five hundred bullock waggons were used by merchants for transporting goods between Benares and Pātaliputra and the sea-coast.

as better, being less expensive and troublesome, and consequently productive of larger profits. But Chānakya points out several difficulties of communication by water, namely, that it is liable to obstruction; it is not available in all seasons, and it is more liable to dangers and less easy to defend.[1] Trade routes (baṇik-patha) are divided by Chānakya under four heads, namely, those going north towards the Himālayas; those going south beyond the Vindhya mountains; those going west; and those going east. The northern and the southern routes were both regarded as very important, for the principal products of the north were elephants, horses, fragrant substances, ivory, wool, skins, silver, and gold, while in the south conches, diamonds, gems, pearls, and gold and other metals could be obtained in abundance.[2] The Buddhist books give us a more detailed description of the trade routes. From these we know that an important route went from Srāvastī to Pratishthāna, the principal stopping places being Māhismatī, Ujjayinī, Vidisā, Kosambī, and Sāketa. Another road ran from the north to the south-east from Srāvastī to Rājagriha, and the stopping places were Setavya, Kapilavastu, Kusinagara, Pāvā, Hastigrāma, Bhāndagrāma, Vaisālī, Pātaliputra, and Nālanda. This road probably went on to Gayā and there met another road from the coast of the Bay

[1] Arthasāstra, Bk. VII. ch. 2.

[2] Ibid.

of Bengal.[1] The Greek writers speak of a road which went from Pushkalāvatī (Pesketaotis) near Attock through Takshasilā, Bukephala, and crossing the Hyphasis to Pātaliputra. Another road went from Pushkalāvatī to Indraprastha (near modern Delhi) and then to Ujjayinī. These and many other roads connected different parts of the country with one another and with the seaports. The Indian caravans were perhaps met at border-stations by western caravans bound for Persia, Tyre, and Egypt. The northern route crossed the Himālayas and went to Tibet and China.

The main waterways were the Indus and its tributaries in the Punjab, the Jumna and Ganges with their tributaries and branches in Middle India, and the Brahmaputra in the east. The rivers of the Deccan and South India were also useful to some extent as waterways. Besides these natural water routes, the navigation canals probably afforded some facilities of communication in certain parts of the country.

The government, however, did not confine their attention to inland navigation, for we know that merchants sailed along the coasts, and even made ocean voyages to Persia, Arabia, Egypt, Burma, the islands of the Indian and Pacific oceans, and China. Foreign commerce perhaps began before the advent of the Āryans in India. It is believed that a large

[1] Vide Rhys Davids, Buddhist India, p. 104.

maritime trade was carried on between India and the Accadian-Semitic Empire of Assyria. Many centuries later, Solomon (in the tenth century B.C.) and his ally Hiram used to send every three years ships of Tarshish to India, and these ships used to take back Indian produce. In the Rig-Veda, there are several references to sea-voyages undertaken by men "eager for gain."[1] The Baudhāyana Dharma-sūtra also mentions maritime navigation (samudra-saṁyāna) and taxes levied on maritime commerce (samudra-śulka).[2] At the time of Alexander's invasion, Indians were expert sailors, and it was Indian pilots who guided Alexander's vessels.[3] The author of the Periplus says: "Native fishermen appointed by Government are stationed with well-manned long boats called trappaga and kotumba at the entrance of the river whence they go out as far as Surastrene to meet ships, and pilot them to Barygaza. At the head of the gulf, the pilot immediately on taking charge of a ship, with the help of his own boat's crew, shifts her clear of the shoals, and tows her from one fixed station to another."[4]

For the safety and convenience of sea-going vessels, harbours were constructed by the governments at suitable places. The seaports on the coast of the

[1] Rig-Veda, I. 48, 3, and I. 116, 5. Cf. Atharva-Veda, V. 19, 8, where the ruin of a kingdom in which Brāhmanas are oppressed is compared to the sinking of a ship which is leaking.

[2] I, 1, 20; II. 1, 41; I. 10, 13.

[3] Arrian (McCrindle), p. 163.

[4] Periplus of the Erythraean Sea.

Arabian Sea attained to positions of considerable importance and renown. Bharukachha (Sans. Bhṛigu-kshetra, Gr. Barygaza, modern Broach) was the greatest seat of commerce in Western India. Three other important ports were Patala and Barbarikon, near the mouth of the Indus, and Surashtra (modern Surat) at the mouth of the Tapti. Ujjayanī is mentioned in the Periplus as an inland port. From this town were "brought down to Barygaza every commodity for the supply of the country and for export to our own (i.e. Greek) markets onyx-stones, porcelain, fine muslins, mallow-coloured muslins, and no small quantity of ordinary cottons."[1] The two great seats of commerce in the interior of the Deccan (Dakshināpatha)[2] were Pratishthāna (Paithāna) and Tagara-pura (Tangara, identified with Tair, now a small village). The seaports on the Malabar coast were Nelkunda and Mouziris (Murjari). The latter was a city "at the height of prosperity, frequented by ships from Ariake and Greek ships from Egypt." The coast of the Bay of Bengal, on account of the usual roughness of the sea, did not offer much facility for the construction of harbours and the growth of seaports, but there were two towns of considerable importance on this coast, namely, Mansala (Masalia, modern Masalipatam) in the Madras

[1] Periplus of the Erythraean Sea, p. 122.

[2] The other inland ports mentioned in the Periplus are Naoura (Onore) and Tundis (Tundi).

Presidency and Gange near the mouth of the Ganges.[1] At the time of Fa Hian's visit,[2] Tāmraliptī [3] in Bengal was a very important seaport, and had an extensive traffic with South India and Ceylon. The prosperity of Tāmraliptī was great in Hiuen Tsiang's time. "Wonderful articles of value," says the Chinese traveller, "and gems are collected here in abundance, and, therefore, the people of the country are in general very rich." [4]

The principal exports from India were: topazes, sapphires, silk, fine linen, muslin, silk thread, indigo, coloured cloths, cotton, rice, oil, cattle, clarified butter, and soapstone. Besides these, Pliny speaks of the large quantities of gold and silver which were taken from the mines on the other side of Mons Capitolia (Mount Ābū), and he estimates the capital expended every year in the purchase of Indian goods at fifty million sesterces (a sum equal to about £500,000) and says that twenty ships passed yearly out of the Red Sea to India.[5] The chief imports were Italian, Laodicean and Arabian wines, brass, tin, cloths of various kinds, slaves, cloves, honey, coarse glass, red sulphuret of antimony, and gold and silver

[1] Periplus, p. 132.

[2] We also read of 'Thīna' as an important port in Burma.

[3] It was from this port that Fa Hian sailed for Ceylon. The vessel in which he went carried 200 men, and astern of this great ship was a smaller one.

[4] Beal, Buddhist Records. I-Tsing also mentions it as a flourishing port.

[5] Pliny, Hist. Nat. VI. 23.

coins.[1] From China, India imported certain kinds of woollen and silk fabrics.[2]

As large numbers of boats were required for the transportation of goods, the construction of vessels became a very important industry, and this was undertaken either by, or under the auspices of, the State.[3] Ships and boats (nau) are mentioned in the Rig-Veda and the Atharva-Veda. The ships with which Alexander was supplied on his return from India numbered eighty thirty-oared galleys, but the whole fleet did not fall much short of two thousand. The author of the Periplus says: "The ships which frequent these parts are of a large size, on account of the great amount and bulkiness of the pepper and betel of which their lading consists."[4] Chānakya speaks of various sorts of boats, and Bhoja in the Yukti-kalpataru, mentions twenty-four different kinds.

The Commerce Department of the State, besides keeping the means of communication open and safe, and collecting the trade dues, performed other important duties. It encouraged the importation of foreign merchandise by a remission of taxes in proper cases, and it not only protected the foreign merchants but secured to them certain special privileges.[5] Megasthenes says: "Among the Indians, officers are

[1] Periplus of the Erythraean Sea.

[2] Arthasâstra, Bk. II. ch. 11.

[3] Vide Arthasâstra, Bk. II. ch. 16.

[4] Periplus of the Erythraean Sea, p. 136.

[5] Arthasâstra, Bk. II. ch. 16.

appointed even for foreigners, whose duty is to see that no foreigner is wronged."[1] The Superintendent of this department facilitated the exportation of goods not required for home consumption. He acquainted himself with the values of goods in different countries, and encouraged the production of such goods as might be profitably exchanged for foreign goods. He also furnished the merchants with information relating to such matters as conveyance charges, expenses on the road to any foreign country, the dangers of the journey, the history of towns, and the trade customs of different places.[2] Sometimes, merchants formed combinations amongst themselves for the purpose of raising prices to an excessive extent.[3] In such cases, it was the duty of the Superintendent to fix the prices of commodities. According to Chānakya, prices were to be fixed after determining the amount of capital outlay and the total cost of production, including such charges as the payment of tolls, road-dues and other taxes, the cost of labour,

[1] Fragment I. Megasthenes adds: "Should any of them lose his health, they send physicians to attend him, and take care of him otherwise, and if he dies, they bury him, and deliver over such property as he leaves to his relatives. The Judges also decide cases in which foreigners are concerned with the greatest care, and come down sharply on those who take unfair advantage of them."

[2] Ibid.

[3] Chānakya says: "The more greedy among the merchants often oppress the people by forming combines and making profits of cent. per cent. (pane panaśatam)." The Nītivākyāmrita says: "Merchants left to themselves charge high prices for their goods, and, therefore, the King should regulate prices." Ch. VIII.

and the expenses of conveyance. When the prices were fixed by the government, a profit of five per cent. on local goods and of ten per cent. on imported commodities was allowed.[1] In case of an over-supply of goods, it was the duty of the Superintendent to control the production until the stock was exhausted. Balances, weights and measures were manufactured and sold by government, and any person using false weights, measures or balances was severely punished. The State also took steps for preventing the adulteration of goods, especially of food articles.[2]

Transactions were carried on, and values estimated, in terms of coins of various substances and denominations. Gold coins were perhaps rarely used, silver and copper coins forming the bulk of the medium of exchange.[3] The silver *karsha* and the copper *karshā-paṇa* were the coins mostly used.[4] Originally, it seems, the coins were guaranteed as to weight and fineness by punch marks which were tokens of merchants, or of guilds, or of the bullion-makers; but later on, coins were struck chiefly by royal authority. In Chānakya's time, gold and silver coins were issued in abundance from the royal mints.[5]

[1] Arthasāstra, Bk. IV. ch. 2.

[2] Arthasāstra, Bk. IV. ch. 2.

[3] Many of the Smriti works mention gold coins.

[4] The silver coins were paṇa, ½-paṇa, ¼-paṇa, and ⅛-paṇa, in Chānakya's time. Arthasāstra, Bk. II. ch. 12.

[5] Some of the Smriti works refer to the Karshāpaṇa as a silver coin, while others regard it as a copper coin. The Sukranīti refers to silver Karshas. In Prof. Rhys Davids' opinion, the Kahāpana was a copper coin in early

There was also a considerable use of instruments of credit, and promissory notes were not unknown.[1] We are not exactly aware what banking facilities there were in the country, but we know that loans were frequently given.[2] Gautama, one of the early law-givers, mentions the practice of lending money at interest (kusīda).[3] Brihaspati mentions six different kinds of interest, viz. Kāyika (bodily), Kālika (periodical), Chakra-vṛddhi (compound interest), Kārita (stipulated interest), Śikhāvṛiddhi (hair-increase), and bhogalābha (interest by enjoyment).[4] This lending of money at interest was permitted only to Vaisyas. Usury, however, was strongly condemned. Bodhāyana quotes the following verse in condemnation of usury: "Weighed in the scales the crime of killing a learned Brāhmana against (the crime) of usury; the slayer of the Brāhmana remained at the top, the usurer (vārdhushi) sank downwards."[5] Almost all the law-books, therefore, insist on a limitation of the rate of interest. According to Gautama and Vasishtha the legal rate of interest is $1\frac{1}{4}$ per cent. per month, or 15 per cent.

Buddhist times. He says: "Though the Kahāpana would be worth, at the present value of copper, only five-sixths of a penny, its purchasing power then was about equal to the purchasing power of a shilling now." Buddhist India, p. 101.

[1] Arthaśāstra, Bk. II. chs. 12-14.

[2] Prof. Rhys Davids says: "The great merchants in the few large towns gave letters of credit on one another." Buddhist India, p. 101.

[3] Gautama, X. 6.

[4] Brihaspati, XI. 55.

[5] Bodhāyana, I. 5, 10, 23. This verse is also quoted by Vasishtha, II. 42.

per annum. Manu and Chānakya also regard this as the proper rate. Where, however, no security was given, or in cases where no periodical interest was taken, or the loan was returned in kind, higher rates of interest might be demanded. According to some law-givers, the interest demanded from the members of the higher castes was to be less than from those of the lower. On this point Vasishtha quotes the following verse: "Two in the hundred, three, four and five, as has been declared in the Smriti, he may take as interest by the month according to the order of the castes."[1] Some of the law-books also lay it down that interest should cease after a time, and that no debtor should ever be compelled to pay more than double the amount of capital in case of gold and three times in the case of grain.[2] The fact that usury was strongly condemned must have made the lending of money at interest rather unusual, and it was perhaps this circumstance which prompted Megasthenes to say: "The Indians neither put out money at usury, nor know how to borrow. It is contrary to established usage for an Indian either to do or to suffer a wrong, and therefore, they neither make contracts nor require securities."[3]

[1] Vasishtha, II. 48.
[2] Vasishtha, II. 44.
[3] Megasthenes, Fragment XXVII.

CHAPTER XIX

RELIGION

THE Sanskrit word 'dharma' is usually rendered into English by 'religion.' But the two words are not exactly the same in meaning. The essence of religion is creed; of dharma, conduct. Thus 'dharma' is wider in its signification than religion. It includes the ideas of virtue, piety, duty, and law. Somadeva Sūri, in his Nītivākyāmrita, defines 'dharma' as that which promotes the greatest good of society.[1]

In the early Vedic times, no sharp line of distinction was drawn between the religious and the political activities of the people. Sacrificial meetings were often converted into assemblies for the discussion of matters of military, civil, and judicial interest. Gradually, however, it must have been

[1] Nītivākyāmrita, Ch. 1. Prof. Rhys Davids defines 'dharma' as "what it behoves a man of right feeling to do—or, on the other hand, what a man of sense will naturally hold." Buddhist India. The Mitāksharā mentions the following six kinds of 'dharmas' or duties: (1) Varṇa-dharma, or duties of castes; (2) Āśrama-dharma, or duties of orders; (3) Varṇāśrama-dharma, or duties of the orders of particular castes; (4) Guṇa-dharma, or duties of persons in accordance with their qualities; (5) Nimitta-dharma, or duties on particular occasions; and (6) Sādhāraṇa-dharma, or general duties (i.e. those to be observed by all)."

found necessary to separate the political functions of the State from the religious concerns of the people, and the rise of the caste-system perhaps helped this process of separation.

The connection of the State with Dharma in the Brahmanic period was of a peculiar kind. The religious rites and ceremonies, and the ethical rules of conduct, were settled and declared by the Brāhmanas. In these matters the State did not interfere. But it was the duty of the King and his officials to enforce the observance by the people of their respective duties. The King was thus the protector, but not the head, of religion.

After Asoka's conversion to Buddhism, it became a sort of state religion in Northern India, and that great monarch assumed a position not very far removed from the headship of the Buddhist Church. He settled disputes between members of the various orders, and even arrogated to himself to look after their private concerns. In the Kosambī Edict, Asoka instructs his high officers in these words: "The way of the church must not be quitted. Whosoever shall break the unity of the Church, whether monk or nun, from this time forth shall be compelled to wear white garments and to dwell in a place not reserved for the clergy."[1] He made Dharma a special department of the State, and appointed officials called Dharma-mahamātras and Dharma-yutas to have

[1] Vide also the Sārnāth Edict and the Sānchī Edict.

charge of that department.[1] In Rock Edict V. Asoka says: "Now in all the long time past, officers known as the Censors of the Law of Piety never had existed, whereas such Censors were created by me when I had been consecrated thirteen years." He convoked religious assemblies from time to time, and one of the Great Buddhist Councils is believed to have been held during his reign. His officers of religion paid constant visits to different parts of the country to instruct the people in 'dharma,'[2] and he himself undertook tours of piety (dharma) wherein were practised "the visiting of ascetics and Brāhmanas, with liberality to them, the visiting of Elders, with largess of gold, the visiting of the people of the country, with instruction in the Law of Piety and discussion of the Law of Piety."[3] Asoka, however, did not rest content with instructing his own people in 'dharma,' but adopted measures for the preaching of Buddhism in foreign countries. In Asoka's opinion, the chief conquest was the conquest by the Law of Piety, and this was won by him not only among such

[1] 'Dharma-mahamātras' is translated by Mr. V. A. Smith as "superior officers charged with the supervision of the Law of Piety." He also accepts Mr. Thomas's translation of 'dharma-yutas' as "subordinate officers of religion." Vide Asoka, Rock Edicts, footnotes.

[2] Before the appointment of the special officers of religion, the ordinary State officials had the duty of instructing the people in 'dharma.' In Rock Edict IV. we read: "Everywhere in my dominions the subordinate officials and the Commissioner, and the District Officer, every five years must proceed on circuit, as well for their other business, as for this special purpose, namely, to give instruction in the Law of Piety."

[3] Rock Edict VIII.

settlers within his own dominions as the Yonas and the Kambojas, among the Nābhāpamtis of Nābhaka, among the Bhojas and Pitinikas, among the Āndhras and Pulindas, but also in the realms of the Cholas and Pāndyas, in Ceylon, and even in such distant countries as Egypt, Cyrene, Macedonia, Epirus, and Syria.[1]

This missionary work in connection with Buddhism was continued after the death of Asoka. Religious teachers, proceeding from various centres of religious influence, carried a knowledge of the doctrines and discipline to different foreign countries. The conversion of Kanishka to the Buddhist faith led to the still wider diffusion of Buddhism in Central Asia and Tibet. From these countries a knowledge of Buddhist doctrine spread to China, and, in the first century A.D., at the request of the Emperor of China, a band of Buddhist missionaries headed by Kāsyapa Mātanga was sent to that country. During the following centuries a constant communication was kept up between India and China, and Buddhism made rapid progress in the latter country. From China the religion travelled to Japan, which soon became strongly attached to Buddhism. The religion of the Buddha continued to spread, till it became the

[1] Rock Edict XIII. (Shāhbāzgarhī text). With reference to the character of this conquest Asoka says: "And again, the conquest thereby won everywhere is everywhere a conquest full of delight. Delight is found in the conquests made by the Law. That delight, however, is only a small matter. His Sacred Majesty regards as bearing much fruit only that which concerns the other world."

faith of a greater number of human beings than had ever before—or have since—adopted the creed of any single religion.

After Asoka the position of the head of the church was claimed by very few—if any—monarchs of India. Kings, however, in many parts of the country, continued to lend their active support to Buddhism by constructing Vihāras and Sanghārāmas,[1] by erecting images of the Buddha, by endowing Buddhist institutions, and by holding Buddhist religious assemblies. Under the sanction of Kanishka, the third Buddhist Great Council was held, at which the teaching of the three Pitakas was arranged according to the doctrines of the various schools. King Harshavardhana assembled every year the Sramanas from all countries, and bestowed on them gifts of all kinds. He ordered the priests to carry on discussions, and himself judged of their arguments, whether they were weak or strong.[2] He rewarded the good and punished the wicked, degraded the evil and promoted the men of talent. He showed great reverence and honour to priests who were learned and were distinguished for purity of life; but if any one disregarded the rules

[1] At the time of Hiuen Tsiang's visit, there were 100 Sanghārāmas and 10,000 priests in Kanauj, 50 Sanghārāmas and 10,000 priests in Magadha, 100 Sanghārāmas and 20,000 priests in Mālava, and 100 Sanghārāmas and 5,000 priests in the Mahārāshtra country.

[2] On one such occasion, Hiuen Tsiang "established the standard of right doctrine without gainsaying"; and after this the King persuaded him to go on a procession on an elephant attended by the great Ministers of State. Bk. IV.

of morality, him he banished from the country, and would neither see him nor listen to him.[1]

Once in every five years, Harshavardhana held the great assembly called the Mokṣa Mahāparishat. On such occasions he emptied his treasuries to give all away in charity. Hiuen Tsiang witnessed one of these assemblies, and he gives a beautiful description of it. The kings of twenty countries assembled with the Sramanas and Brāhmanas, the most distinguished of their country, with magistrates and soldiers. The ceremonies lasted several days. One day a golden statue of Buddha was carried in procession, attended on the left by Harshavardhana himself, dressed as Sakra and holding a precious canopy, and on the right by Kumāra-rāja, dressed as Brahmā and waving a white chāmara. Each of them had as an escort 500 war-elephants clad in armour; and in front and behind the statue of Buddha went 100 great elephants carrying musicians, who sounded the drums and raised their music. King Harsha, as he went, scattered on every side pearls and various precious substances in honour of the three objects of worship. After the feast, the men of learning assembled in the hall and discussed, in elegant language, the most abstruse subjects.[2]

From about the fifth century A.D. Buddhism began to decline in India. Brahmanism, which had so far

[1] Hiuen Tsiang, Buddhist Records, Bk. V.

[2] Ibid.

flourished side by side and in friendly relations with Buddhism, began now to receive greater encouragement at the hands of the rulers, some of whom even went the length of persecuting the more corrupt forms of the religion of the Buddha. The tenets of Jainism also became gradually more and more popular, and helped in a considerable degree to supplant the Buddhist doctrines.

In Ceylon, Buddhism took a firmer root than in India, and remained a sort of State Religion until recent years. Many of the Kings of Ceylon claimed the headship of the Church. Devānampiya Tissa, under whom Buddhism was spread throughout the island, assumed the power to regulate the affairs of the Church. Another King, Kassapa IV., took upon himself the duty of purifying the religion and enforcing discipline among the priests by the expulsion of immoral men and the appointment of new priests in the vacant places.[1] King Parākrama Bāhu introduced unity in the offices of the church.[2] He also held a great trial of the priests, and unfrocked those who were found guilty of unworthy conduct. Nissamka Malla also introduced many reforms in the church organisation.[3]

So much about the credal side of dharma.[4] The more important side of 'dharma,' as has already been

[1] Mahāvamsa, Ch. LII. [2] Ibid. Ch. LXXVII.

[3] Vide Epigraphia Zeylanica.

[4] In Pillar Edict VI. Asoka says: "I devote my attention to all communities, for all denominations are reverenced by me with various forms of

remarked, consisted in right conduct. This aspect, although present in Brahmanism, became more prominent in Buddhism, and was strongly emphasised by Asoka. The true ceremonial, in Asoka's opinion, was the ceremonial of Piety—which consisted in purity of mind, gratitude, steadfastness, mastery over the senses, truthfulness of speech, toleration, liberality, proper treatment of dependents and servants, obedience to father and mother, right behaviour towards friends, comrades, relations, ascetics, and Brāhmanas, and abstention from the slaughter of living creatures.[1] It was always considered the duty of the State to offer facilities for the performance of their duties by the people. And the State itself had certain active duties to perform in the domain of 'dharma.' One of these was the relief of the poor, the helpless, and the afflicted. For this purpose there were almsgiving establishments and puṇyaśālās. Very often gifts of property and grants of revenues were made by the State for the support of religious teachers and learned men. With regard to such grants, Vishnu says: "He (the King) must not suffer any Brāhmana in his realm to perish through want; nor any other man leading a pious

reverence. Nevertheless, personal adherence to one's own creed is the chief thing in my opinion."

[1] Vide Rock Edicts IV. and VII. and other Edicts. With reference to Asoka's religious work, Prof. Rhys Davids remarks: "But how sane the grasp of things most difficult to grasp. How simple, how true, how tolerant, his view of conduct of life."

life. Let him bestow landed property upon Brāhmanas. To those upon whom he has bestowed (land) he must give a document destined for the information of a future ruler, which must be written upon a piece of (cotton) cloth, or a copper plate, and must contain the names of his (three) immediate ancestors, a declaration of the extent of the land, and an imprecation against him who should appropriate the donation to himself, and should be signed with his own seal."[1]

Asoka appointed many high officers to superintend his establishment for the distribution of alms in Magadha as well as in the other provinces.[2] He also established hospitals and dispensaries, for men as well as for animals, throughout his wide dominions.[3] On the roads he had banyan trees and mango-groves planted, and at every mile he caused wells to be dug and rest-houses to be erected.[4] From numerous inscriptions we know that this kind of charitable work was continued by successive monarchs. The Gadhwā Stone Inscription of Chandragupta Gupta II., for instance, tells us that that monarch erected a perpetual almshouse for the Brāhmanas of a certain

[1] Vishnu, III. 79-82. Endowment of lands or taxes granted by one King was, as a rule, maintained by his successors. In an inscription of a recent date (1204 A.D.) occurs the following passage: "The slayer of a cow or of a Brāhmaua may perchance find atonement in the Ganges and other holy places; but in the case of the appropriation of the possessions and goods of Brāhmanas, there can be no (atonement) for man." Inscriptions from Belgaum B. (ed. by L. D. Barnett).

[2] Pillar Edict VII. [3] Rock Edict II. [4] Pillar Edict VII.

place.[1] The Sānchī Stone Inscription records the gift by the same monarch of the income of a village for the support of Bhikshus. In the Bilsad Stone Pillar Inscription of Kumāragupta mention is made of the dedication of a religious almshouse of large dimensions and beautiful structure to the use of those who are eminent in respect of virtuous qualities.[2] According to Hiuen Tsiang, King Harshavardhana "in all the highways of the towns and villages throughout India created hospices (puṇyaśālās) provided with food and drink, and stationed there physicians, with medicines for travellers and poor persons round about to be given without stint." [3]

Charitable establishments in aid of 'dharma' were erected and maintained not only by the State, but also by guilds of merchants and pious individuals. In Fa Hian's time, Kings, ministers, and people are said to have vied with each other in making gifts to the poor and to religious persons.[4] The same benevolent spirit was observed by Hiuen Tsiang as subsisting in the seventh century. At this time the Nālanda Monastery was known as the "charity without intermission" monastery, where myriads of priests were entertained, and people from every part hospitably received.[5]

[1] Corpus Inscriptionum Indicarum, Vol. III.

[2] Corpus Inscriptionum Indicarum, Vol. III.

[3] Buddhist Records, Bk. V.

[4] Fa Hian, Ch. XI.

[5] Life of Hiuen Tsiang, p. 110.

Education was another activity connected with religion. From very early times, teachers and scholars were supported by the State, either by periodical allowances or by gifts of lands, incomes of villages, and proceeds of taxes.[1] Under the patronage of Kings, famous seats of learning grew up in different parts of the country to which scholars flocked in thousands and tens of thousands. Education received a great impetus after the spread of Buddhism. Under Brahmanism education was mainly confined to the higher classes of society, but Buddhism proclaimed the equality of all mankind, and Buddhist monarchs thought it necessary to make arrangements for the instruction of the multitude.

The congregation of learned men at the seats of learning gave rise to Universities. The first important university of ancient times was Taksha-silā. The Jātakas speak of Taksha-silā as a great centre of learning, where the pupils were taught by teachers of world-wide fame.[2] At the University of Taksha-silā eighteen branches of learning were taught in separate schools, each of which was presided over by a special professor. The subjects taught there included not only philosophy, theology, and literature, but also sculpture, painting, and handicrafts. Taksha-silā continued to flourish till about the first century before Christ. In the early centuries of the

[1] Vide Sukranīti, Ch. II. sls. 122-123.

[2] Vide, for instance, the Bhīmasena Jātaka, in Cowell's Jātaka, Vol. I.

Christian Era, there grew up in Berar the University of Dhanya Kataka.[1]

But the most important of the Indian Universities was that of Nālanda. The Nālanda Vihara was, according to Hiuen Tsiang, established by a King of Central India, and a long succession of Kings continued the work of building, using all the skill of the sculptor, till the whole is truly marvellous to behold."[2] The lands in its possession contained more than 200 villages, these having been bestowed on the monastery by Kings of many generations.[3] In this university the teachers were men of conspicuous talent, solid learning, exalted eloquence, and illustrious virtue,[4] whose fame had spread through distant regions. From morning till night the teachers and pupils engaged in continuous discussion. Learned men from different cities went there in multitudes to settle their doubts, and the streams of wisdom and knowledge spread far and wide. Hiuen Tsiang gives a detailed description of the course of studies at this university, which included both sacred and profane subjects. The pupils started with the study of the siddha-vastu (or the book of twelve chapters), and then they were instructed in the five chief Vidyās, namely, Śabda-vidyā, or the science of sounds; Śilpa-vidyā, or the science of mechanics, etc.; Cikitsā-vidyā, or the science of medicine; Hetu-vidyā, or

[1] Journal of the Buddhist Text Society, Pt. IV. vol. vii.

[2] Hiuen Tsiang, Bk. X. [3] Takakusu, I-Tsing, p. 65. [4] Ibid.

the science of causes; and Adhyātma-vidyā, or metaphysics. The Brāhmanas also studied the four Vedas.[1]

The monastic University of Odantapuri was perhaps founded in the fifth or sixth century A.D., but it rose to fame during the reigns of the Pāla Kings of Bengal.[2] It had a splendid library, which was destroyed by the Mahomedans at the time of their first invasion of Bengal. Another University which was established under the patronage of the Pāla Kings was that of Vikrama-sīla. It is said that the University was composed of six colleges, and employed more than a hundred professors. There were numerous religious establishments and hostels attached to the University for the residence of monks and pupils. Vārānasi in Northern India and Kānchī in the south also flourished as seats of learning for many centuries.

[1] Buddhist Records, Bk. II.

[2] Journal of the Buddhist Text Society, Pt. IV. vol. VII.

CHAPTER XX

LOCAL GOVERNMENT

We know practically nothing of the system of village government which existed in India in pre-Āryan times. A distinguished scholar has, however, tried to establish the following points :

The Dravidians, when they assumed the government of countries originally peopled by Kolarian tribes, retained the village communities established by their predecessors, but reformed the village system. They made each separate village and each province formed by a union of villages more dependent on the central authority than they were under the Kolarian form of government. Under the Dravidian rule, all public offices beginning with the headships of villages were filled by nominees appointed by the State instead of being elective as among the Kolarians. The Dravidians set apart lands appropriated to the public service in every village, required the tenants to cultivate these public lands, and stored their produce in the royal and provincial granaries, this being the form in which the earliest taxes were paid.

They also in the Dravidian villages made every man and woman bear his or her share in contributing to the efficiency of the government, but this system was not followed in the same completeness in the Kolarian villages, where the people were not so ready as the Dravidian races to submit to strict discipline, to which the Dravidians had been accustomed long before they entered India.[1]

A discussion of these points would take us beyond the scope of the present work, and we shall therefore confine our attention to the Āryan system of village administration. In the early Vedic times, the villagers themselves managed the simple affairs of the village;[2] but the States being small, there was hardly any distinction between the Central and the Local Government. In course of time, however, it was found necessary to have a separate organisation for the management of local affairs; and as the States grew larger and larger in size, the distinction between the two kinds of governmental activity became more and more marked.

Originally, it seems, the villages were completely self-governing. They were practically free from central control. The grāmanī[3] (headman) and other village officials were appointed by the community and

[1] F. J. Hewitt's article in the Journal of the Royal Asiatic Society, Vol XXI.

[2] Prof. Macdonell says: "The village does not appear to have been a unit for legal purposes in early days, and it can hardly be said to have been a political unit." Vedic Index, I. p. 246.

[3] The word 'grāmanī,' leader of the village, occurs in the Rig-Veda.

were accountable to them.[1] But gradually they were brought under the control of the King.[2] By the time of Manu, the village officials had become government servants, and the Local Government system had become subordinate to the Central Administration. Manu describes this organisation in these words : "Let him appoint a lord over (each) village, as well as lords of ten villages, lords of twenty, lords of a hundred, and lords of a thousand. The lord of one village himself shall inform the lord of ten villages of the crimes committed in his village, and the ruler of ten (shall make his report) to the ruler of twenty. But the ruler of twenty shall report all such (matters) to the lord of a hundred, and the lord of a hundred shall himself give information to the lord of a thousand."[3] Vishnu also speaks of the appointment of a headman for each village, and of heads of ten villages and of hundred villages, and lords of provinces (deśādhyakshāḥ).[4]

During the rule of the Maurya Emperors, the process of centralisation was carried much further.

[1] Prof. Rhys Davids says : "From the fact that the appointment of this officer (i.e. the headman) is not claimed by the King until the later law-books it is almost certain that in earlier times the appointment was either hereditary or was conferred by the village council itself." Buddhist India, p. 48.

[2] In Prof. Macdonell's opinion, "the grāmaṇī's connexion with the royal person seems to point to his having been a nominee of the King rather than a popularly elected officer. But the post may have been sometimes hereditary, and sometimes nominated or elective ; there is no decisive evidence available." Vedic Index, I. p. 247.

[3] Manu, VII. 115-117.

[4] Vishnu-Smriti (Jolly's Sanskrit text), Bk. III.

Under Chānakya's system, villages were classified as of the first, second, or third rank.[1] Each village had a headman (grāmika, grāmādhipa, or grāmakūṭa) whose duty it was (1) to delimit the boundaries of the village and of the different plots of land within the village; (ii) to divide the village lands into cultivated lands, uncultivated lands, plains, wet lands, (flower) gardens, vegetable gardens, fenced lands, dwelling-houses, assembly halls, temples, irrigation works, cremation grounds, charitable houses, places of pilgrimage, and pasture lands; (iii) to enter in his books all sales, gifts, charities, and remissions of taxes which take place within the village; (iv) to divide houses in the village into revenue-paying and non-revenue-paying, mentioning the amount of taxes, rates, etc., payable by each; (v) register the number of inhabitants distributed by castes, and following different occupations, such as agriculture, pasturage, trade, arts, manufactures, manual labour, and menial service, together with an account of the conduct and character, income and expenditure, of each inhabitant.[2]

During the centralised administration of the Maurya Emperors, the village assembly lost much of its power and prestige. Some local matters, however, continued to be decided by this assembly.

[1] The Sukranīti says that a piece of land which is one kros (two miles) in area, and which has an income of 1,000 silver karshas, is called a 'grāma.' A pallī is half of a grāma, and a half of a pallī is a kumbha. I. 193.

[2] Arthasāstra, Bk. II. ch. 35.

It was a popular body consisting of the elders of the village (grāma-vṛiddhāḥ). There was no fixed number of members, and the attendance varied according to the nature of the business that was to be transacted. The members were not elected, but chosen by a sort of natural selection. They were usually men who, by their age, character, and attainments acquired the confidence of the villagers, and their opinions were supposed to represent the collective wisdom of the village. These village elders not only decided administrative matters, but formed a court of justice for the decision of small civil suits, such as the boundaries of lands, and for the trial of petty criminal cases like larceny and assault. They also looked after public property, e.g. that of temples, and the interests of infants, and attended to the question of poor-relief.[1] Decisions of the village assembly were, as a rule, unanimous; but when any difference of opinion arose, the matter was decided in accordance with the view of the majority, provided the majority consisted of honest persons.[2] Disputes about the boundaries of two villages were decided by the elders of the neighbouring villages.

The headman was the president of the village assembly as well as its executive official. Presumably, he was the leader of the village both for civil purposes and for military operations.[3] He was also the

[1] Arthasāstra, Bk. II. ch. 1. [2] Ibid. Bk. III. ch. 9.
[3] Vedic Index, I. p. 247.

connecting link between the village administration and the central government of the country. The headman possessed extensive powers, among them being the power to send out of the village thieves and adulterers. He was usually a hereditary officer, and he either remunerated himself out of the land-revenue and other taxes collected from the village, or had the use of a plot of land free of rent. It was the duty of the villagers to help the headman in the discharge of his duties and to pay his expenses.

The Sukranīti mentions, besides the headman, five other officers of a village, namely, the superintendent of police (sāhasādhipati), the collector of the land-revenue, the clerk, the collector of tolls, and the watchman (prātihāra). The village officials were held responsible for the internal security of the villagers. If, for instance, a theft occurred in the village, and the officers failed to catch the thief, they had to compensate the owner for the property stolen.[1]

In their corporate capacity the villagers constructed and maintained works of public utility, and undertook measures tending to the improvement of the village; and those who took the lead in such matters received honours and rewards from the King.[2]

[1] Āpastamba, II. 10, 26, 6-8.

[2] Arthaśāstra, Bk. III. ch. 10. Prof. Rhys Davids, alluding to the accounts given of village administration in the Buddhist books, says: "Villagers are described as uniting of their own accord to build Mote-halls and Rest-houses and reservoirs, to mend the roads between their own and adjacent villages and even to lay out parks." Prof. Rhys Davids draws a beautiful picture of the simple life of the villagers of ancient times. He says: "None

So far as their domestic affairs were concerned, the villagers, it seems, were not subject to vexatious interference from the central authorities. But every village formed an integral part of the general administrative system of the country. Above the village headman was the Circle Officer (Gopa) who was in charge of a number of villages, usually from five to ten in number, and whose duty it was to supervise the work of the headmen. A number of Circles formed a Division or District which, according to Chānakya, was to comprise one-fourth of the province (janapada).[1] The ruler of a Division or District (Sthānika) was subordinate to the Governor of the Province, who himself was subject to the Central Administration. In the Central Government, all matters relating to local administration were under the immediate control of one of the Ministers. Manu says: "The affairs of these (officials), which are connected with (their) villages, as well as their other affairs, shall be inspected by one Minister of the King (who must be) of a cheerful disposition and never remiss."[2] Under Chānakya's system, the Collector-general was to be in charge of this department.[3]

of the householders could have been what would now be called rich. On the other hand, there was sufficiency for their simple needs, there was security, there was independence. There were no landlords and no paupers. There was little if any crime." Buddhist India, p. 49.

[1] Arthasāstra, Bk. II. ch. 35.

[2] Manu, VII. 120.

[3] Arthasāstra, Bk. II. ch. 35.

Some of the South Indian and Ceylon inscriptions throw much light on the system of village government in those parts of the country. The Vevalakatiya Slab-inscription of Mahinda IV., King of Ceylon (1026-1042 A.D.), although comparatively recent, is particularly interesting in this respect. From this inscription we learn that within the village (of Dasa-gama) justice was administered by means of a Communal Court composed of headmen and responsible householders, and the village assembly was empowered to carry into effect the laws enacted by the King-in-Council and promulgated by his Ministers. It investigated all crimes committed within the village, exacted the prescribed fines from the law-breakers, and inflicted other kinds of punishment. But the most interesting points in the inscription are those which relate to the collective responsibility of the inhabitants of Dasa-gama for producing offenders within a limited time, and the fines imposed on the whole community in case of failure.[1] We give a few extracts from this inscription :

" . . . Touching the dasa-gama . . . , each headman (of these villages), as well as those headmen and householders who have given security for Kibi-gama, shall ascertain (the facts) when in any spot within this (district) murder or robbery with violence has been committed. Thereafter they shall sit in session

[1] Vide Epigraphia Zeylanica, Vol. I. No. 21, Editor's Note.

and enquire of the inhabitants of the dasa-gama (in regard to these crimes) . . .

"If the (offenders) are not detected, the inhabitants of the dasa-gama shall find them and have them punished within forty-five days. Should they not find them, then the dasa-gama shall be made to pay (a fine of) 125 Kalandas (weight) of gold to the State.

". . . Holders of villages and of paman lands shall divide among themselves in accordance with former usage the proceeds of (the . . .) fines and other minor (?) fines . . ." [1]

The capital city and the larger towns had separate organisations of their own for purposes of local government. In the Rig-Veda we find mention of the Purapati, or lord of the city. Manu says: "And in each town let him appoint one superintendent of all affairs (sarvārtha-cintaka) elevated in rank, formidable, (resembling) a planet among the stars." [2]

This Superintendent was perhaps the President of the City Board. From Megasthenes we know that the government of the capital city was conducted by a Municipal Board consisting of thirty members, divided into six Committees of five members each. The members of the first Committee looked after everything relating to the industrial arts. Those of the second attended to the affairs of foreigners. The third Committee enquired into births and deaths, with the view not only of levying taxes, but also in

[1] Epigraphia Zeylanica, Vol. I. No. 21. [2] Manu, III. 121.

order that births and deaths might not escape the cognizance of Government. The fourth Committee superintended trade and commerce. Its members had charge of weights and measures, and it was their duty to see that the products in their season were sold by public notice. They also issued trade licenses, no one being allowed to deal in more than one commodity unless he paid a double tax. The fifth body supervised manufactured articles, which were to be sold only in public. What was new was to be sold separately from what was old, and there was a fine for mixing the two together. The sixth Committee consisted of members who collected the tenths of the prices of the articles sold. Such were the functions which these Committees separately discharged. In their collective capacity they had charge of the general affairs of the city, and looked after such things as the keeping of public buildings in proper repair, the regulation of prices, the care of markets, harbours, and temples.[1]

It is worthy of notice that Chānakya makes no mention of the Municipal Board or its Committees. Perhaps under his regime the old municipal method of administration was superseded by a system in which government officials controlled all the affairs of the cities. In Chānakya's system, the chief official of the city was the Nāgaraka. Under him were four Sthānikas or Divisional officers, each of whom was in

[1] Megasthenes (McCrindle), Fragment XXXIV.

charge of a quarter of the city. Under the Sthānikas were the Gopas, each of whom attended to the affairs of ten, twenty, or forty families. The chief duty of the city officials was to see that the householders and traders were not in any way disturbed in their respective avocations. It was also their business to provide medical aid to the sick, to take note of persons entering or leaving the city, to take precautions against the outbreak of fires, to look to the cleanliness of the city, to watch the movements of suspicious characters, and to prevent the commission of crimes.[1]

[1] Bk. II. ch. 36.

APPENDIX

TRANSLITERATION OF THE SANSKRIT ALPHABET ADOPTED BY THE GENEVA CONGRESS.

अ	*a*	घ	*gh*	प	*p*
आ	*ā*	ङ	*ṅ*	फ	*ph*
इ	*i*	च	*c*	ब	*b*
ई	*ī*	छ	*ch*	भ	*bh*
उ	*u*	ज	*j*	म	*m*
ऊ	*ū*	झ	*jh*	य	*y*
ऋ	*ṛ*	ञ	*ñ*	र	*r*
ॠ	*ṝ*	ट	*ṭ*	ल	*l*
ऌ	*ḷ*	ठ	*ṭh*	व	*v*
ॡ	*ḹ*	ड	*ḍ*	श	*ś*
ए	*e*	ढ	*ḍh*	ष	*ṣ*
ऐ	*ai*	ण	*ṇ*	स	*s*
ओ	*o*	त	*t*	ह	*h*
औ	*au*	थ	*th*	ळ (in Pali *ḷ*-)	*ḻ*
क	*k*	द	*d*	ं (*Anusvāra*)	*ṁ*
ख	*kh*	ध	*dh*	ँ (*Anunāsika*)	*m̐*
ग	*g*	न	*n*	: (*Visarga*)	*ḥ*

INDEX

ABDICATIONS of Kings, 90 & *n.* 3
Abettors of Crime, punishment of, 167
Abul Fazl, on Hindu Polity and Law, 13 *et alibi*
Absolutism in State-sovereignty, never attained, 40
Accounts Department, Officials of, 121-2, 184-5
Administration, under Monarchic rule, 47-52
  Size of Territory in relation to, 30-1
Administrative Law Courts, 146
  Systems, sources of information on, 2 *et sqq., passim*
Adulteration, State action as to, 272
Agni Purāna, the, on Politics, 5 *et alibi*
Agreements, Invalidation of, 166
Agriculture, State relations with, 257-8
  Superintendents of, 124, 257-8
Aindra Mahābhisheka sacrifice, 90, 93
Ajanta caves, 249
  Paintings in, 86 *n.* 3
Ajātasatru, of Magadha, 48, 59, 95
Ayeen-i-Akbery, of Abul Fazl, on Hindu Politics, &c., 13, *passim*
Alexander the Great
  Fleet of, 270
  Indian campaigns of, 7, 31, 44, 45, 235, 236, 240
    Difficulties met, at Forts, 217
    Historians of, on Indian Politics, 7 *et alibi*
    Political divisions at date of, 57-8
    Results on Administration, 47
Alliances, 190-1
  Treaties making, 192-3
Almsgiving, State, 282, 283
Almshouses, establishment of, 282, 283-4
Ambashthas, the, democracy of, 44
Ambassadors
  Functions of, 193
  Interchange of, 186-7
  Qualifications desirable in, 194-5
  Sanctity of Person of, 194
Ambhi, of Taxila, and Alexander, 236 *n.* 2
  Kingdom of, 57
Ānanda, 95
Āndra Kingdom, Army of, 196
  Country, and Fortified towns of, 57
  Suzerainty of, 60
Anga, and Capital, 55
Angas, the, as Sources of Law, 132
Anus, the, 54, 55 *n.*
Appeal, Courts of, 145, 149
  Right of, 149, 168
Arab Invasions, 238
Arbitrators, functions of, 147-8
Architecture, Hindu, 246 *et sqq.*
Aristocratic Governments, 45
Aristotle, contemporary with Chānakya, 10
Arjuna, 230
Armour, 204, 206
Armoury, the, 206
  Superintendent of, 123-4
Armies, *see also* Military Organisation
  Best kind, according to Chānakya, 198
  Sections of, 197 *et sqq.*
    Subdivisions of, 200-1
  Sizes of, instances of, 166-7

Arsakas, Country and Capital of, 56
Arthasāstra, the, of Chānakya, on Public Administration, 8 *et sqq., et alibi*
Authenticity, origin &c., of, 9 *n.* 1
Books apparently based on, 12-14
Meaning of the title, 8-9
Political doctrines of, 9 *et sqq.*
Āryan States, primitive, 38-9
Increase of, 54
Sizes of, 30-1
Āryas, the, Conquest of, and rule in India, 2 *et sqq.*, 219-20, *et alibi*
Social distinctions among, growth of, 16, 17 *et sqq.*
Tribes of, in Punjab, 15 & *n.*
Āryāvarta, Source of Laws, 135
Asia, Central, Buddhism in, 278
Asoka, King, Buildings by, 246, 247
Conquests of, 222
Dominions of, extent of, 59-60
Edicts and Inscriptions of, 49, 84 *nn.* 2 & 3, 222, 247, 276, 277, 282 *n.* 1
Foreign relations of, 186-7
Government by, 40, 49, 50-1
Irrigation works of, 253
Ministerial responsibility under, 116
Position of the State under, 40
Provinces of, 49
Religious ascendancy of, 79 *n.* 2, 276-9, 282
Training of, 89-90
Virtues of, 83-4
Āsrama-dharma System, the, 23
Assakenoi, the, and other nations mentioned by Megasthenes, 57
Assam, fleet of, 200
Assemblies (*see also* Councils, Public Assemblies, & Village Assemblies), 94-7
Moksa Mahāparishat, described, 280
Two kinds of, 95
Vedas on, 97
Assyria, maritime trade with, 267
Asvamedha sacrifice, the, 90, 92-3
Attack, in Battle, 213-4
Audit of Public Accounts, 122, 185
Avanti, and its Capital, 56
Avantivarman, King of Kasmir, and Irrigation work, 254
Rule of, 87
Ayodhyā, city of, 240

BALANCE of Power, Chānakya, &c., on, 195
Balances and Weights, State Control of, 292
Superintendent of, 124
Bali, Hindu architecture in, 255, 256
Barbarikon, seaport, 268
Barygaza, trade of, 268
Battle-array, various kinds of, 210 *et sqq.*
Battle fields, choice of, 209-10, 230
Benevolences, 179
Bengal, Pāla Kings of, territories of, 61 & *n.* 2
Universities of, 287
Berar, University in, 286
Betting, Fines on, 175
Bharata, first Monarch to bring all India under Āryan influence, 48
Bhāsa, poems of, 6
Bhāskara, of Nilantha, the, 13
Bhilsa Topes, the, 248
Bhīma, 230
Bhoja, King of Dhara, 13 *n.* 1
Bimbisāra, of Magadha, 59
Birth, not original ground for Caste-grouping, 19
Births and Deaths, Enquiries into, 296-7
Bodh-Gaya, Asoka's Temple at, 247
Bows, 204, 205, 207-8
Brahmana Caste or Brahmanas, Architecture of, in extra-Indian lands, 254-5
Ascendancy of, 21
Duties of, 20
Exemption of, from Taxation, 178
Immunity of, from certain forms of Punishment, 171
Judges generally of, 144, 171-2

Brahmana Caste
Kings of, 70
Origin of, 18
Religious domination of, 276
Custom, force of, as Law, 135
Brahmanism, recrudescence of, 280-1
Right conduct, enforced by, 282
Brahmāvarta, Customs of, as Laws, 133
Brewing, State control of, 262
Bridges, 252
Cambodian, 255-6
'Brihaspati Sūtra,' the, 11 *n.* 2
Broach, seaport, 268
Bucklers and Shields, 206, 208, 209
Buddha, the, in praise of Popular Assemblies, 95-6
Buddhism, in Ceylon, 79 *n.* 2, 278
Reforms introduced by Various Kings, 281
Decline of, 280-1
Education encouraged by, 285
Spread of, by Missionaries, 277-9
Buddhist Age, attitude to Brahmanas during, 23, 282-3
Chief Tribes at rise of, 44 *n.* 4
Forms of Government common in, 43
Religion and the State in, 276 *et sqq.*
Architecture &c., in Ceylon &c., 254-5
Art, objects of, 248
Great Councils, 277, 279
Religious books, on Indian Politics, 2, 6
Building-regulations, 245-6
Buildings, Taxes on, 175
Bureaucracy, the, Training, Qualifications, &c., 128-9

CABINET, the, functions &c., of, 113, 114, 115, 185
Calingae, the, Capital of, 57
Cambodia (*see also* Kāmboja), conquest of, 224
Public Works in, 255
Roads and Bridges, 255-6
Camps, Choice of Sites for, 209, 210
Canals, 252-5
as Trade-routes, 266
Capital Cities, descriptions of, 240 *et sqq.*
Local government of, 296-7
Revenues derived from, 175-6
Caste Associations, 97
Caste-privileges, 151, 170-1, 274
Caste-system, origin of, 16, 17 *&* *n.* 1, 18 *&* *n.*
Political effects of, 69-70, 97, 276
Castes, duties of, 20
Cattle-breeding by the State, 258
Cavalry, 196, 197
in Action, 208
Value of, 199
Cave-dwellings, 250
Cave-temples, 249, 250
Censors of the Law of Poetry, 277
Ceremonial, Asoka's views on, 282
Cession of Territory, 234-5, 237
Ceylon,
Administration of Justice in, 146 *n.* 4, 147
Buddhism in, 79 *n.* 2, 278, 281
Conquests of, Chola, &c., 61, 224
Councils in, 104, 105
Inscriptions in, 69 *n.* 3, 104, 295
Value of, 8
Irrigation-works in, 255
Kings of, as Heads of the Church, 79 *n.* 2, 281
Public Works in, 255
Queens of, Regnant and Consort, 69 *&* *n.* 3
Village government in, 295
Chaityas (Buddhist Temples), 248, 249
Chakravarti, *see* Suzerain
Chālukya Empire, 61
Chānakya or Kautilya, alternative names of, 9
Famous book by, on politics, 8 9
Minister and "maker" of Chandragupta, 8 *n.* 3, 10 *n.* 1, 59, 116, 118, 237
Political aim of, 222, 237
Chandragupta Maurya, 7
Administrative machinery devised by, 49
Cavalry of, value of, 199

Chandragupta Maurya
Chānakya's relations with, 8 *n.* 3, 10 *n.* 1, 59, 116, 118, 237
Conquests of, 222, 237
Empire of, 31, 47, 48, 59
Cities in, 240
Financial system under, 175 *et sqq.*
Greek contemporaries of, 10
Irrigation-works of, 253
Megasthenes' Embassy to, 186
Naval Department of, 200
Sūdra descent of, 70 *&* *n.* 1
Chandragupta Vikramāditya, Empire of, 60
Chargés-d'affaires, 193
Chariots of War, 106, 199
Men carried by, 204
Superintendent of, 125
Charitable Establishments, 284
Works, of Kings and others, 282-4
Charities, Superintendents of, 125
Chedis, the, Country of, 56
Chief Judge, the, 114
Qualifications of, 144 *n.* 3
Chief Justice, the, 142-3
Chief Superintendents of Public Finance, 122, 184-5
China, Buddhism in, 278
Imports from, 270
Relations with, 187
Chinese Pilgrims' accounts of India, 7-8 *et alibi*
Chola Empire, 61
Buddhism in, 278
Circles of States, 189, 195
of Villages, administration of, 294
City officials, in Chānakya's day, Titles and Duties of, 297-8
Cities, Chief Buildings in, 244
Construction and adornment of, 240 *et sqq.*
Civil and Criminal Cases, how dealt with, 145-6, 152, 166-7
"Civil List," ancient view of, 73, 179 *&* *n.* 2
Clan, evolution of, into Tribe, 38
Clan and Vassal system of Rajput Government, 52
Clans, confederate, 54, 55
Class Distinctions, absent in Early Vedic Times, 16
Early Āryan, *see also* Caste system,
Evolution of, 18 *et sqq.*
Climate as Factor in Conditions of States, and Character of Peoples, 30-3
Coastal Trading, 267
Coinage, 272
Collective Responsibility of
Police, 125-6
Villagers, 27, 252, 292, 293, 295-6
Collector General, the, 113, 183, 294
Salary of, 129
Colour-line, the, as Basis of Caste-system, 17 *&* *n.* 1
Commander-in-Chief, the, 114, 202
Salary of, 129
Subordinates of, 202-3
King as, 78
Commerce
External, 266 *et sqq.*
Internal, 264-6
Interior centres of, 268
Principal seaports for, 268-9
State Department of, 264, 270-2
Superintendent of, 123
Commissariat, Department of, 203
Committees of
Departments, 127
Military Affairs, 203
Municipal Boards, 296-7
Conduct, Right, chief arm of 'Dharma,' 275, 282
Prominence of, in Buddhism, 282
Conquered Territory
Acquirement of, 222
Treatment of, 136
Laws maintained, 231-2
Conquerors, Chānakya's advice to, 50 *n.* 1
Conquest, delight in, of ancient Kings, 220-1
Conquests, external and internal, 224

Corporal Punishment, rarity of, 166-7
Councils, in Ceylon, 104-5
  Domestic, of Rajput Chiefs, 53
  Great, or Royal Assembly, 79, 97
    Functions, &c., of, 97-100
  of Ministers, *see* Privy Council
  North Indian, 96 *et sqq.*
  South Indian, 103-4
  Town, 53
  Village, 53, 96 *n.* 3, 291-2, 295
Counter-suits, 157
Courts of Law and Justice
  Administrative, 146
  Appeal, 145, 149
  Chief, 142-3, 145-9
  Local, 145-7
  Movable and Stationary, 141-2
  Principal and Lower, Jurisdiction of, 145-7
  Relations between different kinds of, 148-9
  Village, 53, 146-7, 292, 295
Cows, Superintendent of, 124-5
Credit, essential to Agriculture, 257
  Instruments of, 273
Criminal cases, 145-6, 152
  Punishments given, 166-7
Crown Lands, Revenues from, 180
Crown Princes, Training of, 89-90
Cultivators, Loans to, 257
Culture-State level, reached under Asoka, 40
Custom, as Basis of Law, the Sishtas as authorities on, 133, 134-5
  Validity of, divergent views on, 136-7
Custom (Customary Law), 150, 151

DAIRY-FARMING, State, 238
Dasa class, the, 26-7, 170
Dasaratha, states ruled by, 58
Dasyus, the, 16 & *n.* 3
  Āryan conflicts with, 219-20
Death-sentences, rarity of, 166
Debts, recovery of, 166
Deccan, struggles for, of Chālukyas and Rāshtrakūtas, 61
Defence, weapons of, 206, 208
Defendant, the, in Lawsuits, 156 *et sqq.*
Departmental Officials, 121 *et sqq.*
Despotism, foreign to Aryan peoples, 74
Devānampiya Tissa, Head of Buddhism in Ceylon, 281
Dhanya Kataka, University of, 286
Dharma, definitions of, 275 & *n.*
  Two sides of
    Credal, 275, 276 *et sqq.*
    Social, 257, 281 *et sqq.*
Dharma-sāstras, the, dates of, 4 & *n.* 1
  Meaning of, 9
  Origin of, 134
  Sources of Law, 133
Dharma-sūtras, the, 4, 34
  Dates of, 4 *n.* 1
Diamonds, 123, 260, 265
Didda, Queen of Kasmir, 69
Dilīpa, type of a Virtuous King, 83
Dīpavamsa, the, date and historical value of, 6 & *n.* 1
Diplomatic Agents, classes and powers of, 193-5
Direction of Military Affairs, organisation of, 202-3
Distance-Pillars on roads, 251
Divine origin of the State, theory of, 35-6 & *nn.*
Division or District, composition of, 294
Documentary Evidence, 161
Domestic Councils of Rajput Chiefs, 53
Dravidians, the, 17 & *n.* 2
  Village government by, 288-9
Druhyus, the, 54, 55 *n.*

EDICTS (*see also* Epigraphs) of Asoka, 49, 276, 277 *et alibi*
  Royal, Legal force of, 78, 139-40, 150
Education, spread of, under Buddhism, 285
  State support of, 285
Egypt, Buddhism in, 278
  Indian relations with, 186, 187
Elective Kingship, 64-8

Elephants, as Kingly mounts, 86 *n.* 3
Military use of, 195, 196, 197
Equipment, 208
Men carried by, 204
Value of, 199-200
Superintendent of, 124-5
Ellora caves, the, 249
Engineering, in Asoka's day, 247
Envoys, 193
Epics, Hindu, 2, 3
Dates of, 4 *n.* 1
Epigraph Records, on Politics, &c., 8, 84 *& nn.* 2-4, 105, 146, 147, 222, 223, 247, 282 *n.* 1, 283, 284, 295
Evidence, in Lawsuits, 158-9, 161, 162-3
Excise Duties, 175
Expenditure, Public, allocation of Funds for, 181
Heads of, 181-2
Exports, the chief, 269

FA-HIAN, and other Chinese Pilgrims, on Indian Life, &c., 7-8 *et alibi*
Family, the, 23
as Basis of State-organisation, 38
Position in, of
Father, 24-5
Other members, 25
Slaves, 25 6
as Social unit, 24
Famine, unknown in India, in Megasthenes' day, 32
Female Guards of Kings, 81 *n.* 2
Feudalism, and the Rājpūt system, 52
Fighting from Heights, 214
Finance, Public, Minister of, *see* Treasurer-General
Authorities on, 5, 173 *et sqq.*
Circumstances affecting, 182-3
Expenditure, heads of, and allocation of Funds, 181-2
Officials controlling, 183 *et sqq.*
Revenue, sources of, 173 *et sqq.*
Fines, Legal, 166, 175
Fire-arms, 206-7
Fiscal Minister, *see* Collector-General
Fleet of Alexander the Great, 270
Food Adulteration, State check on, 272
Forced Raising of Revenue, 178-9
Foreign Commerce, 266 *et sqq.*
Countries, relations with, 186 *et sqq.*
Invasions, instances of, 235 *et sqq.*
Policy, main consideration in, 190
Rulers, classification of, by Chānakya, 187-9
Forest Revenue, the, 177
Forestry, State control of, 258-9
Forests, Superintendent of, 123
Forts, 215 *et sqq.*
"Frightfulness" in War, Elephants as Instruments of, 199
Not imposed on Non-combatants, 230-1
Functions of the State, differentiation of, 40

GAMBLING, Fines on, 175
Game Laws, 259
Gandhāra (Kandahar) and its Capital, 56
Kings of, caste of, 70
Gangaridae, the, 57
Army of, 196
Elephants in, 196, 197
Gange, seaport, 269
Gangetic nations, *temp.* Alexander the Great, 57
Gardens, Groves, and Flowers in Cities, 241, 242, 243
Gautama Buddha, caste of, 23
Gems found in India, 260, 265
Gold, Silver, &c., sources of, 260, 265
Golden Age, the, and its decline, 34-5
Gopas, City Officials, 298
Government Officials
Classes and Duties of, 121 *et sqq.*
Pay, 129-30
Pensions, 130
Selection, 128
Supervision, 127-8, 129
Governmental Systems, 42 *et sqq.*
Governors of Provinces, titles of, 49
Grand Assembly, the, 100

Grants to Religious Teachers and Learned men, 282-5
Grazing Dues, 177
Great Buddhist Councils, 277, 279
  Council, or Royal Assembly, functions of, 97-100
Great Council or Royal Assembly, 97-100
  Countries, 6th century B.C., 55-7
Græco-Indian Provinces, cession of, 234-5, 237
Greece, Political relations with, 186, 187
Greek lands accepting Buddhism, 278
  Monarchs, Ambassadors to and from, 186-7
  Travellers, on Indian Politics, &c., 7 *et alibi*
Group-government of Villages, 290
Guilds, 97
  Buildings of, 250
  Charitable Establishments of, 284
  of Producers, State-controlled, 263
  Classes, procedure, and value of, 263-4
Gujrat, Saka conquest of, 238
Gunpowder, and similar compounds, 206-7
Gupta Empire, rise and fall of, 59-60, 238
  Inscriptions, 8
  Period of Architecture, 250-1

HAIR-CROPPING, as Legal Punishment, 167
Harbours, 267
Harshavardhana, King, army of, 197
  Conquests of, 223
  Defeat due to Elephants, 199-200
  Empire of, 60-1
  Government as exercised by, 50-1
  Great Assembly, quinquennial, held by, 280
  Hospices built by, 284
  Misrule of, 87
  Nomination of, by Ministry, 68
  Support of, to Buddhism, 279-80
  Treaty of, with the King of Kamarūpa, 191
  Virtues of, 83, 84-5 *& nn.*
Headmen of Villages, duties, powers, and status of, 53, 289, 290, 291, 292-3, 295
  Officers over, 294
Hereditary Kingship, 64, 65
  Departures from, 67-8
  Soldiers, 198
High and Low Justice, among Rājpūts, 52-3
High Priest, *see* Purohita
Hill-fort, old, structure of, 217-18
Hill-tribes, aboriginal, 38
Hindu Art, at Home and Abroad, 240 *et sqq.*, 254-6
  Temples, splendour, of, 250
Hiram, trade of, with India, 267
Historical Literature of India, 6-7
Hiuen Tsiang, on the bases of Indian Monarchical Government, 52
Horse-sacrifice, performed by Kings, 90, 92-3
Horses, Superintendents of, 124-5
Hospitals for Men and Animals, set up by Asoka and others, 283, 284
Hun Incursions, 60, 90, 238
Hunters as Forest guards, 259 *& n.* 1

IMPERIAL Unity, object of and difficulties impeding, 47, 48-9, 62, 236, 239
Imports, chief, 269-70
Income of the State, sources of, 173 *et sqq.*
India, Conquests of Kings generally limited to, 224
Indian people, characteristics of, 171, 172, 227-8
Individual, the, status of, 19, 20, 39, 41
  Stages in life of, 23
Indus Valley peoples, *temp.* Alexander the Great, 235-6
Industries, 257 *et sqq.*
Infantry, in Action, 208-9
  Classes of, 197-8
  Equipment and weapons, 207-9
Inland Navigation, 266
Inscriptions, *see also* Epigraphs
  Ceylonese, on Councils, 104-5
  Historical value of, 8

Inspecting Officers, 127-8
Institutes of the Sacred Law, 132
Intelligence Department, the, 126-7
Intercaste Marriages, in early times, 18-19
Interest on Loans, 273-4
Inter-relations of Government, from Village to Central Administration, 294
Inter-state Jealousies in regard to Foreign Invasion, 236, 239
Intervention by unauthorized Persons, in Courts of Law, 144
Invaders, Chānakya on, 233
Invasion, Lessons of, 235
  Policy of the Invaded, 232-3
Iron Pillar near Delhi, the, 261-2
Irrigation, 252-5
  Officers of, 253, 254
    Superintendent of, 124

JAINAS, cave-dwellings of, 250
  Religion of, books of, on Indian Politics, 2, 6
    Growth of, 281
Japan, Buddhism in, 278
Jārasandha, King of Magadha, conquests of, 220
  Struggles of, for Suzerainty, 48
Jātakas, the, on Politics, 6
Java, conquest of, 224
  Hindu architecture in, 255, 256
Javelins, 208, 209
Jayagangā Canal, the, 255
Judgment, delivery of, 165
Judges, duties of, 162-3, 168 *et sqq*
    Numbers essential to form a Court, 143
    Punishments of, for unrighteousness, 169-70
    Qualifications of, 144 *n.* 3
    Uprightness of, 171-2
    Usually Brāhmanas, 144, 171-2
    Various Classes of, 142
  Kings as, *ex officio*, 77-8, 81-2, 141, 142-3
  of Principal Courts, 145
    the Chief, 114
      Qualifications of, 144 *n.* 3
Judicial Functions of Village Assemblies, 295
  Investigation, 164
  Procedure, 5, 149 *et sqq.*
  System, Vedic and Post-Vedic, 141 *et sqq.*
Jury System, 143-4
  Unofficial interveners, 144
Justice, administration of, in Vedic times, and after, 141
    by Rajputs, 52-3
    by Village Assemblies, 245
  Brāhmanas, as roots of, 141 *n.* 2
  Efficiency of, factors of, 171
  Evolution of, 141
  King as fountain of, 141
  Open to all residents, 170
Justices, Itinerant, 147

KĀLIDĀSA, poems of, 6
Kalinga, army of, 196
  Asoka's conquest of, 222
  Chola conquest of, 61
Kāmandaki-nīti, the, 12
Kāmboja, and its Capital, 56
Kambojas, Kshatriya clan, occupations of, 46
Kanauj, City of, described, 243-4
  as Suzerain State, 60-1
Kānchī, University of, 287
Kanishka, conversion of, to Buddhism, 278, 279
Kānva Kings, caste of, 70
Kāra-ganga river, altered course of, 255
Kārli caves, the, 249
Kashmir, or Kasmir, conquests in, 238
  Irrigation in, 253-4
  Kings of, history of, 6
  Queens-regnant of, 69 & *n.* 2
Kasis, the, 54
  Country and Capital, 55
Kassapa IV., of Ceylon, Buddhist Reforms of, 288
Kāsyapa Mātanga, Buddhist missionary to China, 278
Kautilya, *see* Chānakya
Kauravas, the, battle-array of, 210-11
  Partition between, and the Pāndavas, 69

Keeper of the Royal Seal, the, 114
Kerala State, South India, Assemblies of, 103-4
Khāndavaprastha, City of, described, 241
  Pāndava palace at, 241
King, the, Actions of, Ministerial responsibility for, 116
  Authority of, limitations on, 39, 40, 48, 50, 103, 104, 113
  Bad, instances of, 87-8
  as Commander-in-Chief, 78
  Conquering, instances of, 220-1
  Daily routine of, 81 *et sqq.*
  Difficulties of, 87
  Duties of, 3, 5, 63 *et sqq.*, 102
  Functions of, 77-9, 81 *n.*2, 90 *et sqq.*
  Good, instances of, 83-5 *&* *nn.*, 87
  Graded ranks of, 88
  as Head of Society, 79
  Insecurity of, 88, 116, 117
  Insignia of State of, 86 *&* *n.*3
  as Judge, 77-8, 81 *n.*2, 141, 142-3, 149
  as Legislator, 78, 139-40, 150
  Oaths of, 74, 75
  Qualities desirable in, 79-81
  Relations of, with
    Brāhmanas, 22
    Land of the State, 73, 179 *&* *n.*2
    Ministers, 68, 74, 75, 77, 106 *et sqq.*, 113, 117-18
    Religion, 39, 78, 79, 276 *et sqq.*
  Revenues allocated to, considered as Payment, 73, 179 *&* *n.*2
  Succession of, 64-8
  Support given by, to Buddhism, 279-81
  Training of, 89-90
King's Court of Justice, Procedure of, 142-3
  Jurisdiction of
    Appellate, 145, 149
    Original, 145
Kingdoms, 54
  Partitions of, 68-9
Kingly Office, ancient writings on, 45 *et sqq.*, 63, 64, 70 *et sqq.*
Kingly Office
  Ceremonies connected with, 90 *et sqq.*
  Origin of, 70
    Legends of, 71
King-making and deposing by Ministers (*see also* Chānakya), 68, 116, 117
Kingship, divine origin ascribed to, 70
  Distinction between, and the "divine right of Kings," 72
  Nature of, in India, 72 *et sqq.*
Kings of Ceylon, relations with Buddhism, 281
Knowledge, four branches of, 1
Kolarians, the, 17 *&* *n.*2
  Village government of, 288-9
Korat-Mekong Road, Cambodia, 255-6
Kosalas, the, 54
  Country and Capital, 55
  State of, rise and fall of, 57
Krishna as Oligarch, 43 *&* *n.*1
  as Plenipotentiary, 193
Kshatriya caste, best armies chiefly composed of, 198
  Duties of, 20
  Kings usually belonging to, 69
  Occupations of, 46
  Origin of, 18
  Reformers belonging to, 23
Kshudrakas, the, opposition of, to Alexander, 236
Kukuras, oligarchy of, 46
Kumārugupta, stone inscription of, 284
Kumāra-rāja, 280
Kurus, the, alliance with the Pānchālas, 54, 55
  Country and Capital of, 56, 58
  Oligarchy of, 46
Kushān conquests, 238
Kutsa, 48

LABOUR, Payment by, of Taxes, 178
Lakes, artificial, 252, 253, 255
Lalitāditya, achievements of, 87
Lances, 208, 209

Land, the, not owned by Kings, 179
Land and Water Trade-routes, 264 *et sqq.*
Land-holding, of Villagers, 27
Land-Taxes, 176
 Importance of, 179
Lands, Grants of, to
 Officials, 130
 Religious teachers and the Learned, 282-3, 285, 286
Law, above the King, 74 & *n.* 2
 Ancient idea on, 131
 (Beyhar), Abul Fazl's summary of, 13
 Civil and Criminal, 5
 Origin ascribed to, 132
 Sources of, Vedas, &c., 132 *et sqq.*
 Sacred, 131, 132, 133, 150, 151
 Secular, 131, 150-1
 Evolution of, 132
Law-Member of Council, 140
Lawsuits, Causes giving rise to, 152-3 & *n.* 3
 Different kinds of, 153
 Rules concerning, 151-3
Legal Remedies, 166
 Representation, when allowed, 165
Legislation
 Direct, impossible, 131, 137
 Indirect, 137 *et sqq.*
Legislative Assemblies, *see* Parishats
 Power, not owned by early Kings, 78
Libraries containing books on Chānakya's doctrines, 13
Lichchavis, the, Country, Confederacy, and Capital of, 55
 Oligarchic rule among, 44, 46
Life, Individual, Stages in, 23
Lilāvatī, Queen of Ceylon, 69
 Elected and Deposed by Ministers, 117
 Slab Inscription of, on her Council, 105
Loans, Interest and Usury, 273-4
 to Cultivators, 257
Local Administration, Ministerial Control of, 244
 Courts of Justice, 145-7
 Government by
 Central Officials, and Minister, 49, 294
 Local Rulers, 50
 Rajput, 52-3

MACHIAVELLI, comparison of, with Chānakya, 11 *n.* 1
Madrakas, oligarchy among, 46
Madras, Chānakya-sūtra found at, 13
Magadha, Empire of
 Army of, 196
 Capitals of, 55
 Rise and fall of, 57, 59, 60, 238
 States included in, 47
Magical weapons, 206
Mahābhārata, the, date of, 4 *n.* 1
 Cited on Aryan life and Indian politics, 3 & *n.*
 Duties of each caste, and common to all, 20 & *n.* 4
 Origin of the State, 34-5
 List given in, of Nations in, or near, India, 58-9
Mahāpadma Nanda, of Magadha, 48, 59
 Sūdra caste of, 69-70
Mahāsammata, tradition of, 66 & *n.* 4
Mahāvamsa, the, date of, 6 *n.* 1
 Value as Chronicles, 6
Māhmūd of Ghaznī, invasion of, 243
Māhmud, Sultan, invasion by, 238
Mahomedan conquest, political results of, 62
 Empire, political conditions rendering possible, 238-9
Mālava (Avantī), and its Capital, 56
Mallakas, oligarchy of, 46
Mallas, the, Clans and Country of, 55
Malloi, the, and other Democratic Tribes of the Punjab, 45
 Country of, 57
 Opposition shown by, to Alexander, 236
Man, in relation to Society, as organised by Caste, 20

Mandavya-durga, hill-fort, structure of, 217-18
Manu, Code of (*passim*), date and origin of, 4 *n.* 1
 on Duties of different castes, 26
 on the State as Divine in origin, 36
Maritime Trade, 266 *et sqq.*
 Taxes on, 267
Marriages, Inter-caste, in early times, 18-19 *nn.*
Masalipatam, seaport, 268
Matipura, Sūdra King of, 70
Matsya, country, 56
Maurya rulers, 7
 Centralisation of authority under, 290-1
Maya, Dānava architect, 241
Mazaga, fortifications of, 217
Maze array of Kauravas in Battle, 210
Megasthenes as Ambassador, 186
 on India affairs, 7, *et alibi, passim*
Mercenary Soldiers, 197, 198
Merchants, Foreign, privileges accorded to, 270-1
Metallurgy, State control of, 261
 Hindu skill in, 261-2
Metals, &c., Superintendent of, 123
Meteorology in regard to Agriculture, 258 *&* *n.* 2
Milinda Panha, the, on Politics, 6
Military Organisation, 196 *et sqq.*
 Directing Body and Sub-Committees, 203-4
 Equipment of Soldiers, 207-9
 Methods of Fighting, 208-9
 Training of Soldiers, 202
Mīmamsā, as source of Law, 133, 137
Mines and Mining, revenues derived from, 176, 269
 State control of, 259-60
 Superintendent of, 122-3
Mining, in warfare, 214
Ministers, Chief and other, Ranks, Titles, and Offices of, 111 *et sqq.*
 Duties of, 110
 Good and Bad, 119-20
 King's relations with, 68, 74, 75, 77, 106 *et sqq.*
Ministers
 Number of, 110-12
 Powers of, 116-19
 Qualifications desirable in, 106-7 *et sqq.*
 Responsibility of, 68, 114-15, 117
  Stories illustrating, 115-16
 Usually Brahmanas, 108
Mints, Royal, 272
 Superintendent of, 123
Missionary work of Asoka, 277-8
 Later activities in, 278-9
Mitra and Varuna, legend of, 21-2
Mokṣa Mahāparishat Assembly, described, 280
Monarchy, 45-6
 Constitutional, 51
 Growth of, 46-7
 Limited, nature of, 50-1
 Vedic, Elective, and Hereditary, 64, 65, 66, 67
Monasteries, Buddhist, 248
 Architecture of, 249
 Royal support to, 279
Money-lending, 273-4
Mount Abu, mines beyond, 269
Mudrā-Rākshasa, the, and other books elucidating Politics, 6-7
Muhammad Ghori, conquest by, and establishment of Mahomedan rule, 238
Muhammad Kāsim's invasion of Sindh, 238
Municipal Boards of Capital cities, Duties of Committees of, 296-7
Murjari, seaport, 268

NĀGARAKA, Chief City official, 297
Nālanda Monastery, honourable title of, 284
 University of, 286
  Studies at, 286-7
Nations, Lists of, at various dates, 54 *et sqq.*
Naval Affairs, Department of, 200, 203
Nelkunda, seaport, 268
Nepal, partition of, 69

Nitisāra, of
Kāmandaki, date, &c., 12 & n. 1
Sukracharya, date, &c., 12 & n. 1
Nitimayūkha, the, 13
Nitiprakāsikā, the, weapons referred to, in, 13
Nitivakyāmrita, the, of Somadevi Sūri, 12, 14
Non-Combatants, uninjured by Troops, 230-1
Non-tax Revenue, 177-8
Nyāya, authority on Laws, 133, 137
Nysa, form of Government at, 43

OATHS of
Kings, 74, 75
Witnesses, 161, 163
Octroi or Tolls, 124, 175-6
Odantapuri, University of, 287
Offence, weapons of, 204-5, 206-9
Officers of the Army, 201, 202-3
of Religion, under Asoka, 276, 277
Official Buildings, 244
Officials, Families of, Subsistence Allowances to, 130
District, titles of, 49
Village (*see also* Headman), 289, 290, 291, 293
Principal, *see* Ministers
Subordinate, 121 *et sqq.*
Oligarchic Governments, 42-6
Ordeal, the, in Criminal Cases, 163-4
Ores, the principal, 260, 265
Orissa, Hindu temples in, 250
Overseers, or Inspectors, 49

PAITHĀNA, commerce of, 268
Palaces, 244, 246-7
Pāla Kings of Bengal
Territories of, 61 & 2 n
Universities of, 287
Pāli Pitakas, the, list of great Countries in, 55-7
Palimbothra, city of, described, 241
Pānchālas, the, connection of, with Kurus, 54, 55
Country and Capital of, 56
Oligarchy of, 46
Panchatantra, the, and other tales, elucidating Politics, 7
Pāndavas, battle-arrays of, 210
City of, 241
and Jarāsandha, 220
Pāndyans or Pāndyas, army of, 197 n. 1
Buddhism among, 278
Women-rulers of, 69 n. 3
Parākrama Bāhu, King of Ceylon, Buddhist reforms of, 281
Public works of, 255
Parasu-Rāma, 21
Parishats, *see also* Moka Mahaparishat
Composition and functions of, 133, 137-9
Parthian conquest of Sindh, &c., 238
Passports, Superintendent of, 125
Patala, seaport, 268
Two-King Rule at, 45-6
Pātaliputra, city of, 24
Asoka's Palace at, 246-7
Peace-making; various forms of Agreement, 233-5
Pearls, 123, 260, 265
Pensions 130
Perjury, punishment of, 161
Persia, political relations with, 107
Physical surroundings of the State, 29 *et sqq.*
Piety, Law of, Asoka's action and views as to, 277-8, 282
Pigeons, official and military use of, 201, 259 n. 1
Pilots, 267
Plaintiffs, share of, in Trials, 155 *et sqq.*
Plato, possibly contemporaneous with Chānakya, 10
Plenipotentiaries, 193
Poetical Works, giving light on Indian Politics, 6-7
Police, the, duties of, 125-6
Efficiency of, 171, 172
Chief of, Salary of, 129
Police-State character, of early Indian State, 39-40
Policy of Indian Ruler toward Foreign Rulers, Six Sorts of, 189-90 *et sqq.*

Political Divisions at different periods, 54 *et sqq.*
Theorists, criticised by Chānakya, 11
Politics, as an Art, 1
Sources of Information on, 2 *et sqq., passim*
and Religion, gradual separation of, 274, 275
Position in, of Brāhmanas, 21
Science of, origin of, myth on, 3 *n.* 1
Polity (Rajneet), 13
Poros, King, 236 *n.* 2
Armour of, 206
Army of, 196
Disposition in battle, 214
Kingdom of, 57
Power, Balance of, 195
Prasii, the, Megasthenes on, 57
Pre-Āryan races, origin of, 17
Status of, at Āryan conquest, 17, 38
Prices, State regulation of, 271-2
Priests, *see also* Purohita
Buddhist, relations with
Ceylonese Kings, 281
Harshavardhana, 279-80
Prime Minister, the, powers, duties, and responsibilities, 68, 112-13, 117-18, 119 *n.* 2
Salary of, 129
Prisoners, liberation of, on great occasions, 232 & *n.* 1
Privilege, before the Law, according to Caste, 151, 170-1, 274
Prince-ruled States, 42
Privy Council or Council of Ministers, 97, 100, 101 *n.* 2 *et sqq.*
Members of, Salaries of, 129
Law member, 140
Promissory Notes, 273
Property, restoration of, by the Courts, 166
Provinces, government of, 49
Public Assemblies, 43 & *n.* 4, 45
Decline of, 97
Public Works, building and care of, 240 *et sqq.*
Revenue derived from, 177
Publicity of Trials, 151
Punjab, the, Alexander's successes in, 31, 44, 45, 235, 236, 240
Āryas of, tribal division of, 15 & *n.* 1, 54, 55 *n.* 1
Chief nations of, in Brāhmanic period, 54-5 & *n.* 1
Cities of, conquered by Alexander, 240
Climate, soil, and inhabitants, Megasthenes on, 31-2
Democracies in, 44-5
Purānas, the, dates of, 4 *n.* 1, 5 & *n.* 1
on Politics, 2, 5
Sources of Law, 132, 133
Value of, 5
Purohita, or Chief Priest
Importance of, 112-13
Salary of, 129
Pūrus, the, 54, 55 *n.*

QUEENS, regnant, and consort, 69 & *nn.* 2, 3

RAILS (buildings), 248
Rainfall, official observation of, 258 *n.* 2
Forests in relation to, 259
Rājā, title, meaning of, 44
Rājanyas, *see* Kshatriyas
Rājās, local, status of, 50
Rājasthān, 62
Rājasūya sacrifice, the, 90-2
Rājatarangini, the, of Kalhana, historical value of, 6
Rajendra Chola, conquests of, 61
Rājpūt conquests, 61-2
Mode of Government, 5-23
Rājyavardhana, assassination of, 68, 116
Prowess of, 90
Rākshasa, fidelity of, 119 *n.* 2
Rāma, type of a Virtuous King, 83
Rāmāyana, the, *cited* on Āryan life and politics, 3 *et passim*
Date of, 4 *n.* 1
Rāshtrakūta nation, conflicts of, 61
Reforms of Buddhist Kings of Ceylon, 281

Regiments, distinctions of, 201
Religion, 275 *et sqq.*
State connection with, 276 *et sqq.*
Asoka's officers of, 276, 277
Religious Associations, 97
Edifices, Buddhist, 248
Asoka's, 247
Institutions, Superintendents of, 125
Remedies, legal, 166
Republics, 42, 43 4
Reservoirs (Tanks, Lakes, &c.), 252, 253, 255
Responsibilites of
Judges, 168 *et sqq.*
Ministers, 68, 116, 117
Police, 125-6
Villages, 27, 252, 292, 293, 295-6
Rest Houses, 251, 283
Re-trial of Cases (*see also* Appeals), 168
Revenues, sources and administration of, 173 *et sqq.*
Classification of, by Chānakya, 175 *et sqq.*
Rig-Veda, the, on Āryan Conquest and Rule, 2
Rings, or Combines, of Merchants, State interference with, 271
Rites (*see also* Sacrifices), private and public, 5
Rivers as Trade-routes, 266
Roads, 251
Cambodian, 255-6
Rock-cut Caves, 249, 250
Royal Assembly, *see* Great Council
Royal Family, Salaries of, 129
Royal Progresses, 85 *n.*, 277
Royal Revenues, regarded as Pay for Kingly Duties, 73, 179 *&* *n.* 2
Ruler of State, evolution of, from Head of Family, 38
Rules of Conduct, two classes of, sanction for, 131-2

SABARCAE and other tribes, Democracy of, 44
Sabhā form of Assembly, 95
Sabuktagin, invasion by, 238
Sachivatantra system of Government, 51 *&* *n.* 3
Sacred Law, the, 131, 132, 133, 150, 151
Sacrifices performed by Kings, 90 *et sqq.*
Saka conquest of Sindh, 237-8
Sākiyas, government of, 43 *&* *n.* 4
Salaries of various Officials, and of Royal and other Persons, 129-30
Salt, Government control of, 262
Samiti form of Assembly, 95
Samudragupta, the Conqueror, King of Magadha, conquests of, 93, 222-3
Empire of, 60
Nomination as King, by his father, 68
Sanchi Topes, the, 247, 248
Sānghārāmas, *see* Monasteries
Sankaravarman, exactions of, 87
Sanskrit Alphabet, transliteration of, 299
Sasiguptas, and Alexander, 236 *n.* 2
Sāstras, the, as rules for Kings, 51, 74
Saurasenas, the, Cities of, 57
Saurāshtras, the, Country and cities of, 58
King of, and his army, 196-7
Sculpture, Buddhist, 247
Seamanship, *temp.* Alexander the Great, 267, 270
Seaports, 267-9
Secular Law, 131, 150
Evolution of, 132
Seleukos Nikator, ambassador of, to Chandragupta, 186
Defeat of, by that King, 31, 237
Self-help, as Extra-judicial remedy, 167-8
Self-satisfaction, as a Source of Law, 133, 136-7
Sentences, Legal, 165
Servants, Legal Protection of, 26-7, 170
Shipbuilding, 270
Shipping, Superintendent of, 124
Siam, Conquest of, 224
Hindu architecture in, 255

Siege-warfare, 214-15, 225
Signalling, military, 201
Silver, *see* Gold, Silver, &c.
Sindh, Conquests and invasions of, by
  Alexander the Great, 235
  Muhammad Kasim, 238
  Parthian power, 238
  Saka race, 237-8
Sishtas, the, Sources of Law, 133, 134-5
Size of States, advantages and the reverse, of, 31, 46-7
Slaughter-houses, Superintendent of, 125
Slavery, Indian form of, 25-7
Slings as weapons of war, 209
Smritis, the, dates of, 4 *n.* 1
  on Politics, 2, 4-5
  Sources of Law, 133-4
Social environment of the State, 15 *et sqq.*, 55 *n.* 1
  Life and Customs, authorities on, 3 *et sqq.*
Society, Good of, the aim of 'Dharma,' 275
  Subordinate to Law, 131
  in Vedic age
    Structure of, 16
      Gradual changes in, 16
      Origin of caste-system, 16-18 *& nn.*
Soil as affecting
  Character of Peoples, 31-3
  Conditions of States, 31-3
Solomon, trade of, with India, 267
South India, Temples of, 250
  Village government in, 295
Spies, 126-7, 194
Spirituous Liquors, Superintendent of, 125
Stambhas, 248
State, the, origin of, various views on, 34 *et sqq.*
    Theocratic organisation of, frequent, 39
  Indian
    Activities of, in Right Conduct, 282 *et sqq.*
    Character of, 39
    Functions of, 40
    Power of, Extent of, 39, 40
State, the (*cont.*)
  Character of
    Rights in, of Individuals, 39, 41
    Seven Limbs or Elements of, 63 *& n.* 2
    Size of, as affecting Administration and Strength, 31, *cf.* 42 *et sqq.*
    Sphere of action, 39-40
Sthānikas, or City Divisional Officers, 294, 297-8
Stone Architecture, 246-7
Story-Books, light given by, on Politics, 7
Stūpas, 247, 248
Subjects, duties and rights of, 3
  Relation of, to Kings, 64-8, 172 *et sqq.*, *passim*
Subordinate Officials, 121 *et sqq.*
Subsistence Allowances, 130
Sudarsana (artificial) Lake, 253
Sūdra caste, duties of, 20
  Kings belonging to, 70
  Manu's views on, 26 *n.*
  Origin of, 18
Sugandhā, Queen of Kasmir, 69 *n.* 2
Sukranīti, the, 12
Sumatra, conquest of, 224
  Hindu architecture in, 255, 256
Sunga Kings, caste of, 70
Superintendents of Cities, 296
  of Departments, 121 *et sqq.*
  Salaries of, 129-30
Supply Services, military, 201
Surasenas, Country and Capital of, 56
Surāshtras; Kshatriya clan; occupations of, 46
Surat (Surashtra), seaport, 268
Sureties, 167
Surrender, rules of, 228-30
Sūryamatī, Queen, rule of, in Ceylon, 69
Suyya, irrigation-works of, 254
Suzerain rule, 47-9
Swords, 204, 208, 209
Syria, Buddhism in, 279
  Relations with, 186, 187

TAKSHA-SILĀ, University of, 285
Tamil works on Politics, 7

Tāmralipti, seaport, importance of, 269
Tangara, commerce of, 268
Tanks, &c., 252, 253, 255
Tārāpīda, cruelty of, 87
Tārīkh-i-Hind, of Alberuni, on India before Moslem conquest, 8 *et alibi*
Taxes and Taxation, 173 *et sqq.*
  Classes exempt from, 178
  Principles regulating, 180-1
  Remission of, in furtherance of Foreign Trade, 270
  Revenue from, 177
Territorial expansion
  Causes, 46-7
  Commencement of, and steady progress, 59
Territory
  Cession of, by the Vanquished, 234-5, 237
  as Material Basis of the State, 29
    Climate, Size, and Soil, in regard to, 30-3
  Views on, of Chānakya, and others, 29-31
Theft, Responsibility as to, of
    Police, 125-6
    Village communities, 292, 293
  Rarity of, 172
Theocratic character of early States, 39
Tibet, Buddhism in, 278
Titles of Kings, according to grades, 88
Tolls Levied on
    Goods entering cities, 124, 175, 176
    Land-routes, and Water-ways, 177
  Superintendent of, 124
Topes, 247, 248
Tours of Piety, made by Asoka, 277
Town Councils, 53
Town-planning, 244-5
Towns, classes of, 244-5
Trade
  Mediums of, 272-4
  Municipal control of, 297
  and Trade-routes, 264 *et sqq.*
Trade Unions, 97
Tradition, as given in the Smritis, as Basis of Law, 133-4
Trans-Hyphasis region, aristocratic rule in, 45
Transliteration of the Sanskrit Alphabet, 299
Transport Service, military, 201
Trasadasyu, the first Emperor, 43
Treasurer-General, the, 113-14
  Duties of, 183-4
  Salary of, 129
Treasury, the, conditions favourable to, and the reverse, 182-3
  Superintendent of, 122
Treaties
  Alliances made by, 192-3
  Nature of, defined by Chānakya, 192
  of Peace, various forms of, 233-5
Tree-planting by Roads, 251, 283
Trench-warfare, 214
Trials, Publicity of, 151
  Stages in, and procedure, 154 *et sqq.*
Tribal evolution, 38
Tribes of the Punjab, in Vedic times, 54, 55 *n.*
Troops, arrangement of, in battle, 210 *et sqq.*
  Classes of, 197
  Equipment of, *see* Weapons
  Sections of, 197
Turvasas, the, 54, 55 *n.*

UJJAYINĪ, city of, described, 242-3
Universities, famous, 285-7
University and other Libraries, containing books on Chānakya's doctrine, 13
Usury, condemnation of, 273-4

VAISAMPĀYANA, the Nītiprakāsikā attributed to, 13
Vaisya caste, duties of, 20
  Kings of, 70
Vaivasvata Manu, the first King, 37
Vājapeya sacrifice, the, 90, 92
Vajjians, the, Assemblies of, 95-6
  Country and Clans of, 55
Vārānasi, University of, 287
Vardhamāna Mahāvīra, caste of, 23

Vatsa, and its capital, 56
Vedas, the, dates of, 4 *n.* 1
Cited, *passim*, on
Elective Kingship, 64-5
Indian Politics, 2-3
Public Assemblies, 94
Famous Kings named in, 63 *n.* 1
as Sources of Law, 132, 133
Vedic Age, Social structure in, 16
States, sizes of, 30, 31, 42
Warfare, organisation of, 204 & *n.* 2
Videhas, the, Country, Confederacy and Capital of, 55
Village Assemblies, powers and duties of, 53, 96 *n.* 3, 291-2, 295
Courts, 53, 146-7, 292, 295
Government
Āryan, 289 *et sqq.*
Ceylonese, 295
Dravidian, 288-9
Kolarian, 288-9
South Indian, 295
Officials (*see also* Headman), 289, 290, 291, 293
System, 27-8
Villages, Circles of, administration of, 294
Classification of, 245, 291
Collective duties of, 27, 252, 292, 293
Vihāras, 279, 286
Vikramāditya, King of Srāvastī, and his Ministers, 115-16
Vikrama-sila, University of, 287
Virajas, Ruler of the World, 35
Vrijji, Country, Clan-Confederacy and Capitals of, 55
Oligarchic rule of, 46
Vrishnis, the, oligarchic government of, 43

WAGERS, in relation to Lawsuits, 154
War, legendary origin of, 220 *n.* 1
and Peace, Minister for, 114
Warfare, essentials of Success in, 224
Laws of, 228 *et sqq.*
Preliminary considerations, 224-5
Speeches to Soldiers, 225-7
Three kinds of, Chānakya on, 224-5
Variant views on, 221-2
Water, provision of, Merit acquired by, 252-3, 255, 283
Water-storage, 252-5
Waterways, main, 266
Weapons of War, Authorities on, 13
Classification and Lists of, 204 *et sqq.*
Weaving, State Control of, 262-3
Superintendent of, 124
Weights and Measures, Superintendents of, 124
Wells, provision of, 252, 283
Witnesses in Law Cases, 159-61
Women Sovereigns, 69 & *nn.* 2, 3
Word of Honour, Treaties made by, 192
Works of Mercy, 282 *et sqq.*

YADUS, the, 54, 55 *n.*
Yasodharman, King of Malava, conquests of, 223
Empire of, 60 & *n.* 2
Yona, and other settlers in Asoka's realm, Buddhism of, 278
Yudishthira, King, 230, 257
Abdication of, 90
Conquests of, 48, 220-1
Elected by the People, 68
Grand Assembly held by, 100
Type of Virtuous King, 83
Yue-chi conquests, 238
Yuktikalpataru, the, of King Bhoja, date of, 13 & *n.* 1